Love, Sex & Tragedy

Simon Goldhill

LOVE, SEX & TRAGEDY

How the Ancient World Shapes Our Lives

THE UNIVERSITY OF CHICAGO PRESS

The University of Chicago Press, Chicago 60637
First published in 2004 by John Murray (Publishers), London NW1 3BH
A division of Hodder Headline

13 12 11   5

ISBN: 0-226-30117-6 (cloth)
ISBN: 0-226-30119-2 (paper)

Library of Congress Cataloging-in-Publication Data
Goldhill, Simon.
  Love, sex & tragedy: how the ancient world shapes our lives / Simon Goldhill.
    p. cm.
  Includes bibliographical references.
  ISBN 0-226-30117-6 (cloth : alk. paper)
    1. Civilization, Modern—Ancient influences. 2. Civilization, Classical. I. Title: Love, sex, and
tragedy. II. Title.
  CB430.G65 2004
  909'.08—dc22

                                                    2004048024

♾ The paper used in this publication meets the minimum requirements of the American National
Standard for Information Sciences—Permanence of Paper for Printed Library Materials, ANSI
Z39.48-1992.

Contents

A Life in Ruins

Melina Mercouri, the dazzling actress who became Greece's most famous Minister of Culture, knew how to work her audience. She stood up to address a grand international conference. 'Forgive me,' she said in a heavy Greek accent (though she spoke English well enough), 'but I must first say few words of Greek.' She paused while the delegates settled back resignedly, and then, with brilliant slowness, began. 'Democracy. Politics. Mathematics. Theatre . . .'

To speak of culture in the modern West is to speak Greek. All the highest forms of artistic production self-consciously look back to the classical world for their origin and authority. Modern theatre finds its ideals in ancient theatre, and traces its defining history back through Roman comedy to Greek tragedy. Opera began as the attempt to rediscover the power of those ancient theatrical performances. Novels, epics, poetry, all have their ancient parents. Art draws its models from the classical body, and constructs its museums like classical temples. To be as beautiful as Venus, to enchant like a Siren, to strut like an Adonis, to be as strong as Hercules – these images ground our imagination and our language.

But it is not only in high art that a classical inheritance is evident and pervasive. Men and women fight and die for democracy, as citizens of the West celebrate and promote democratic values in their rhetoric and actions. These days, democracy is the club it is necessary for a state to belong to if it is to count as fully civilized. Democracy too finds its roots and principles in ancient

Athens of the classical era. 'Politics', as the politician Mercouri knew, was a Greek invention.

Even at the most personal level of our lives, it is hard to escape the pull backwards towards the classical. 'Lesbian' means what it does because the Greek poet Sappho, a woman who loved women, lived on the island of Lesbos; 'Greek love' is there to be held up in any discussion of homosexuality; a soulful friendship is called a 'Platonic relationship'. From the classical pillars outside the high-street bank to sweaty exercise in the gymnasium, to our very ideas of what a perfect stomach should look like, the inheritance of the ancient world is part of the fabric of our everyday modernity.

A classical inheritance is all around us and in us, recognized or unrecognized. Yet there has been no period since the Renaissance which is as intent on forgetting the classical past as today. The images and language that flooded the minds of previous generations now need a guidebook. A painting of a classical myth must have an explanation on its museum label, every classical reference in a poem needs a footnote. What for centuries was the foundation of Western culture, a shared resource of the imagination, has been systematically uprooted in modern educational systems across the West, with inevitable consequences for public culture. Modernity has come to mean amnesia – amnesia about the past, about cultural tradition, about the passions and interests of our own history. Like adolescents who believe themselves the first to discover swear-words and sex, and who can only stare with incomprehension at their parents' desires, modern culture finds it hard even to notice that it is forgetting its inheritance.

One consequence of this amnesia is that the inheritance of the past can easily be seen as trivial or irrelevant. If one looks at the most superficial signs of this inheritance, it clearly *is* trivial. Classical columns outside a bank represent little more than a hoped-for grandeur and respectability, and the advertising hoardings which use classical images are only manipulating a token of classiness. 'Lovely as Venus' is a cliché. This book is not interested in this superficial circulation of images of the past, for all that they are readily identifiable hints of a long tradition. It is not a guide to how ancient myths appear in modern art and literature, nor is it concerned with Disney's 'Hercules', nor with 'Xena, the Warrior Princess'. Nor are there discussions of modern productions of ancient dramas. There aren't even jeremiads against the education system and its politicians. My focus is not the pieties which classics so often attracts. Rather, this book is about why classics matters.

Every chapter of this book is dedicated to showing why learning about classics makes a fundamental difference to understanding the major concerns of modern Western life – a fundamental difference to our self-understanding. The questions to be explored are the most basic and important concerns of our public and private life. How does the past form our identity today? How much are our sexual desires and our perceptions of our bodies the product of cultural expectations, or a true sign of nature? How should we understand the role of religion in society, especially with regard to marriage and the family? What does it mean to be a citizen of democracy? What do our leisure activities say about us and our society? Myth and history, sex and the body, religion and marriage, politics and democracy, entertainment and spectacle: these are basic building-blocks of the modern self. The motivation which drives this book is the need to reassert the importance of understanding classics for understanding these building-blocks, now above all, as educational and artistic amnesia seeps further and further through contemporary culture. What matters here is how classics is integral to the making of the modern self.

The range of these questions is very large indeed, but the grounding principle of the book is simple. It can be summed up in a single idea – taken, of course, from an ancient writer: 'If you do not know where you come from, you will always be a child.' This assertion comes from the Roman statesman and orator Cicero, and his words hiss with aggressive scorn. When he says

'you will always be a child', he does not mean in a state of inno-
cent bliss, like some romantic dream of a time before corrupt
culture can sully the natural condition of man. He means that you
will spend your life without power, without authority, without the
ability to act fully in the world or to understand properly how the
world works. A Roman father could put his own child to death
with impunity, and be praised for his austere Roman virtue when
he did so. A child is at best a disempowered adult in waiting. That
is the sort of life Cicero threatens us with.

For Cicero, it is essential to know where you come from: you
must know what happened before you were born. Not knowing
where you come from is a life sentence – not just a condemnation
of ignorance, but a declaration of incapacity. What Cicero means
by 'knowing where you come from' goes right to the heart of why
classics matters to us today.

Our family is one place we come from. Families matter in
Rome. Cicero himself did not come from one of the grand
families of Rome. He constantly showed both the pride of the
self-made man and the snobbery about class and breeding that
holding your position at the top of Roman society required. Good
Roman households had the death masks of the ancestors lined up
in the hallway as a public display of status. A Roman man lives
among the dead who made him the man he is. For the modern
post-Freudian world, too, a family drama, stretching into the
past, defines the modern person, and finding one's roots, one's
family history, is a narrative of self-discovery. We carry our death
masks inside our minds. Knowing about how we relate to our
families is central to any story of self-understanding. But for
Cicero there is much more at stake in knowing where you come
from than a question of personal identity.

Public life also defines a person. Cicero's political career strad-
dled the bloody civil war which ended the Roman Republic and
established Augustus as the first emperor of the Roman Empire.
Mark Antony, Cleopatra's lover, and the leader of the losing side
in that civil war, had Cicero assassinated, not least because Cicero

had made such brilliantly hostile speeches against him. Antony had Cicero's hand cut off and brought to him, the hand that had pointed at him so often in the Senate and written such aggressive words. Cicero lived in interesting times. He gave his life for his politics. In a time of civil war, politics affects the life of every citizen, and changes in the constitution have a radical impact on lived experience. The journey of Rome's political transformations defined Cicero's public and private life. This political narrative is the basis of Cicero's sense of history, and how he played his role as hero of the state.

'Knowing where you come from' was a fundamental issue for any player on the political stage of Rome. But as a political ideal it has also scarred the history of the modern West. The politics of race and nationalism make the question of origin a cause for violent conflict, just as passionate self-identification with religious and ideological groups motivates murderous hatred. 'Knowing where you come from' is a fraught political ideal for anyone who faces daily violence on the streets. Each personal story has its own politics. For Cicero and for us today, 'where you come from' is an insistent political question.

But self-understanding demands more than this political history. For cultural identity also makes knowing where you come from a charged question. When different cultures come into hostile contact with each other, every border-crossing, every border-control becomes a scene of self-assertion and power – conditions all too familiar in the global interaction of today, as they were when the Roman Empire was expanding.

Rome came to dominate the Mediterranean with astounding rapidity. But its conquest of Greece was particularly unsettling for the conquerors. With Greece, the Romans came into contact with a people who had themselves colonized parts of Italy many years before. Even more unsettling was the fact that Greek culture seemed so superior to Roman. Greece had had centuries of philosophy, theatre, medicine and literature when Rome's founders were still sucking milk from a wolf. In Horace's famous image, 'captive Greece captured its wild conqueror and brought its culture into the Latin land'. Romans learnt about culture from Greece: they stole its statues, translated its philosophies, consulted its doctors, and borrowed its literary forms. They learnt to speak Greek. Romans may have sniffily dismissed the weakness, effeminacy and opportunism of 'those little Greeks', but they were hopelessly drawn into the cultural orbit of Greece. No one facilitated this process more than Cicero. He translated Greek texts into Latin, made Latin philosophy possible, collected Greek sculptures, and through his letters in particular offered an image for future generations of a cultivated Roman man, a public figure, who spent his leisure time passionately engaged in exploring a Greek heritage for Rome. Even the Romans looked back to Greece – which is why much of this book is focused on ancient Greece rather than on Rome. 'Knowing where you come from' must include one's cultural inheritance. Cicero is obsessed with what makes a Roman Roman.

Cultural identity is equally a modern obsession – and a battleground which stretches across a huge terrain. Nationalism makes culture an issue which leads people to reach for their guns, metaphorically or literally. The question of what makes an American an American (or the English English and so on) is articulated both at the hurtful level of petty prejudice or social form and at the grander level of social regulation and political process. When such concerns of cultural identity intertwine with religious identity – what makes a Muslim Muslim? – or with racial issues – is there a black culture? – the resultant explosive mix has the potential for confusion and destructiveness, which the modern city knows all too well. Contemporary Western society's difficulty with cultural difference makes the question 'Do you know where you come from?' a pressing one for society.

There are different ways of telling a person's story, as contexts and questions shift. A personal, familial identity, a political identity, a cultural identity, overlap and interplay in each of us, and Cicero invokes all of these ways of understanding a person, when he demands that we know where we come from. But his blunt declaration is also trying to *do* something to his audience – something more pointed and more urgent than just offering a general reminder that being a grown-up means having a complex life-story. Cicero is trying to make his readers take up a position with regard to history – history conceived in all these broad ways. He is asserting that history makes such a difference that, if you do not work to understand it, you cannot lead a full life, an adult life, in society. History changes who you are, makes you who you are. If you do not know that history, then you cannot really be self-aware. That *is* a bold claim; and this book aims to show that it is true.

There is a stunning moment in Euripides' most celebrated tragedy, the *Bacchae*, or rather a stunning double moment. In one of the early scenes, the young ruler of Thebes, Pentheus, is faced by the god Dionysus whom the mortal fails to recognize. He thinks the god is an Eastern charlatan leading the women of the city into a dangerous and sexually corrupting cult – and he intends to lock the god into the palace's gaol. The god, ever in control, taunts the young man, and at one point declares flatly, 'You do not know what your life is, nor what you are doing, nor who you are.' Pentheus replies with a smug literalism: 'Pentheus, child of Agave, whose father is Echion.' That is, he gives his name, his family, his position, as an answer to the question 'Who are you?'

At the terrible climax of the play, Pentheus is caught spying on the women whom Dionysus has sent maddened into the hills. His mother, Agave, grabs him. The terrified Pentheus tears off his paltry disguise and pleads, 'I am your child, mother, Pentheus, whom you gave birth to in the house of Echion. O mother, pity me . . .' But Agave, in her madness, seizes his arm and pulls it from its socket, and, with her sisters, rips the boy apart in bloody and horrific bare-handed slaughter. When he needs most to assert and prove who he is, he tries the self-same markers of identity – his name, his mother's name, his position, and so forth – and they have no power, no recognition. He is pulled apart, his body, his self, dismembered.

The tragedy demonstrates with shocking vividness that if you think the answer to the question 'Who are you?' can and should be answered with a name, a family, a role, then you haven't yet begun to understand 'what your life is, nor what you are doing, nor who you are' – as the god Dionysus taunts us all. It's not by chance that the *Bacchae* has proved an immensely popular play in the last hundred years, a century which has thrown up so many challenges to the smug self-confidence that thinks the question of what it means to be a human being is an easy one. It's a play which insists that 'Who do you think you are?', 'Where do you think you come from?', 'Where do you think you are going?' are always unsettling and difficult questions for all of us.

The temple at Delphi had a remarkable inscription above its entrance: 'Know yourself.' Delphi was the most celebrated oracle in the Greek world, which the Greeks visited to ask the most important questions about their own futures. Individuals asked about their families and their fortunes; states raised matters of political policy. For both individuals and states, the inscription gives a stark warning. Self-knowledge is the first and last necessity, if you are to understand the questions and answers of your life. This injunction from the god at Delphi has lost none of its power. Without self-awareness, without self-understanding, there can only be a fragile grasp on the questions that matter.

This book is about why classics, the study of the cultures of ancient Greece and Rome, plays an essential role in answering those central questions about what it means to be a human being in today's society. Its claim is not only that history matters for understanding who we are and how we are. More specifically, it reveals how the *ancient* world matters profoundly for our self-awareness in modern life. The modern self cannot be fully or properly appreciated without its buried life, its ancient grounding, its formation through inherited ideas and images. Self-understanding requires the uncovering of those foundations.

I

WHO DO YOU THINK YOU ARE?

I

The Perfect Body

When Clark Gable took off his shirt in the film *It Happened One Night* (1934), two extraordinary things happened. First, the clothing industry was altered for ever. Because he wasn't wearing an undershirt, thousands and thousands of men decided never to wear an undershirt again, and within a year a string of clothing manufacturers went into liquidation. Second, thousands of people gazed at the bare torso of the star who was the sexiest man alive.

It is almost impossible for a modern generation of movie-goers to recapture the shock and the eroticism of that moment. Today, there is almost no part of a man's body that cannot be seen on the screen or in the magazines, and we may be more familiar with Russell Crowe's chest than our own. But it was extremely rare at that time for a film star to bare his body. In *Casablanca* (1942), Humphrey Bogart keeps his shirt on. In the war films and westerns that were the meat and drink of the industry, a soldier or a cowboy is always shot, but archetypically he is wounded only in the arm. It's a cliché of the genre. The sleeve of a shirt can be ripped off, a dramatic moment assured, but the body is kept decorously hidden. A whooping Indian or another 'native' might have a bronzed and naked torso, but not one of our boys. When Noël Coward is shipwrecked in the wonderfully patriotic naval adventure *In Which We Serve* (1942), he never even undoes his top button.

It was only in the late 1960s and the 1970s that things started to change systematically. War films like *M*A*S*H* (1970) – a cynical, funny, outrageous response to the conflict in Vietnam – is typical. It showed the body mangled, fleshy, bloody and exposed. From these years on, whether you look at love stories or heroic tales, there is more and more exposure of the body. From *Rocky* to *Gladiator*, now a hero has to be bare-chested.

This is not the first time that the image of the hero has moved from clothed to unclothed (or vice versa). The story of Perseus and Andromeda is one of the most frequently painted Greek myths, especially the scene where Andromeda is chained to a rock, waiting to be eaten by a sea-monster, only to be saved by Perseus who flies in to kill the beast and marry the girl. In ancient pictures, it is Perseus who is nude – as Greek heroes usually are – except for a helmet, his winged sandals and often a billowing cloak. Andromeda is usually rather decorously robed (Figure 1). But when the story becomes popular again for European artists in the Renaissance, the classical Perseus appears dressed in

1. Perseus and Andromeda

armour and tunic, and Andromeda becomes more and more exposed, until her long hair and wispy silks provide no more than a frame to display her naked body to the viewer. Titian (Figure 2) so highlights the naked Andromeda that the viewer's eyes are quite distracted from the swooping and very much dressed Perseus in the background. To be heroic Perseus now needs his armour, while the female body is vulnerable – to male eyes as

2. Perseus and Andromeda *by Titian*

much as to the sea-monster. The idea of acceptable or normal nudity has radically changed.

There is a history to how the male body has been displayed. It is not just a question of how much of the body a viewer is allowed to see, but also of what a body is meant to look like: a torso in *Gladiator* or *Rocky* doesn't look like Clark Gable's. There are images of the body all around us – from the pictures of men in film, on TV or in magazines to the medical writer's body, the novelist's representations, the legal system, grand art and smutty graffiti. All these images of the body tell us how to be, how to

13

think about ourselves, how to see who we are. But where do these images of the perfect body stem from?

The simplest answer is Greece. Since the Renaissance and its rediscovery of Greek art, there has been a long tradition of taking the ideal of the male body from Greek sculpture. The slim but well-muscled torso, the elegant symmetry of form, the balanced turn of the head or twist of the athlete's shape, have produced an image so firmly lodged in the Western imagination that it is hard to look at it freshly or in any historical context. For anyone who goes to the gym, who worries about thinness, or getting in shape, or their muscle tone – or even for anyone who just knows what a good body is – there's a history stretching back to ancient Greece that will change the way your body looks to you.

In the modern West, we are bombarded with images of the body. For the classical Greek citizen, too, images flooded the eyes and filled the public and private spaces of the city in a quite remarkable way. When the Athenian strolled in the market place, the buildings all around were decorated with grand, state-funded paintings of the warriors and battles of the past. There were huge statues of the heroes of democracy, and towering over the city was the Acropolis with the Parthenon and its other temples, decorated with friezes depicting crowds of human figures. All around stood a forest of statues – of athletes, dead heroes, generals, civic benefactors, gods. Lining the avenues, placed around sanctuaries, carved in relief on temples and tombs, on porticoes and civic buildings, were stone and bronze representations of the male form. When the Athenian sat at home to drink wine, his pots and cups were decorated with beautifully painted pictures – an army of perfect bodies. The major cities and civic arenas of classical Greece were crowded with hundreds of images of exercised and buffed masculinity.

The perfect body gave the Greek citizen a difficult model to live up to. To get the body in shape needed training, and that meant, first of all, the gym. The gymnasium was one of the fundamental signs of Greek culture. You could be sure you were in a Greek city if you saw a theatre, a symposium, a political debate – and a gym. It was a prime place for thinking about the body, and for performing with it. The modern preoccupation with the gym, often seen as a sign of contemporary city life, finds its real origin here, in the ancient Greek city. Our preoccupation with bodies and exercise is not new at all, but another classical inheritance. Choosing your gym, worrying about your appearance, exercising the body, adopting a diet, hiring a personal trainer – this is all good ancient Greek civic activity.

The gym was the place where a Greek citizen went to work out. Men only. A citizen should go to the gym regularly, even on a daily basis, and particular groups went to particular venues. Socrates, Plato says, used to like hanging out at Taureas' Gym near the Temple of the Queen of the Gods, where some very upper-class Athenians exercised – but he was easily persuaded into other gyms by an invitation from a good-looking young man. The citizen would strip. (Unlike the modern gym, all exercises were practised naked – though the penis was tied back for running races.) He would rub oil into his body or have it rubbed into him by his servant, and then he would exercise – run, or wrestle, or jump, or practise for other competitions like javelin or discus throwing. Boys, at least those of the best sort, had their tutors along to keep an eye out for them, and professional trainers coached the more serious athletes. Finally, the oil and dirt would be scraped off with a metal strigil, or scraper. The oil flask and the strigil are what men would stroll purposefully with, like a sports-bag and tennis racket.

Modern advertising was epitomized up to the 1970s by Charles Atlas, who used the title of 'the world's most perfectly developed man' to support his promise that exercise will 'make a man' of you, as it had for him. (Atlas claimed that it was actually a statue of Hercules in New York's Metropolitan Museum of Art which inspired him to attain 'the perfect male body'.) The ancient gym was central to the whole performance of masculinity in the

15

ancient city: it truly 'made you a man'. This meant, first, honing
your body as a preparation for war, since real men all fought in
the city's army and navy. The second-century essayist Lucian captures the cultural ideal of what a man in the gym should look like:

The young men have a tanned complexion from the sun, manly faces;
they reveal spirit, fire, manliness. They glow with fabulous condition-
ing: neither lean or skinny, nor excessive in weight, but etched with
symmetry. They have sweated off all useless flesh, and what's left is made
for strength and stamina, and is untainted by any poor quality. They
maintain their bodies vigorously.

The ideal form is neither too thin nor too fat, but perfectly balanced. On show are not just physical qualities, but 'manliness' and
'spirit', shining from 'manly' faces. Their bodies display what sort
of men they are, and how they live. This all-round perfection of
masculinity is what athletics promises you, and why you go to the
gym. But without exercise, a man's body, says Lucian, will end up
like this: 'It'll have either a white and lazy flabbiness, or a pale
scrawniness, like a woman's body, bleached from the shade, quivering, and dripping with sweat, and panting . . .' The threat to a
man's body is being 'like a woman' – the reverse of all that is good
about the real man. Lucian gives a checklist of negative qualities –
pale, scrawny, flabby, quivering, weak and wet – to set against the
qualities everyone should aim for: tanned, firm, symmetrical,
vigorous and dry. The message is clear: exercise hard, or suffer
the humiliation of a bad body, which means being a bad citizen.

Classical artists depicted the athlete's ideal body which Lucian
so enthusiastically described. The frieze in Figure 3 formed part
of a base on which there once stood the statue of a man, which
acted as a grave-marker. The six bodies are displayed as though
in an anatomical textbook, starting on the left with a full frontal
view, and rotating around to a view from the rear. (The rotation
does give the sculptor a few problems with the fifth body in particular.) The body should be, as Lucian insists, lean but well

built – bulked up from exercise but not fat or over-muscled like a modern body-builder. The muscles should be well defined ('etched') with a six-pack stomach and cut pectorals, and the torso should reveal an iliac crest, the sharp line or fold running above the groin and up over the hip, a physical characteristic that can be revealed only when the muscles are very strongly developed but the body is exceptionally lean – and which Greek sculptures emphasize in a way impossible to achieve in real life. Thighs are powerful, calves sharply articulated, penis small (always), and, since these are beautiful young men, they have no beards yet, but they do have carefully done hair.

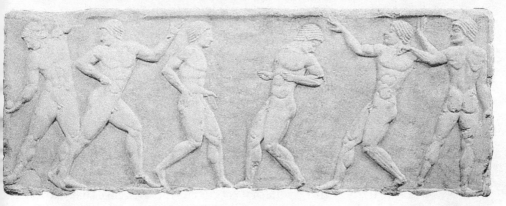

3. 'Anatomical' frieze from a funerary monument

The gym was where a citizen found out what sort of a man he was – by competing with other men, by displaying his body, by making his body more manly. The gym put masculinity on trial, and not just in the athletic activities. It was also a key place for erotic encounters, where the beautiful boy became known as a beauty, where men vied for the attention of beautiful boys, where men gathered to talk, strut and watch each other. It was where you saw other men, and where you viewed others and yourself against the image of the perfect body. The gym made the body a topic of conversation, display, desire and worry as well as of exercise and care.

The Roman statue in Figure 4 adds the theory to the practice. It is a copy of one of the most famous statues in the ancient world, the *Doryphoros*, or 'Spear-carrier', made by Polycleitus in the fourth century BC. Polycleitus was also a writer on sculpture, who was the first to develop a 'canon' of beauty – that is, he outlined in theoretical mathematical terms the perfect proportions a man should have if he is to be the perfect specimen of manhood. This procedure was followed by Leonardo da Vinci in his sketches of the proportions

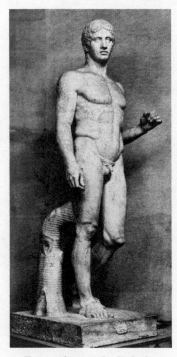

4. Doryphoros *by Polycleitus*

of the human form, which test the divine mathematics of beauty. It was also adopted, with less theoretical disinterestedness, by Charles Atlas, who advertised himself as the 'ideal male specimen for the 20th century', and who posed in an imitation of Polycleitus' statue (Figure 5). Polycleitus summed up his theoretical principle of balance and harmony with the word 'symmetry' – a term obviously echoed in Lucian's admiration for the perfect body. Although scholars have argued whether the *Doryphoros* actually does embody that canon (most think it does), the typical Greek turn to theory is crucial. It is not just that the gym made people especially conscious of the body. There was also an artistic credo, which offered abstract rules for the perfect body, rules by which you could evaluate a body, real or sculpted, and discuss it.

The ideal form was sculpted and painted innumerable times, flooding the cities of Greece with a body image that took some living up to. While it is more usual nowadays for female models to provide a bodily form for modern Western women that almost no one can match, in Greek culture it is the ideal male body that stares out from temples, pots and paintings as a relentless and impossible yardstick for men. A real man's body needs a lot of work and care to produce and maintain.

Nudity was essential to the culture of the ancient gymnasium. It is one rather obvious difference between Charles Atlas and the *Doryphoros* in their displays of what is a perfect form – as it is between the ancient Perseus and Titian's hero. Modern surprise at Greek nude exercise immediately indicates how habits of bodily display are culturally specific. But attitudes to the nude body in Rome are even more provocative. Going to the bathhouse was as important to a Roman as going to the gym was to a Greek. People met in the bathhouse not only to enjoy the hot baths, cold baths and steam rooms, but also to gossip, and occasionally to take light exercise – again, in the nude. As with any modern health club or spa, social boundaries need special care when socializing involves taking your clothes off, and the bathhouse had its protocols and rituals. But what has always seemed shocking to the Judaeo-Christian tradition is the fact that women went to the baths too.

5. Charles Atlas

It has often been wondered, of course, whether there were women-only sessions, or whether upper-class bathers were segregated. It does seem that some baths may have been reserved for men or for women; and some baths did have times for single-sex bathing. But mixed bathing was certainly a normal activity in Rome. Plutarch, a gentleman and a scholar, is typical of the ancient Greek response when he confesses to being profoundly shocked by such improper practices. When modern gentlemen and scholars too express their surprise and outrage at Roman mixed bathing, it is evident how tricky it is to step outside our own culture of nudity, our own expectations of the display of the body.

Outrage is not the only response to Roman mixed bathing. The suggestiveness of the baths particularly excited the imagination of

Victorian artists like Alma-Tadema: several of his most obviously titillating paintings take the bathhouse as their setting. *The Tepidarium*, the 'Warm Room' (Figure 6) is a wonderful example: the woman's flushed face and dreamy expression, together with her exposed position on her sensuous rugs, are designed to invite the viewer's fantasizing gaze. The strigil in her right hand implies she has been exercising and needs scraping down. The feather fan sensuously maintains a measure of decorum (although to Kenneth Clark it suggested pubic hair). Even in ancient Rome itself, where going to the baths was an everyday event of leisure and pleasure, serious moralists often complained about the loose morals and lax behaviour which they thought went on there. And louche poets wrote poems about the baths that gave the moralists all the ammunition they needed.

The worry about nudity is not only its obvious sexual potential, however. Nudity is often thought to be the natural condition when we are most simply ourselves, but it is also the state when

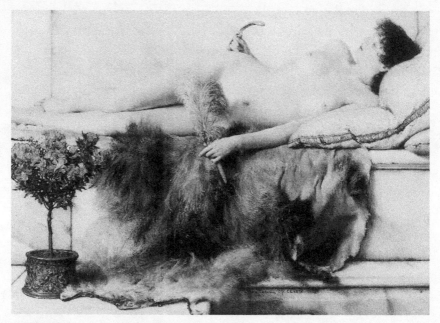

6. Tepidarium *by Alma-Tadema*

we can least well tell the social, intellectual, moral condition of the person in front of us. Roman culture, even more than modern society, was obsessed with visible signs of status, honour and position, strongly and clearly marked out. Nudity hides the clothes, jewels and other badges of office which let the world know who *this* citizen is. A shared space where nakedness in fact concealed a man's status might well have produced anxiety. Clothes do make the man.

The ancient practices of nude display may seem somewhat strange to modern eyes. No less surprising is the fact that in both ancient Athens and the Roman Empire there was a flourishing business in health manuals, diets and exercise handbooks. A whole series of experts, from doctors to athletic coaches to personal masseurs, vied with each other. From the fourth century BC, there are several diet books, or 'Regimens', collected in the Hippocratic Corpus, which give advice on what to eat, how often and when to bathe, how much exercise to take and of what types, how long to sleep, and how much sex to have. The Greek word for such regimens is *diaite*, from which comes the English word 'diet'. The diet books that still keep topping the bestseller lists today are no modern phenomenon. The ancient Greeks, equally obsessed with the body beautiful, were also anxious for expert advice.

These diet books have long sections on what different foods do to a man's digestion, and long arguments about how to cure various conditions by carefully organized regimens of life. If, for example, you have headaches, feel lethargic, constipated and occasionally feverish – a condition called 'Surfeit' – then:

after a vapour bath, purge the body with hellebore, and for ten days gradually increase light and soft foods, and meats that open the bowels, so that the lower belly can overcome the head by drawing the humours down and away. Practise slow jogging, long enough early-morning walks, and wrestling with the body oiled. Do eat lunch and take a short sleep after lunch. After dinner just a stroll is enough. Bath, oil yourself, make the bath warm, and keep away from sex. This is the quickest treatment.

This advice is a mixture of specific medical actions, such as having a vapour bath with hellebore to purge the system, and of more general rules for life like 'Do eat lunch and take a short sleep after lunch.' It aims to regulate the citizen's daily life from sex to jogging, according to the doctor's scheme of things. Greece didn't just give us democracy and theatre: it also gave us personal trainers and faddish diets.

The citizen's body is public property. Naked in the gym, relaxed at the symposium, walking in the street, speaking in the assembly or in the law court, the citizen's body was there to be watched and commented on. How to stand, how to walk, how to *appear* a man in your physical demeanour are shared concerns. Other men look at and judge the citizen's body: a citizen's sense of self depends on that evaluation. Socrates was always useful, according to Xenophon, the fourth-century writer, as he seeks to prove with this story. 'Seeing that Epigenes, one of his companions, was in poor physical condition for a young man, he said, "You've got the body of someone who just isn't engaged in public matters!"' Epigenes retorts that he is a private citizen and not active in public life, but Socrates rebukes him strongly: 'You should care for your body no less than an Olympic athlete.' When he sees the young man in poor physical condition, Socrates naturally concludes that his body instantly and obviously testifies to the shameful fact that the young man isn't participating in the public life of the city with the proper public spirit. He goes on to explain how as a soldier in particular or even just as a man 'there is no activity in which you will do worse by having a better body'. Consequently, he concludes, you must work 'to see how you can develop the maximum beauty and strength for your body'. And that won't happen by itself: 'You have to care for your body.'

Xenophon epitomizes the logic of caring for the body. The citizen must train his body to make it as beautiful and strong as possible, in order to have success both in war and in all other public activities. Socrates will walk up to someone and complain about the flabbiness of his body and nag a man because he just isn't toned enough. Unlike modern philosophers, fixed in the classroom and seminar, he is out on the street, actively changing people's lives. Socrates gets involved because the flabby citizen is a public matter, a matter of public concern. Fat is a political issue.

The influence of ancient Greece on the modern male body is profound. What looks sexy and what is thought healthy depend hugely on the Greek ideals embodied in classical sculpture and art. The perfectly honed, muscled, lean and symmetrical male body is developed as an ideal in the ancient world's art, medical texts and other writings. Despite the Christian tradition which despises the body as sinful, and longs for a spiritual, non-materialistic life, this image of the trained and cared-for body has become fully lodged in the imagination of Western society, an instantly recognizable icon of beauty and health. We are meant to know what a good body is. We may know that different cultures have different ways of defining the good body. We may be well aware that body images are manipulated by powerful media, which have always provided fantasies of bodily perfection, whether a buxom woman painted by Rubens or a gamine model in *Vogue*. But we still feel that we know what a good body is. And the fact that we think we do know shows how powerfully Greek myth still works in contemporary Western culture.

In today's culture of the body, this longing for Greece is rarely made explicit. But the connection between an idealized Greece, the perfect body and athletics was made absolutely clear when modern Europe reinvented the Olympic Games, at the end of the nineteenth century. The Frenchman Baron Pierre de Coubertin is always credited as the founder of the modern Games. An adept self-publicist, he was happy enough to claim the invention for himself quite often too. Coubertin was in love with the athletics of the British public schools – he read *Tom Brown's Schooldays* like a holy text; and he also hoped to make his own compatriots more capable of resisting the German war-machine by a programme of 'sporting education', a hope which echoes the ancient Greek sense of athletics as the best preparation for war. But the glue that truly held together the nascent Olympic movement was an unabashed and powerfully felt Hellenism, a love of ancient Greece. Olympia, wrote Coubertin, was 'the cradle of a view of life strictly Hellenic in form'. German archaeologists had excavated Olympia to reveal the actual site of the Games; Heinrich Schliemann had found Troy and its treasures; the passion for antiquity was at its height. The opportunity to live a Hellenism fully with one's own body, in Greece, in a festival that so evoked the glories of the past, provided an irresistible force that brought the Olympics into existence.

The obsession of the nineteenth century with all things Greek changed physical culture. While the Olympic movement was being refounded – and well into the early decades of the twentieth century – a cult of the physical flourished in Germany in particular. Groups met to hike, to exercise and to swim or work out together, sometimes in the nude. The Romantic love of nature produced a particular German fixation on The Woods and The Mountains, which joined with a passion for Hellenism to make 'exercise' a charged idea for German nationalism. Nude gymnastics was a sign of nationalist fervour. In fact, public nudity is still acceptable in Germany in a way quite different from the rest of Europe and America, and there are parks in Berlin, for example, where nude sunbathing is still normal.

But, as the century progressed, this cult of the body fed into the most worrying sides of German nationalism and its aggressive promotion of the trained Aryan physique. The strongest link between the nineteenth-century Romantic love of Greece and the violent Aryan passions which linked the cult of the body to Nazi ideology is provided by Friedrich Nietzsche. His idealizing of the

German spirit, his theories of power and his praise of the morals of the superman, who dominates his inferiors, all had a profound effect on the nationalism that culminates in the Nazi party before and during the Second World War. Even if the argument has often been made that such a use of Nietzsche by German fascism is a drastic abuse of the philosopher's own true political stance, there can be little doubt that reading him provided a justification and inspiration to many ideologues of the twentieth century.

Nietzsche epitomizes the impact of the Greek body on the Western imagination in a trenchant and odd paragraph. 'The Germans', he claims, 'have joined anew the bond with the Greeks, the hitherto highest form of man.' Here is the ideologically charged claim that the German race descends from the Greeks, and that as the Greeks were the highest form of man, so Germans aspire to that pinnacle, their own true inheritance. 'Today we are again getting close to all those fundamental forms of world interpretation devised by the Greeks . . . We are growing *more Greek* by the day.' But for Nietzsche it is not just in our thinking that we can become more Greek: 'We are growing *more Greek* by the day; at first, as is only fair, in concepts and evaluation, as Hellenising ghosts, as it were; but one day in our *bodies* too.' We can, 'as Hellenising ghosts', think ourselves into a Greek frame of mind, but the crucial and ultimate goal is to become Greek 'in our *bodies* too'. We need to become physically Greek. It's almost as if by doing ancient philosophy we will all get iliac crests and a six-pack. This longing for a Greek body is summed up in ringing terms by Nietzsche: 'Herein lies (and has always lain) my hope for the German character!' In short, to be truly German, for Nietzsche, means becoming Greek 'in our *bodies*'.

The connection between the ancient body, German nationalism and modern ideals in Olympic athletics is brilliantly captured in Leni Riefenstahl's infamous *Olympia*, a documentary about the Berlin Olympics of 1936, a film made for Goebbels' Ministry of Propaganda. Its huge success in Nazi Germany makes it part of a

7. *From Leni Riefenstahl's* Olympia

grim politics of the body, whatever its creator may have intended for it. But the film reveals the longing for the Greek body in the most striking imagery. Part one of the documentary, called 'Festival of the Nations', begins with a lengthy prologue in which ideologically laden images of ancient Greece are lovingly evoked. The camera shifts from views of the Acropolis to other romantic ruins, and finally to close-ups of white marble statues. Not all are athletes, but the final image is the celebrated classical statue *The Discus Thrower*, sculpted by Myron. In the film, the image begins to rotate and fades into a modern athlete, who throws the discus with muscular poise and power (Figure 7). The modern athlete is literally seen as the embodiment of the ancient sculpted ideal. Nietzsche would have loved Riefenstahl's image of the transformation of the ancient discus thrower into the modern German athlete. So taken was Hitler with *The Discus Thrower* that in 1938 he pulled every diplomatic string possible to buy the statue for Germany. The Italian Culture Minister was overruled and the statue went to Berlin (it was quietly repatriated in 1948). Riefenstahl's image clearly had a powerful impact on the Führer.

Nietzsche and Riefenstahl form part of a long and continuing tradition of trying to live up to the Greek body. Like the Greeks themselves, we surround ourselves with images of the masculine form, trained by exercise and diet, the object of public scrutiny, longing and failure. This embodiment of Greek myth runs through the Western cultural imagination, and lives on as an inheritance in us all. The gym, the torso, the pose, the diet – the fascination of the Greek body is displayed all around us still. 'Being Greek in our *bodies*' may seem like Nietzsche's fantasy. But it is an ideal that many people, consciously or unconsciously, still share today.

2

A Man's Thing?

The modern preoccupation with the body beautiful lives out a myth from ancient Greece. But this striving for the perfect body reflects only one side of a far more complex story of how the Greeks and Romans put the human form on display. The way we differ from the ancient world is also profoundly telling about the taboos and anxieties which shadow the modern sense of the self.

The influence of the most splendid classical statues on our imaginary bodies is evident. But the buffed torso in our galleries gives a distortingly blinkered view of how the body was represented in the ancient world. In locked drawers and secret cabinets around the world, museum curators keep the penises that have been knocked off statues, along with the other objects which the Christian tradition has covered with fig-leaves, or tried to turn their pious eyes from. What the ancients did with erect penises is very revealing because it is so different from modern society's approach. When it comes to the phallus, the ancient body offers a different sort of mirror in which we can see more clearly who we think we are.

The curators and moral policemen have the law on their side, in modern England and in most modern Western countries at least. For years, the definition of hard-core pornography in English law has related to the display of the erect penis. It's the one thing you cannot show on television or in the newspapers. On British television, you can broadcast simulated sexual intercourse, sadistic violence and naked women (after nine o'clock at night), but even in a medical programme a man's erection is not allowed.

The basic aim of the law is to ban images or writings that have a 'tendency to corrupt and deprave' those who see or read them, especially the young and vulnerable. So, for the good of society as a whole, all such obscenities should be censored. Or, as the internet and video industry make censorship harder and harder to maintain, the circulation of such images should at least be restricted to 'adult' viewers *as* pornography. And the proof case for the law, as far as imagery is concerned, is the erect male member. On the next few pages, however, you will see some pictures of erect penises. But this will not be pornography, and this book will not corrupt your mind, nor will it make you depraved. It's classics. And it's art.

8. Caristyas' monument on Delos

Figure 8 might seem rather tame. It shows two decorated columns each topped by the remains of what were once very large erect penises complete with testicles and pubic hair. They stand either side of the entrance to a small sacred site, dedicated to Dionysus, on the island of Delos. When historians of religion see erect penises, they usually say rather vaguely 'fertility symbol', and turn their eyes as quickly as possible towards more elevated subjects. But that reaction is more than usually inadequate in this case. For the column to the forefront of the picture is decorated with sculptures and an inscription that tells us a more precise story about what this monument is doing and why it stands in this rather cultured Greek civic context. It was set up just after the end of the fourth century BC by a man called Caristyas to celebrate the fact that he had funded a series of victorious plays in the local drama competition. There's many a Hollywood starlet who might appreciate the irony: this penis memorializes a successful theatrical impresario.

The monument itself may be particular to Caristyas, but it would have been quite unsurprising in form and content to Greek eyes. On both sides of the column, there are matching carved reliefs of a naked Dionysus flanked by his entourage including a maenad, one of the wild female celebrants of his rites. Dionysus is the divinity who is the patron of theatre as well as of wine, and Caristyas' victories were in a dramatic festival of Dionysus. These images are absolutely standard versions of the revels of Dionysus, often used to celebrate theatrical success in this period.

The picture on the front of the column may be more striking to modern eyes (Figure 9). Here is a

9. Caristyas' monument (front view)

cockerel with a man's penis for a head. But this image isn't odd in Greek terms. A phallus with wings, for example, often flaps around on the scenes painted on Greek pots (though modern scholars don't know quite what to make of this 'phallus bird', except to hazard the not very bold suggestion that it might have 'erotic overtones'); women are shown carrying these phallus birds or riding on them. But in this case the cockerel/phallus is immediately recognizable as a cult statue from the worship of Dionysus on Delos. The Delians celebrated a famous festival, the Phallophoria, in honour of Dionysus, in which a splendid procession carried to the main sanctuary of Dionysus a specially made statue of a bird with a phallus for a head. Caristyas wants his victory celebrated in a way that links his success into the island's religious ceremonies.

Using representations of an erect penis in civic ritual would be distinctly baffling in the modern state, but carrying huge phalluses was part of Dionysiac worship across the ancient world. At the height of Athenian political power, foreign allies were required to send a phallus to be marched in the procession of the Great Dionysia, the festival at which tragedy and comedy took place. This was a grand political occasion, full of ceremonial pomp and attended by visitors and dignitaries from all over the Greek world. Athenians saw nothing odd in a procession at their most splendid state ceremonial of huge models of erect penises.

And why not? All they had to do was look round the city. By the front doors of houses stood 'herms', statues of the god Hermes, the divinity who guarded transitions. But unlike the beautifully carved drapery or etched muscles of classical sculpture's greatest hits, these figures were just a head on a square pillar, and, jutting out of the pillar, a large erect penis. Sometimes the head was left off altogether. Herms were also placed at crossroads throughout the Athenian countryside, and on each one a little moral motto, such as 'Do not cheat a friend', was inscribed. These herms had been set up by the state as a way of mapping out the territory of Athens under the state's own political and moral control. Part of religion, part of politics, part of the state's organization and territory, the phallus was an everyday sight – an integral feature of the symbolic world by which ancient culture expressed itself.

Other gods too, especially Dionysus, had cult statues that were similar to these herms: a block, a head, an erect penis. In Roman culture, Priapus was just such a phallic figure, though he often had more of a developed human body. Priapus, however, in the Roman imagination wielded his phallus like a weapon to protect gardens and orchards from thieves. His phallus was a threat and a sign of power – and Roman masters did indeed boast of raping male and female slaves by way of punishment, or merely by way of asserting their authority.

Not all Roman uses of the phallus involved such obvious aggression. In the ashes of Pompeii, excavators found bell-pulls for front doors in the shape of penises, and lamps in the shape of

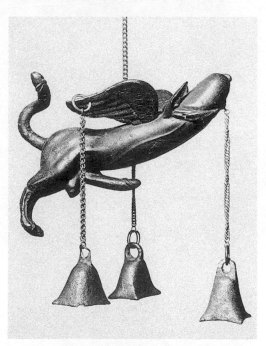

10. Roman bell pull

grotesque and exaggerated genitalia. Figure 10 shows just how ornate and, well, how *phallic* these objects can be. Here a set of three bells hangs from a flying erect penis, one from each of the wings, and one from the tip of the penis, like a bizarre modern sexual fetish. But this winged phallus also has a phallus of its own, equally erect. What's more, it has a tail, and the tail is also in the shape of a penis, though a very curly one. This is not just a penis in a public space, but someone's bizarrely fantastical penis-on-a-penis-on-a-penis *objet d'art*. It's hard to know how normal, how tacky or how funny this bell set would be to Roman eyes. How exactly should one ring it?

11. Amphora with a herm

The phallus was part of the furniture of ancient religion and social life. It was part of the grandest civic ritual and part of day-to-day experience. It is also ripe for all the jokes and outrages that such a powerful symbolic image can attract. Figure 11 illustrates one representation of a herm, with a not very sophisticated joke. It decorates a vase made in classical Athens, and shows both a herm and an altar. The herm has an outsized phallus, and his expression seems pointedly uncomfortable. The god is impotent to stop a bird flapping in his face – and his outsize penis emphasizes the derisive treatment of the cult statue as an everyday perch. The image is well suited to this wine amphora, a pot that was designed to be used at a male drinking party, a symposium, where such jokes were at home. The contrast with the modern world is worth underlining. When a scholar in a religious studies department in America in the 1990s published a book entitled *God's Phallus*, he lost his job. The modern world, even when it likes religious humour, doesn't much enjoy jokes about the sexual body of divinity.

It is more difficult, however, to look at the young female figure in Figure 12, although it is beautifully carved. For the easily shocked modern reader, this needs a little more care. It's a real eye-opener. It is a herm of a bearded, ugly god with horns who must be Pan, the unruly and disruptive god of the countryside, who causes 'panic'. In front of the herm is a young female figure

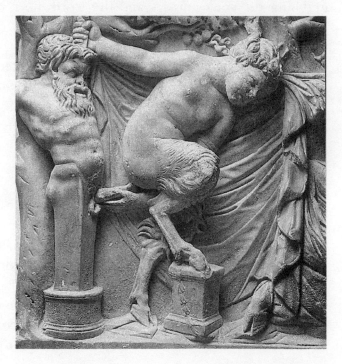

12. *A Panisca on a Roman sarcophagus*

who has the lower limbs of a goat – a girl Pan, a 'Panisca'. She has one hoof raised on a small pedestal or altar; and the background of drapery and the trailing fronds of fruit trees also suggest an elegant rural shrine. But with her right hand she is grabbing the statue's horn while with her left she is guiding the god's phallus into her.

This relief isn't just a smutty image, however. First of all, there are several jokes that make the image work in a surprisingly complex way, to match the skilful carving. Whereas Pan is trad-itionally a raper of nymphs, shepherd boys, goats, here he is being used by a female for *her* pleasure. Pan normally chases girls who could be metamorphosed by their fear into reeds and end up cut and blown as Pan-pipes. Here the god is of stone, and it's the girl who, quite unpanicked, is doing what she wants with his static form. It's a standard stereotype of ancient comedy that women constantly need sexual gratification: here we see how the Panisca improvises in the rural shrine with suitably rustic flair. She is grabbing the god's horns – and the word 'horn' in Greek and Latin, as in modern English, is a regular dirty pun: this is a 'horny' picture. The pun is, as it were, made visible by her two hands with their positioning. Even the god's typically distorted features take on a particular smirk from his treatment at the hands of the girl. It is important that the figures in this image aren't simply human, and that she can't be your sister, lover, wife, friend. It would be much more embarrassing or inappropriate or simply rude for a Roman viewer, as for a modern one, if this little scene was staged by people like us. The mythic nature of the scene helps make it possible, and funny, and not just a crude sexual gesture.

But what makes this image really surprising, or even shocking, for a modern viewer is that it is carved on a Roman sarcophagus. It is not a lascivious image from a brothel or a bedroom, but part of an elaborate stone carving as the final resting place of a wealthy second-century Roman. This is an object for the most sacred and difficult of rituals, an image for a funeral. This picture is meant to be viewed in a holy and serious frame. It is not an image that would raise eyebrows in this context for a Roman. There are many sarcophaguses with scenes of revelry depicting both mythic and human figures. Our Roman wanted his monument covered with images of the good life, and this witty little mythic vignette of rural delight captures a sense of the pleasures of the world. It would be profoundly odd to see this sort of relief on a modern gravestone.

The erect penis no doubt *can* function as a fertility symbol. It can be used to ward off danger, and it can stand as a sign of male power and dominance. But, more than that, in ancient culture it is carried in public processions, used to make public memorials, put up at doorways and crossroads, used for bell-pulls and lamps, painted, sculpted, handled in religious, political and theatrical contexts as much as in private, relaxed, informal ones. What the modern West stigmatizes as the very sign of obscenity, and bars from viewing because it will corrupt and deprave, is displayed all around the classical world.

This brief tour of the phallus in public art makes it evident how much more there is to classical art than the buffed torso: the difference between the easy ancient display of the erect phallus and its anxious modern concealment is striking. But it is also clear that the difference between modern and ancient attitudes is not just a trivial matter of taste or custom. How the phallus is displayed reveals fundamental aspects about both cultures' sense of the body and sexuality – about what it means to be a person. How we react to the Panisca today inevitably reveals some of our own ideas about the body and sexuality. It shows something about each of us.

So why *is* the erect penis banned from general public sight in modern Britain? Whatever answer is given – there does not seem to be one single reason – it will lead us into all sorts of ideas about sexuality and society. It might be because the lawyers were all men of a certain age and class. It might be because the erection is thought to be a clear sign of desire, in contrast to art, which veils desire. It might be that this is the one most embarrassing thing for men to have displayed. It might be that young children would ask funny questions. What the amazing difference between the ancient world and us reveals is how hard it is to get a clear picture of exactly why we do what we do with images of the body, and what it says about who we are.

3

The Female Body –
Soft and Spongy, Shaved and Coy

This has been a very male story so far. In part, this reflects the ancient material, where almost every writer, painter and sculptor was male, as were the expected or typical audiences for most of what was produced by those male artists. In part, a male emphasis is one rather predictable consequence of focusing on the six-pack and the phallus. But it should come as no surprise that there is also a narrative to be told of the female body on display.

The immediate temptation is to make the male and female stories parallel. That beguiling symmetry of 'his and hers' makes for some revealing pairings. In the realm of English censorship, for example, the law on pornography distinguishes between the erect and non-erect penis, with the added protection of a fig-leaf wherever possible. This has been generally taken as a clear dividing line between the acceptable and the unacceptable. But things are quite different and far murkier when it comes to the female body, and the hunt for unacceptable signs of sexual excitement. Like many a baffled man, the law finds it much harder to recognize the signs of sexual desire in a woman, and has found it equally hard to know what exactly to ban. If arousal is the problem, what is the physical sign of arousal on a woman's body? And what is there on a woman's body which could not arouse a viewing male?

Since the Second World War the boundaries of acceptability have shifted radically and become increasingly blurred, as more and more of the female body is regularly displayed in an extended striptease before a voyeuristic public. For a long time, one fiercely policed dividing line was pubic hair, all sight of which was earnestly airbrushed out of films and magazines. Here's one place we can see the immediate impact of Greek art on representations of the female form. The white marble Aphrodites and Venuses that fired the imagination of artists from the Renaissance onwards never have any pubic hair, although male statues, whether of men or gods, in the same realistic tradition, nearly always do. Neither male nor female statues have anything as vulgar as armpit hair. Ancient habits of depilation can always be invoked to explain this for women at least: women in Greece, we know, did depilate. Some also shaved their pubic hair into neat shapes, or at least some men joked about women who did. But modern artistic traditions have followed the ancient code of no pubic hair for women.

Female images descended from all those Aphrodites are usually bare. The story goes that the Victorian art critic, Ruskin, fed on such images, was so shocked to see pubic hair on his own wife on their wedding night that the marriage was never consummated. For many art historians this way of representing the female form without bodily hair is an 'idealization'. But it is also a fantasy which enacts a form of censorship. It's a distorting veil which makes only some things visible, only some things capable of being seen. The story of Ruskin, whether true or not, reveals the potential for anxiety, that constant handmaiden of fantasy and censorship, which runs through this habit of portrayal. We inherit some of the ancient biases about gender along with the Greek forms of representation.

The removal of bodily hair from these Greek sculptures of females is part of a more pervasive reticence. While naked male statues people the city and countryside of Greece from the earliest days, it was not until the fourth century BC, a couple of generations after Socrates and Pericles, that the first nude female figure, the goddess Aphrodite, was sculpted and put on display. The first naked statue of a female inevitably had a whiff of scandal about it: the people of Kos who had ordered the statue for their city's temple refused to accept it when it arrived. But it was quickly taken on by the neighbouring island of Knidos, and the temple which housed it became one of the most celebrated tourist sites of the ancient Mediterranean. The Aphrodite of Knidos was famous for its ravishing erotic beauty. Men were transfixed by it, and even fell in love with it. According to one all-too-knowing story, one fellow even tried to have sex with it, and, the story-teller adds, you can still see the stain of his semen on the marble on the inside of her thigh. It is a story designed to make a listener stare between the goddess's legs. The statue itself is now lost, but a Roman copy (Figure 13) reveals how the figure is poised as if the goddess has been surprised at her bath, discovered in her nakedness by the viewer. One hand

13. Aphrodite of Knidos

reaches out towards her robe. The other covers her genitals in a gesture which both veils them from the spectator and at the same time draws attention to the place concealed. Her eyes are turned away, coyly or knowingly, from the gazing spectator.

Where male statues stand full-square, open to the gaze of the viewer, the female statue acts out a game of veiling and revealing. Often the female form is draped in clingy clothes, or stands with wispy see-through silks as if in a wind tunnel. With a female sculpture, the viewer is always looking to see how much of the body is open to view.

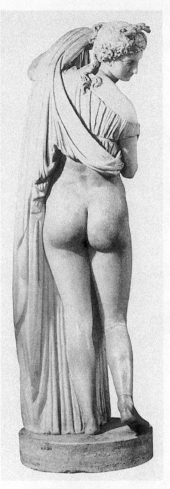

The statue known as *Aphrodite Kallipygos* (Figure 14) offers a different dynamic of display. She stands with her back to the viewer, and she is lifting her robe over her left shoulder to reveal her naked buttocks. The goddess herself looks back over her right shoulder to get a glimpse herself of her own rear. *Aphrodite Kallipygos* means 'Aphrodite with a beautiful arse'. This statue directs its own eyes and your gaze to the carefully revealed and highlighted feature. It needs the lifted robe to frame what is meant to be seen. It directs the viewer's eyes towards the eroticized part of the goddess's body. The goddesses Athene and Artemis are never depicted naked, however, and myths warn us that men like Actaeon who did see them in the bath, even by accident, were ripped apart mercilessly. Looking at Aphrodite raises desire in the viewer – but it is even more dangerous to see other goddesses disrobed.

14. Aphrodite Kallipygos

Displaying the female body, or staring at the nude female form, seems to be a different game from what happens with the male body. When we put the story of the censorship and display of the female body next to that of the male, the juxtaposition helps us understand both. The mutually reinforcing anxieties and social rules can be seen at work. 'Art' allows the spectator to stare at what would otherwise be unacceptable, but it also polices the gaze carefully. The sculpted or painted body treads a fine line between the desired idealism and a worrying realism. If the image of the body becomes too redolent of dirt, or of the messiness of actual sexual activity, it becomes disgusting. When a viewer looks, any awareness of his or her own body – and thus of his or her own sexuality, morality, mortality – needs constant regulation: society always worries about images of the body.

How exactly does looking at pictures corrupt the viewer? When does pleasure in looking become a darker urge? These are the issues that continue to haunt the West's love-affair with images of the body, and they are sharply focused as we look back to Greece's sculptures. We have to put the protocols of male representation next to the protocols of female representation – the man's erect phallus next to the woman's lack of pubic hair, as it were – if we want to appreciate just what looking at bodies means for us.

We can begin to tell a story of male and female bodies on display. But Greek society was fiercely patriarchal and any impression of symmetry between the representation of the male body and that of the female body turns rapidly to an expression of power, with men on top. This is nowhere clearer than in what happens to the female body in medicine. Men's bodies are trained by the diet books and self-control to produce the perfect frame. Female bodies have no such aspiration. As Aristotle sums it up, 'a woman is a natural deformity'. A woman's flesh is by nature wet, cold, weak and passive. She is 'porous and spongy'. (A man, of course, is dry, hot, hard, active.) Medical science's definition of the nature of a woman's flesh defines her condition as permanently inadequate.

Medicine is a master discipline for how the flesh and bones of humans are understood, and Greek medicine remained a model for Western science for centuries. Galen, the leading doctor of the second century AD, was the textbook in European hospitals even after William Harvey discovered the circulation of the blood 1,500 years later; the understanding of 'hysteria', for example, the woman's disease *par excellence*, was always dependent on models of the female mind and body that were deeply influenced by this long tradition. Medicine formulates our grasp of the body, and Greek medicine conceptualized the female body in especially telling ways.

For the ancient Greek medicine of the Hippocratic texts, a woman's body is like a jar, with interconnecting tubes for the flow of blood and juices, tubes which can be dangerously obstructed. So, if you want to check on the fertility of a girl, you should put a piece of garlic in her vagina at night. If in the morning her breath smells, it will show that thankfully her tubes are properly open and there is no blockage to conception. The tube that runs from the nostrils to the womb should be free of obstruction. This connecting passage explains why Greek doctors could think that a woman's voice deepened after she first had sex: the opening of the bottom orifice naturally affects the upper orifice. This link between the mouth and the vagina is still seen in the modern medical vocabulary: doctors refer to the 'labia' (which means lips) and to the 'cervix' (neck) of the womb. A woman's physiology needs scientific explanation – and science gives the reader, and the doctor, power over the world. Medicine is one way in which a woman's place in society is regulated. It changes how we look at women's bodies.

The canon for the perfect body is male. The male body needs regulation, exercise and control, and bestrides the artistic land-scape, four-square, symmetrical, perfected. The female body, a 'deformed man', is permanently insufficient because of its bloody, spongy softness. The 'perfect female body' is almost an oxymoron in Greek medical thought – and this dismissive asymmetry runs through Greek society as a whole. A woman may be sexy, beauti-ful, healthy – but her body is subject to the regulation and control of men. And it cannot form a canon. A woman cannot be looked at in the way that a man can. The inheritance of the images of the body from classical antiquity also comes with a social impact. It is an impact that is obvious in the art galleries and the magazines of today, but it is also felt on the streets and in the institutions of the modern city. 'Why can't a woman be more like a man?' sings Professor Higgins in *My Fair Lady*. The answer to that question and the very way that the question is put have a long history, for which the Greek regime of representing female and male bodies is a fundamental starting point.

There are good reasons why the body feels like the bedrock of existence for all of us. Birth, growth, sickness, death – the human being *is* a physical thing. And what can feel more natural and self-evident than one's own bodily feelings – pain and pleasure, laughter and tears? You can't fake pleasure or pain, to yourself at least. Yet what we have seen of ancient bodies shows how different societies have very particular views of the body, each of which seem natural to the people in their society, even if they can seem strange and even unnatural to outsiders. So what makes the natural seem natural?

Looking at the body through a classical lens highlights how ideas which might seem to be straightforward or self-evident have an enduring history. This history is interesting in itself, but, more importantly, it actually helps create the way the body appears to us. So it may seem just obvious and right that a man whose torso is lean, firm and lightly etched with muscles has a 'good body'. But it isn't obvious or self-evidently right to do so. After all, one might argue that to have such a 'good body' is actually a sign of the vulgar and unattractive labour of a working man, rather like hard and callused hands. We can value softness, plumpness and whiteness in a body because it is a sign of a life of leisure and thus of class, birth and breeding. We can also see the 'good body' as a sign of narcissistic self-obsession, because of the time and effort spent on getting that six-pack. The ambivalence expressed towards body-builders with their excessive, exaggerated musculature derives in part at least from a worry that to spend so much time working on one's own body is somehow wrong, both because of the obsessiveness itself and because the obsessiveness is aimed at one's body, mere flesh. Who really wants to be loved just for their body?

The fact that we think the torso of Apollo and the hands of a lord equal a 'good body' is a product of our cultural history. The longing for Greece in particular is a central factor in this cultural history. The Greek body has become part of our idea of the body. Rubens' idea of a beautiful woman has now become so baffling for a modern audience that it needs explanation. This is not merely a change in taste. Rather, there are interlocking histories of medicine, of art history, of sexuality and display, of social expectation and of religious belief, which together change the idea and ideal of bodily form. Ancient Greece and Rome have provided the images, the fantasies and the models by which this history of change has progressed. The modern imagination, consciously and unconsciously, is full of Greece. How we see the body is part of this cultural history, part of Greek myth in action, in us.

The bodies we watch in film, the bodies we glance at in advertisements, the bodies we read about in novels or in medical textbooks, the bodies we regulate by law and by convention, the bodies of grand art and smutty graffiti, of fantasy and scientific investigation, all these bodies of the imagination surround us with the images by which we live and love. These images are part of a history, a history which concerns how we see and understand the world. If we want to understand that history, to understand *how* we come to be what we think we are, we need to learn to see how that Greek body has continued to run through our ideas of self. Being self-conscious about one's body does not just mean feeling embarrassed about one's appearance. It can also mean recognizing how formative our history has been for us. This should change what you see the next time you look in the mirror. There's a Greek history inside us all, which makes us who we think we are.

4
His and Hers –
A Love Story?

Whenever a perfect body struts on to the social stage, the scene is set for the god of love to inflame the hearts of humans. Classical Athens, the centre of the cultural world of the Mediterranean in the fifth and fourth centuries BC, has always provided the picture of ancient desire which has most provoked later cultures to confusion, fantasy and distaste. The Romans found it alluring and distinctly unsuitable in equal measure; the Christians ranted and raved about its disgusting perversion; the Victorians averted their eyes, or fantasized desperately. Today the social norms and taboos of the Athenian rule-book of desire are less well known. But the question of how the Athenians loved is unusually illuminating for our own most intimate attitudes towards our selves and our bodies.

'Greek love' is a formative element of the Western imagination. There is no modern period or society in the West which has not looked back to ancient Greece to picture and debate how men love men. Sappho from Lesbos is a name which echoes with erotic force across the centuries. The story of modern desire, like the story of the modern body, has a history reaching back to Greece, and, as with the body, this history shockingly highlights both our difference from the ancient world and our inheritance from it.

'Love', the modern cliché always asserts, 'is the same the world over.' But it isn't. And the case of ancient Greece reveals just how odd and particular we are in the modern West (not least when we think we are obviously normal and typical). There is a fascinating love story to be told, and, since Greece will be the main setting of this story, it will be a tale of how men love men. But first I will

47

begin where the modern West always wants to begin: with the story of boy meets girl.

It is one of the quirks of history that a man who had premarital sex with a thirteen-year-old girl and killed himself not long afterwards should have become the archetypal figure of the romantic hero. That Romeo epitomizes the role of the lover in the modern imagination has rather more to do with Shakespeare's play than with the simple facts of his story. In modern culture, the name of Romeo – 'what's in a name?' – immediately evokes the tear-stained sigh towards a balcony and the search for true love across the barriers of social restriction and family feud. This is a story which has been acted and rewritten many times since Shakespeare's tragedy.

In classical Greece there is no equivalent story of the perfect or even the star-crossed young lovers. Classical Greece just doesn't *do* love like that. Even the couple who become the paragons of fidelity for later generations, Odysseus and Penelope, in Homer's *Odyssey* never say 'I love you', or 'I want you', or even 'I have missed you', or any other of the doting expressions a modern audience would demand when a long-lost husband returns from the war. Socrates is exemplary for the Greek husband, when on his deathbed he sends his crying wife away so that he can spend his last hours in discussion with his (male) friends. Monstrous and murderous passions distort the bodies of Greek tragedy's heroines, but never beautiful and delicate love. There is no *Romeo and Juliet* for classical Greece.

The Greek word most often translated as 'love' is *eros*. But 'desire' is much more accurate in most cases. *Eros* is a passionate feeling of attraction for another person. Or for one's city, or for food. When Plato uses *eros* in his dialogue the *Symposium* to express the highest philosophical longings for the Good Itself, longings which transcend the physical and seek the fulfilment of the soul's deepest needs and capabilities, it's easy to see why 'love' has usually seemed the right translation. And many Greek lovers use *eros* for their most profound and melting sensations.

But *eros* is not like 'love' in a Romantic or Christian sense. In a sexual context, it is most often described as a sickness, a burning and destructive fire, which is not wanted by the sufferer at all. As a social force, it can be highly destructive. According to modern song lyrics, 'love makes the world go round', or 'love is a many-splendoured thing'. For Aeschylus, the tragic poet, '*Eros* destroys and perverts all the yoked bonds of society,' and for Sophocles, '*Eros* drags the minds of just men into injustice and destruction.' Tragedy loves to show the violence and misery caused by desire in society. That *Eros* destroys is a general truth which tragedy displays to the citizens of the city. You can cherish 'love', but you should always beware *eros*.

In tragedy an audience might expect everything, including *eros*, to have a tragic ending. Elsewhere, there is that naughty boy with wings – Cupid in Latin, Eros in Greek – who causes trouble, strife and jokes at your expense. Experiencing *eros* is not dignified. It is a commonplace in modern fiction that everyone should want to fall in love. But this idea would most probably be greeted with a bewildered shudder by the classical Athenian – even when the sweet bliss of *eros* is recognized. 'Self-control' is the most prized of virtues, and it means *not* desiring to desire. It also means controlling the unfortunate self as much as possible when and if the regrettable happens and unconquerable desire does strike.

Severe and high-minded philosophers seek fulfilment in contemplation, self-control and deep thoughts. For less high-minded citizens, *eros* can at least be satisfied by a particular physical fulfilment. *Eros* does not last, or rather it is not meant to last. It can be transferred serially and easily to another object of desire. Consummated *eros* is satisfied and finished, whereas love – as modern t-shirts would have it – is for ever. *Eros* is a bitter-sweet, temporary, debilitating disease which makes the translation 'love' rather misleading.

There is one dynamic of *eros* in action which is particularly hard for a modern lover to appreciate and shows the difference between then and now at its most stark. It concerns the ideal of reciprocity. In modern society, to love and to be loved is a standard ideal of romantic yearning. A couple are meant to share equal feelings of passion, affection and respect. A Jane Austen novel requires the hero and the heroine to recognize that they love each other, at least by the last page. We want to walk down the street holding hands. 'Do you love me?' is *the* question in a relationship. There are plenty of lyrics of unfulfilled passion, but, from the knight with his damsel in courtly-love poetry to Fred Astaire and Ginger Rogers, such lyrics are preludes to the anticipated bliss of mutual and shared love. It is only in the later decades of the twentieth century that equal and shared *sexual* desire is expected. Love in Victorian novels takes different routes which trace the moral hesitations about female sexual desire found in Victorian medical writing and social thought. But it is still the case that a person who rejects the ideal of reciprocity is stigmatized – the 'seducer', the 'womanizer', the 'prostitute' and so on. Modern Western society privileges a mutual bonding over time – from young lovers to the elderly couple by the rosy cottage door. Till death do us part.

There is no equivalent ideal in ancient Athenian social or moral expression. It's not that ancient men weren't affectionate or weren't linked in mutual bonds with their wives. Far from it. The relation between husband and wife is repeatedly expressed as a tie of duty, obligation and respect. There is also a mutual expectation of support for the household, for which marriage is the foundation and cornerstone. The strongest and most uncontested imperative of Greek social thought throughout the ancient world is the continuity of the household. The family should continue, secure across the generations – and the security of marriage is integral to that. But feeling *desire* for one's wife can only be a tragic or comic mistake. As the later Latin moralist, Seneca, sums it up: 'to sleep with one's wife like a lover is as disgusting as adultery'.

The moment at which a proper girl is most attractive is as a virgin on her wedding day, and there are innumerable paintings on vases in which a beautiful girl is escorted on her journey to her husband by a little winged Eros (Figure 15). This particular drawing unfolds a circle of images from a vase. It shows all the stages of a Greek wedding. On the far left the bride is seated, being bestowed with attractiveness by a winged Eros. The following six figures are all bringing presents and adornments for the bride – five women and Eros in a little procession. On the right is the groom, the bearded man. He holds the bride's left wrist as he leads her to their new home. Her right arm is held by Eros.

15. Images celebrating a wedding, from an Athenian ointment pot

The god of desire attends the girl at each point of her wedding day. I say 'girl' because the average age of the female at marriage was around fourteen or fifteen, while the average age of the man at marriage was around thirty-five, an age discrepancy which must help keep the man in charge. At this moment, the girl was at the peek of sexual allure to the husband. But, after the wedding day, things change. As a husband, a man's *eros* may be directed to a mistress, a boy, a prostitute, and even – though this was much more dodgy – towards someone else's wife. Explicit and public declarations of passions should exclude your own spouse.

This is true even of the couple who most bravely strive to maintain their household and marriage as an inviolate monument, namely Penelope and Odysseus in the *Odyssey*. Odysseus sleeps with various goddesses on his way home – unwillingly, of course – and Penelope is beset by suitors. But for all their twenty years of suffering, and for all that they do go to bed together at the climax of the story of return, they never once express sexual desire or sexual longing for each other. They don't even use such soft-focus expressions as 'I want to hold him/her/you in my arms.' This silence is not because epic poetry favours dignified reticence. It is a thoroughgoing ideological stance. In Homer, sexual desire is always dangerous for a man, and, in women, always a sign of the corruption of proper order. When a man feels desire in Homer, he should watch out. The evil suitors of Penelope feel desire when they are being tricked towards their death. Paris, the seducer who brings destruction for Troy, is led by his desire for Helen. It is no wonder that Penelope and Odysseus do not talk of desiring each other.

The same pattern is true in the tragic dramas of the classical city of Athens. It's an axiom of modern therapy that learning to express desire is a positive and empowering freedom. But in Greek tragedy, every woman who expresses sexual desire, even for her husband, causes the violent destruction of the household. Any woman who articulates her sexual desire becomes a monster – from Medea, who ends up killing her own children, to Clytemnestra, who kills her husband. In comedy, there are many lusty men, and some even lust after their own wives – but they are, to a man, figures of fun, who are humiliated by their desire, led by their erect penises into scenes of more and more outrageous ridiculousness. For all the shared aim of maintaining the household through marriage, the hierarchical bond of husband and wife leaves no place for a shared and reciprocal sexual desire – at least in the explicit and morally charged world of public expression.

At the heart of the matter stands a particular understanding of masculine desire. The adult male experiences desire – but he neither aims to be, nor does he want to be, the object of desire. He may certainly wish to be treated with respect, honour, duty and so forth, but he does not want to be subjected to another's control. He does not want to be the object of pursuit. Self-control, that prime virtue, means being in control of his wife, his body, his desire, his household. If his wife, his body, his desires or his household get the better of him, he runs the risk of becoming a figure of ridicule, of humiliation, or even being destroyed. A man should not submit himself to another's feelings. This attitude is summed up memorably by a nasty little anecdote in Plutarch. He describes a man who is taunted by his friends because the girl he is sleeping with doesn't really care for him. He replies: 'When I go to a restaurant, I eat fish. I don't care what the fish thinks of me.' Snappily brutal, perhaps, but it captures an archetypal male stance. He is happy to be the subject of desire, and reciprocity doesn't feature. 'Do you love me?' is just not a Greek question.

This lack of reciprocity, linked to the hierarchical power relations between the genders, leads to a vista of marriage which seems particularly bleak to a modern lover. We don't have a single female voice from the classical city of Athens. Not one word of writing from a woman survives (apart from the occasional dedicatory inscription that 'so-and-so gave this'). The few narratives of female desire we have, all told to us by men, end in disaster or violent humour. There are no equivalent stories to the novels of Jane Austen, George Eliot, Virginia Woolf, let alone diaries or personal accounts. Tolstoy wrote that 'all happy families are alike': they don't *have* a story worth telling. So it might be wrong to generalize too grandly from our extant public evidence which is, after all, dominated by tragedy, comedy, law cases and philosophy, all full of unhappy families. But the public picture which emerges of male–female relationships, and particularly the relationship between husband and wife, makes for sobering reading.

Marriage – and all male desire for females – is depicted only by men in the classical city, and it is male concerns we see: how to be self-controlled, dominant, the subject who acts and desires, not the object who flees from an advance. The asymmetry between male and female bodies is lived out in the social expectations of Athenian men and women. The classical city constantly reminds us that the old couple by the rose-covered cottage is not the natural end-point of a love-story, however dominant it remains in modern Western culture. The ancient acceptance and promotion of a lack of reciprocity in love goes against the feelings of modern lovers, the feelings which seem most natural and basic. The cliché that 'Love is the same the world over' is a way of avoiding the uncomfortable thought that our deepest emotions may be structured by social pressures and expectations, and do not just happen. The challenging otherness of the past makes 'Who do you think you are?' an unsettling question.

5
Greek Love

For passionate poetry, profound and soul-searching discussion, great stories and self-aware and sophisticated humour, it's not to marriage we must turn in the ancient world, but to male desire for males. There is no area of Greek life where the differences between modern and ancient culture are more acutely felt, and more stridently argued over, than what's traditionally called 'Greek love' – or, less piously, 'Greek homosexuality'. Both terms carry awkward overtones today, but they are adequate to introduce an aspect of Greek social behaviour which continues to provoke furious debate and fierce personal commitments: for both individuals and for society as a whole, the status of gays is one of the most conflicted areas of contemporary social change.

Again and again serious debate on sexual identity has turned back to Greece, both over the centuries and in the contemporary West. In the late 1990s, for example, the Colorado State Legislature had a long formal debate on the state's anti-discrimination laws, and specifically on whether the legislation should include homosexuals as a category in anti-discrimination clauses. The court took highly publicized evidence from experts on Plato in order to try to find out if 'homosexuality' could be 'natural'. This produced a vitriolic row about what Plato might have meant and should mean for us. The state claimed that Plato and Aristotle showed that homosexuality damaged the family and that it was not in the state's interest to support it. Against that, it was argued that Plato, Aristotle and Greek society gave a quite different picture. 'The legal profession and the public at large', as the

Virginia Law Review put it, must be given 'the full and accurate story about ancient sexual norms'. For Colorado lawyers, Plato was an authority who mattered when it came to male desire.

This sort of debate could be paralleled from almost any period since the Renaissance. As with the aesthetes in Victorian Britain, many a flourishing gay subculture has idealized Greece, and, as with the Colorado Legislature, when arguments turn to the social value of homosexuality Greek society has proved the most significant model to debate. The modern West has found it extraordinarily difficult to think about male desire for males without invoking Greece. This is the area where it is hardest to find a space between fantasy and stigmatization – and where we find modern assumptions about sexuality most revealingly exposed. To describe what 'Greek love' is – the desire of men for men, its institutions and practices – allows us explore the more contentious issue of what 'Greek love' means for us today.

Standard Athenian social expectations provide the rule-book of how proper male desire for males should proceed. The man who desires is called an *erastes*, normally translated 'lover'; and he is a citizen. *Any* free Greek citizen can feel and express desire for males. The fact of desiring someone of the same sex doesn't by itself lead to scandal, shame or indeed to any debate at all – though mocking and sympathy is always on offer to someone in love. The sheer normality of this form of desire is in evidence at all levels of Athenian life. Even a politician appearing in a court of law can talk of his desire for younger men without facing the real or imaginary fury of the moral majority. As in a modern context, a politician has a vested interest in appearing acceptably normal. Here is Aeschines, a fourth-century politician, who is a married man, and acting as a prosecutor in a steamy sex trial: 'my opponents are going to ask if I am not ashamed that I am a pest in the gymnasium and have been a lover to so many boys . . . but I don't find any fault with proper love . . . Nor do I deny that I have been prone to falling in love like that and still do so today.'

For Aeschines, hanging around the gym, picking up boys and being an *erastes* to many of them is a sign of 'proper love'. It is, he declares, what the law says a free man ought to do. Socrates too, also a married man, is repeatedly depicted in Plato as swooning over pretty lads. According to one poet, in political terms an arch-conservative, a perfect day looks like this: 'fortunate is the man who is in love, goes to the gym, goes home, and sleeps all day with a beautiful boy'. A sexual relationship between males is straightforwardly normal.

What the *erastes* desires is an *eromenos*, which is usually translated 'beloved'. This beloved should be what is also called a 'boy', and preferably a beautiful boy. This means a youth just before he begins to grow a beard, but after the onset of puberty. What makes a boy beautiful is 'size' and 'stature', and best is a well-muscled, symmetrical, developed body. What stops a boy being beautiful is hair. The first down upon the cheeks is attractive, but, once a beard starts to arrive, a boy starts being a man and is no longer a proper object of desire. He can now himself play the role of the *erastes*. Bristles mark the dread turning point and are lamented by Greek erotic poets as the creeping and terrible loss of perfect beauty. In the Roman Empire under Hadrian, a Greek called Strato put together a book-length collection of erotic epigrams by many different writers, almost all addressed to boys, which play every conceivable variation on the theme of the coming of unwanted hair. Where English poets advised their loves to 'gather ye rosebuds while ye may', the Greek poet warns his boy not to be stand-offish to him with the crushing threat: 'there are such things as hairs'.

For the Greek man in the classical city, the desire which a free adult citizen feels for a free boy is *the* dominant model of erotic liaison. No other form of masculine contact has the same prestige, the same acceptability or even the same claims of erotic bliss. But sex between men of a similar age, especially when both are bearded, is repeatedly made fun of; or, with moral righteousness, said to be unacceptable; or, with more fervour, hated as just plain disgusting (whatever relations went on under the veil of privacy). The worst man possible, however, is an effeminate adult, who allows his own body to be used for pleasure by another man – the *cinaidos*. No one ever calls himself a *cinaidos*, and it's the sort of high-octane insult that can't even be a joke. You might snicker that all the politicians 'have been buggered' and expect to share a laugh. But to call anyone a *cinaidos* was a violently hostile act. You could, as master, have sex with your own slave boy, and even express desire for him, though the power relations inevitably affected what went on. Having sex with a male prostitute is not very dignified, especially in the eyes of your enemies, but the standard ancient worries about using prostitutes were not like modern moralistic concerns. Rather, eyebrows were raised because going to a prostitute might become financially crippling, or might demonstrate an insufficient self-control, especially when you are bad-mouthing someone you don't like. But all these other types of male desire pale before the model of the citizen and his boy.

There is a fascinating dynamic at work as the beautiful boy grows up into a hairy citizen. For the boy whom the man sees as an object of his desire will grow into a man – who is *not* to be seen as the object of desire, but must play the role of *erastes* himself. Every man knows he was once That Boy. As a result, there needs to be a great deal of care about the boy-who-will-be-a-citizen, an elaborate pattern of protocol and elaborate courtship surrounds the contact between man and boy. It's the sort of rule-book which the Victorians developed for boy-meets-girl – and, like that intricate dance of regulations, the Greek model of polite male courtship was worried over, discussed, followed and ignored with anxious propriety. From the first look across a crowded gym to the final moments of erotic bliss, these steps outline what it was like to be in Greek love.

The initial moment is always *eros* at first sight – the thunderclap of suddenly seeing beauty. Here's Socrates as the boy of the moment comes into the gym of Taureas: 'Charmides seemed amazing to me in stature and beauty, and everyone else seemed to fancy him, they were so thunderstruck and confused when he came into the gym . . . everyone was staring at him like a statue . . . and then I caught a glimpse inside his cloak, and I was set on fire and I was no longer myself . . . it was like I was captured by a beast.' The sight of the boy is a shared, exquisite moment of confusion: everyone fancies him, including Socrates, and everyone stares as if the boy were a work of art. He has the classic qualities of 'beauty' and 'stature'. A second more intimate glance at the boy's body beneath his clothes leaves Socrates helpless and on fire. '*Eros* drips from eyes,' as Euripides put it, and it burns and hurts.

It will need all of Socrates' self-control to show how doing philosophy can damp down the hottest flames of lust. The response to *eros* should be control. The next step of courtship is beautifully captured by Aeschines, with all the self-conscious self-righteousness of the politician in the courtroom. 'The law', he states, allows a free man 'to associate with a boy, to follow him, and consort with him'. That is, when *eros* strikes, a man tries to spend time with his beloved. He follows him round, hopefully to the gym and other social events, displaying desire by 'attendance'. That's not being just moon-eyed and sappy, though. It's often described as an educational process. The lover gives the beloved the benefits of his experience, and teaches him about the world. Proper love is all about self-control, and how to make the beautiful boy a good citizen (especially when you are in court). It's this sort of idealized talk that makes the philosophers so interested in *eros*.

There are many pictures that capture the process which Aeschines celebrates. Figure 16 shows a drinking cup with its images unrolled so that the whole set is visible at once. It gives a set of variations on how a lover 'consorts with and attends' his boy. At the bottom of the cup (Figure 16c) is a refined drawing of an older male. He has a beard, of course, a citizen's clothing over a bare chest, and a staff, often carried by citizens outdoors. He is reaching out to a beautiful youth who is also soberly dressed. The

16a.

16b.

Drinking cup –
men and boys
consorting *16c.*

man and boy are both holding hounds on leashes, and it is normally assumed that this indicates the context of hunting. Hunting is a male activity *par excellence* and it is one of the social areas where older men instruct youths, and they can 'consort together'. It may also be that the older man is giving the boy a gift of the dog, since it is a regular part of courtship for men to give presents. Figure 16b shows three couples. On the left, a bearded man with staff and cloak addresses a youth who wears his cloak around his whole upper body in a gesture of modesty. In the second couple, the middle pair, a similar older man is giving a less reticent boy the present of a hare. (Game, especially hares and birds, is one of the commonest gifts represented.) In the third couple, on the right, the older man is attended by his slave who leads a dog, and he is addressing a seated youth. The third picture, Figure 16a, shows the rest of the cup, which depicts similar figures – but this time on the left a single man watches the exchange taking place next to him. The lover is here offering money to the boy – the purse is clear in his left hand. To the right, another man offers a flower to a boy who looks away towards a leaping puppy – as he is in turn watched by a chastely mantled and upright young man. In Figure 16b we have three symmetrical pairs of lovers, where in each a man 'attends' a boy; in Figure 16a, we have two pairs of three figures, where the third man triangulates the scene into potential competition, potential lack of attention or contact.

Together, these images offer a repertoire of men 'consorting with and attending' boys. They are painted on a cup designed for use in the symposium. As the drinker turns round the images on the outside of it (Figures 16a and b) or drains his wine to see the image at the bottom (Figure 16c), he finds a carefully calibrated reflection of his own social interactions, here at the symposium where men consort with boys and attend on them. The cup shows 'proper love' unfolded.

It's not by chance that Aeschines' moral airbrush doesn't progress beyond this stage of courtship, at least when he's talking about himself. But many writers and painters do. The next steps in courtship are more physical, though no doubt accompanied in the mind of the self-controlled by a more intense care and reflect-iveness. After the gift, perhaps a kiss. The Greek lover spent much time plotting for kisses. This lovely epigram is attributed to Plato, although he almost certainly didn't write it:

> As I kissed Agathon, I stayed my soul at my lips.
> For the poor suffering thing had risen up, to pass through me
>   into him.

This exquisite conceit, that a soul can pass between lovers in the breath of a kiss, has been reused by generations of poets. Socrates is less sanguine, at least as he is portrayed by Xenophon:

'Good heavens,' exclaimed Xenophon, 'what a sinister effect you think a kiss has' . . . 'You are *thick*,' said Socrates, 'do you think that beautiful people don't inject anything into you when they kiss, just because you can't see it? Don't you realize that the beast they call "beauty and youth" is much more terrible than a poisonous spider . . .'

The kiss of a beautiful youth is a bite more harmful than the nas-tiest of spiders, and, if you take the austere philosopher's advice here, as soon as you see a pretty boy you should turn and run.

A kiss, a cuddle, will lead to the final step – what was known as the Business, or the Works – Doing It. But here, too, there is a problem. To what degree can the boy who will become the citizen allow his body to be used by his lover? How far can he go before losing that precarious grip on dignity and status, now or in retro-spect? The perennial question of how far to go is surrounded with euphemisms and hesitation. When a man pursues, a boy should flee. When a man asks a boy, the boy may, under the right circum-stances, 'grant his request'. The 'right circumstances' means a proper and drawn-out courtship with the full expression of edu-cational care. This may culminate in a single burst of bliss, that stolen moment. But what would 'granting a request' involve?

This is, first of all, where the asymmetry of *eros*, its lack of reciprocity, is most visible. The famous cup illustrated in Figure 17, painted by the Brygos painter, strikingly embodies this asymmetry. It shows a bearded man who, for obvious reasons, has put

17. Drinking cup by Brygos

down his outside staff and hat, though he hasn't quite lost his cloak. He is standing with a beautiful, barrel-chested youth, who has accepted his gift, probably of game, which he holds firmly in the sack in his left hand. Both are naked, and seem to be in an affectionate embrace. The boy holds the man's head and stares into his eyes. But where the man shows all the signs of sexual excitement – yet another erect penis – the boy, despite being stimulated by the man's left hand, does not respond in a similar way. Indeed, in all the many pictures we have, from the most circumspect to the most coarse, there is not a single one in which

63

a young man has parallel physical signs of excitement to his lover. Care, acceptance and even affection may be there in a hug, a look, a jump for joy – but the sexual desire travels in one direction only. This picture aims to show a citizen being a man, and a boy being a boy, in the *proper* way. The drinker can drink from this cup, and be satisfied. In the modern era, with our current anxiety about underage sexual abuse, this picture of Greek normality is hard to look at without feeling implicated. It's clear how different a Greek idea of proper sexiness is.

The final act of pleasure, as with the whole dance of courtship, is invested with expectations of proper behaviour. One move that certainly would be too far is oral sex. In both Greek and Latin culture, any person who allows his or her mouth to be used in such a way is thought quite disgusting. The scenes of oral sex on vases are usually orgies and often involve prostitutes, often ugly, often forced. It's simply unacceptable for a proper boy. But what might be most surprising to the modern viewer is that the normal form of Going the Whole Way is what scholars like to call 'inter-crural intercourse' and what the Greeks called *diomerizein* – literally, 'to do the through-the-thighs thing'. The man's penis is inserted between the thighs of his boy. In this way, no penetration of the boy takes place. In the high moral tone set by so many of the legal and philosophical texts, any penetration of a free boy would be called an outrage, a desecration. Figure 18, from a sixth-century-BC wine flagon, makes the final moment fully vivid. The central pair are coupling in what is the standard missionary position for Greek men and boys. The boy is upright and the man leans over his shoulders, knees bent and the position of the penis is very clearly marked as it is inserted between the boy's thighs. This is what scenes of intercourse between men and boys looked like. There are not too many of them on pots – courtship and anticipation is a much more common choice of picture for a man's drinking party. The artwork is rarely as exquisite or as careful with such scenes, and they are probably not the sort of pots that just anyone would care to put out on their table. What does occur on numerous pots is the inscription *kalos ho pais*, 'the boy is beautiful'. This is sometimes made more specific with a proper name, 'so-and-so is beautiful', often with quite a well-known name, celebrating one of the renowned beauties of the day. That's all

18. Wine flagon showing 'intercrural intercourse'

part of the display, scrutiny and wish-fulfilment fantasies that come with the territory of *eros* in the glare of the public life of the city. The 'beautiful boy' is constantly written on the pots and into the erotic lives of the citizens of classical Greece.

It is because Greek love is so different from any modern society's norms that it has proved such a provocative – and inspiring – model for arguments about what normal sexuality is. This elaborate world of courtship and fulfilment, beauty and longing, holds up a mirror which we, like so many before us, can use to reflect on our own culture's attitudes to sexuality. Whenever male sexuality is discussed, the case of ancient Greece insistently questions how we are to understand masculinity.

6

A Man Is a Man Is a . . .

Whenever masculinity becomes a question, the sheer difference of Greek men's sexual behaviour has attracted either outright moral condemnation or longing fantasies of the most idealistic type. Again and again, Greek love is dismissed as outrageous and disgusting; or it fuels dreams of a pre-Christian bliss of free expression. Both of these responses demand a black and white picture of antiquity. Greece is either the pagan world whose vices are rejected to produce modern morality, or it is the lost world before the 'mind-forged manacles' of society shackled desire. Both of these images of ancient sexuality are used to formulate and enforce powerful ideas about what is right and wrong for modern society: both use their oversimplified view of the past to bolster demands on the present.

Riefenstahl's discus thrower living on in the German athlete's body vividly shows the danger of such idealized and oversimplified fantasies of the past, since it is a fantasy with such violent social and political consequences. The pure white image of antiquity's manliness is designed to impress a demand on the present. But the temptation of thinking that the past is simpler and easier than the present can distort even the most genial discussion of masculinity. It is always another time and place 'when men were men'.

But Greece was nobody's childhood. Sexuality was already complex, tortured, funny, silly, confusing and difficult to live through. The rule-book may give us a set of social expectations. But any rule-book of desire is something that is played with,

66

knowingly or unknowingly broken, as well as taken for granted or horribly enforced. In contemporary society, after a century of the women's movement, a century marked by the pressure of war and social change, it has become a standard observation that 'masculinity is under question'. But, already in ancient Greece, the boundaries of male identity were tested, threatened and flamboyantly undermined. Proving yourself a man was already a fragile business. A more nuanced view of the perils of ancient Greek masculinity not only hinders the dangerous idealism of a Riefenstahl, but also should make us very suspicious of any modern claim that 'a man is a man is a man'.

One figure the Greeks loved to use in order to ponder how a man is a man is a man was the satyr. Myth may showcase the heroic male, but it also features these followers of Dionysus who have the hairy tail of a goat, an ugly snub nose and sometimes hairy legs and a goat's horns too. Satyrs are the most common of all decorations on pots for symposiums. They are usually distinguished by their phallic displays, and they do a whole range of things that men might not quite be up to. They are not violent destroyers of marriage like the centaurs, who have to be shown being destroyed themselves – as they are in the Parthenon sculptures from the Athenian Acropolis and other grand civic sculptures. Satyrs do carry off maenads, or try too, but usually they are outrageous in a more homely way. Figure 19 shows satyrs at the symposium. It's painted on a beautiful wine cooler, designed to keep the symposium wine chilled through the evening. The satyr in the middle is doing a balancing trick which shouldn't be tried at home. One of the most popular drinking games at the symposium is called *kottabos*, and it involved balancing a cup on a stick in the middle of the room; each drinker threw the wine dregs from his cup at it from his couch to try and knock it off. The satyrs are setting up a novel form of that game. (Many modern reproductions of this pot piously airbrush out the phallus of the recumbent satyr, which makes the image quite baffling.) It's a classy pot, with fine drawing and an elegant, jolly image. The satyrs have

19. Sixth-century wine flagon with satyrs

their hair neatly tied back in a bun, and the two satyrs who frame the central acrobat have their penises politely tied back. It uses the game, playfully but not perhaps riotously. But not all pictures are so genteel. Figure 20 shows satyrs in a more acrobatic orgy with each other. The image is far less well drawn, and the satyrs have more grotesque faces and bodies. This is not a party for tying back a penis. The figure on the far right, left out of the group sex, seems to be about to have his way with a statue of the sphinx, which remains inscrutable. This image has the satyrs do all the things that proper boys shouldn't do. Each turn of the pot, as the drinker drank, gives one more bad thing, joyfully engaged in. Satyrs are disruptive, and lurk on the dangerous boundary between the human and the bestial.

Satyrs aren't simply mythical, however – because men, good

20. Acrobatic satyr orgy

citizens, dressed up as satyrs. In Athens every year after the tragedies, there were satyr plays. These were short and often uproarious skits with a chorus always made up of satyrs – men dressed in hairy shorts with a penis and tail attached. The satyrs became embroiled in tricks, scrapes and escapades that parodied the serious human world of the tragedies. Furthermore, in many religious processions and festivals of Dionysus throughout the Greek world, men dressed as satyrs, and processed and cavorted.

In Figure 21 we see a man in a satyr mask, this time with a pair of natty spotted shorts to which are attached a tail and an erect penis. This citizen is dancing, hands on hips, in front of a large wine pot trailed with a Dionysiac vine frond. Men play satyrs. And there's the rub. When men get together and drink, when do they become too like a satyr? Satyrs are like parodic men behaving badly. They step on and over the boundaries of male propriety. But they decorate so many pots for the symposium. They are the constant attendants of Dionysus, who is not only the patron of the symposium's wine but also a divine figure who can make a man other than what he is – as wine can. The satyrs are at

21. Man in satyr costume

all the Athenian parties, provoking a question about the limits of behaviour. How freely can a man act at a drunken party? When does he become a satyr? Is *this* what we look like when we have too much of Dionysus' wine? The satyr holds up a sly, embarrassing, funny mirror in which the Greek man must confront his own body and his sexuality.

Some vases make this point wittily enough. Figures 22a and 22b are the two sides of the same pot – and together they ask a question of the drinker. In Figure 22a a satyr carries off a maenad. She has white skin, as women usually do, and garlands in her loosened hair. The satyr's excitement is physically evident, though it's hard to tell how much the maenad is resisting. In Figure 22b, a bearded and properly cloaked man affectionately embraces a woman. They look into each other's eyes and she too has a garland in her hair, though her coiffure is much neater and tidier. This couple are elegantly dressed. The two scenes are linked by the same vines, the same Dionysiac bower. So, as a drinker handles this pot, turning it round, how does he view the two scenes together? Is the affectionate scene of the embracing humans the

22a. Satyr carries off a maenad   *22b. Man embraces woman*

positive, affectionate view of *eros*, and the scene of the satyr the negative image, the horror of rape? Or are they linked more slyly? Should the pair be read together under the title 'what all men are really like'? Or 'one too many glasses of wine and. . .'? The images of this pot ask a question about how male desire gets acted out.

Satyrs, along with fauns and Pans, continue to lurk around in Western art to evoke a sexual licence underneath classical veils. Resplendent in his own spotty costume, complete with horns and shockingly explicit representation of genitals, struts the great Russian dancer Nijinksy (Figure 23). This is a still from his ballet *L'Après-midi d'un faun* ('The Faun's Afternoon'), which was choreographed to Debussy's music and first performed in Paris in 1911. This performance caused a scandal, and the police had to be called in to control the overheated audience. The raw sexuality which Nijinsky evoked terrified and fascinated the Parisians –

and helped make dance for a few years the most revolutionary art-form in Europe. The classical scene allowed the show to take place – and then pushed the boundaries until the audience were in an emotional turmoil. Satyrs are disruptive. They make the pastoral scene a dangerous place to dream in. And for Paris this image of masculinity was all too much.

23. Nijinsky as Faun

But it's not only in myth that masculinity is played with. Plato, whose anatomy of male desire is so influential, creates images of male longing as complex and layered as anything the modern novel strives for. *The Symposium* is the bible of Greek love, but there is no moment in it as memorable or funny as the account of what happens just after Socrates has given his celebrated speech on how the philosopher transcends desiring beautiful bodies by contemplating Beauty Itself. There is a crash at the door, and the drunken figure of Alcibiades stumbles in, supported by a couple of floozies. After Socrates' unworldly idealism, Alcibiades lisps an outrageous and transgressive story about sex which brings everything back down to a very much more worldly level.

Alcibiades was the most attractive and charismatic young man in Athens. The dialogue, written several years after his death, is set when he still had his career ahead of him, a career which was full of treachery, violence, meteoric success and desperate failure. *The Symposium* is set when this dangerous and mercurial anti-hero was young and sexy – and the story he tells is a shocking and frank account of how he tried to seduce the ugly Socrates. Alcibiades, as he tells us himself, was transfixed by Socrates' words, and was desperate to be with him, and knew that 'Socrates is prone to fall in love with beautiful young men and is always hanging around them and getting thunderstruck'– which is exactly how Socrates had described himself in the gym with Charmides. So he tried the usual routine. 'I sent away my attendant . . . and allowed myself to spend time alone with him.' But nothing happened. So 'I invited him especially to come to the gym and work out with me, and I went to the gym with him to try something there.' They exercised and wrestled. But nothing else. Next 'I invited him to dinner, just as if I was a lover plotting for a boyfriend.' At the second dinner, Alcibiades invited Socrates to stay the night. It is dark, they are together: 'I nudged him and said "Socrates are you asleep?" "Not at all," he said. "Do you know what I think?" "No, what?" "I think that you are the only one worthy to be my lover, but you seem to be too nervous to tell me."' Alcibiades' botched and clumsy attempt to bed the philosopher gets nowhere, as the seduction turns into a philosophical conversation. Alcibiades ruefully concludes, 'Nothing at all happened and when I got up after sleeping with Socrates I might have been sleeping with my father or elder brother.'

Alcibiades knows he is the most desirable youth in Athens, the

73

beauty of the age, but he can't persuade an ugly old man with a penchant for loving boys to lay a hand on him even when they lie naked in bed together. What is outrageous about this story isn't just the self-mocking or self-humiliation that such a tale necessarily requires. It's also that Alcibiades had to behave so badly. He had to behave, as he himself comments, like the lover and not the beloved. He is doing the chasing and the asking. He is being outrageously forward – and now he is telling us drunkenly, forwardly, in a mix of self-exposure and self-awareness, about his own badness.

Plato has constructed an extraordinarily layered portrait here. We are being encouraged to look back at the youth of a famously corrupt and opportunistic politician at the moment when, as a sexy and impressionable boy, he could have followed Socrates and become a noble and true soul. But we see Alcibiades himself also looking back to his younger self, when he tried and failed to seduce Socrates sexually. We catch – in retrospect – the drunken moment of Alcibiades' recognition of his own outrageousness, and yet his willing declaration of it – a turning point in the story of his moral decline. Plato weaves together sex and politics, self-recognition and self-deception, story-telling and philosophy, to create a deep sense of how complex an engagement with one's own sexuality can be. The transgressiveness of Alcibiades becomes a way for Plato to write a philosophy of desire.

The Athenian map of masculine propriety has its signposts and roads and fellow travellers, but finding a route through it on the ground can become a more complicated negotiation of traps and lures, promises and mistakes, fantasies and self-deceptions. However much masculinity is bolstered by rules and expectations, there is always some opportunity for a playful or transgressive shimmy round the boundary markers. We surround ourselves with images and fictions of men behaving badly to find the limits of what we find acceptable. We prosecute criminals. And we wonder at figures like Alcibiades, rich, famous, outrageous –

whose attractiveness and transgressiveness are so intertwined, and whose story we love to hear. When Plato becomes a key text in nineteenth-century homosexual culture, it is Alcibiades' wit, self-promotion and flamboyant sense of style as much as the transcendental love of beautiful boys that prove so alluring to Oscar Wilde and his friends.

The fragility of masculinity was an issue in ancient Greece as it is in contemporary Western culture. Yet all too often, despite the Greek sense of the playfulness and dangers of male sexuality, modern society has found it convenient to recognize no more than a simple, pure model of vice or virtue in the past. In the face of the complex world of Greek love, so different from modern norms and expectations, we should at least worry about the self-serving agenda of those ideologues of modern culture who assert so confidently that they know what a man is and should be.

7
Longing for Sappho

The archive of wonderful writing about desire and the repertoire of beautiful images of men's bodies from the ancient world have ensured that 'Greek love' provided a privileged source of ideas for how the West could think about male desire for males, and masculinity in general. The history of female desire in comparison is much less articulate.

The story of how women love women shows strikingly how misleading any idea of symmetry between male and female desire would be. There are no equivalents of the institutions of Greek love, which are basic to male desire. Where men have the gym, the symposium and other public spaces of the city to practise an elaborate ritual of courtship under the watchful eye of the society that supports as well as polices their erotic behaviour, women have no such arenas. Male writers who idealize love of boys describe female desire for females as horrific, immoral, contrary to nature and just disgusting. Even when the second-century-AD satirist Lucian writes a fictional dialogue in which a courtesan called Leaina reveals how she was seduced by a rich woman, Leaina is ashamed and embarrassed by the event, which is described teasingly for the reader, but with a vocabulary of disgust and prurience constantly threatening to break through the surface. This is another reason why 'homosexuality' as a catch-all term is unhelpful for classical Athens. Female homoeroticism remained throughout the ancient world a practice without a name – though with many an insulting description – and a practice with no social status except that of reviled and repressed perversion.

Indeed, it is impossible to find any example from the classical city of a woman who desired another woman sexually. The idea was familiar enough, but it was almost invariably discussed as monstrous by the few Greek writers, all male, who do mention it. In our historical record of classical Athens, with so many cases of men who loved boys, there are no actual examples of any real women who loved women. We can only imagine a hidden world of female desire.

Yet from a time before the classical city, and from an island in the Aegean Sea, one single figure does emerge from that otherwise silenced history, a figure who is a unique icon of modern culture's obsessive use of ancient Greece to picture desire. This is Sappho, and it is she who dominates all our ideas of ancient female desire. Some of her poetry immortalizes her longing for beautiful girls. Following the attraction of Sappho will bring to light much more than just the patron saint of women who love women.

Sappho has become an icon for thinking about sexuality through Greece despite – or perhaps because of – the fact that almost nothing is known about her. Everything we know for sure about her, when put together, scarcely makes up a biographical narrative. She lived around the beginning of the sixth century BC and wrote love poetry on the island of Lesbos, some of which is directed towards females. Everything else that passes for a biography is made up by ancient or modern scholars on the basis of her poetry, or, since there are only a handful of fragments and a couple of poems that can still be read, on the basis of imaginative projection.

The stories come in all shapes and sizes. She fell in love with a man called Phaon, and threw herself off a cliff in suicidal despair; she was a schoolmistress with a group of girls whom she taught; she was short, dark and ugly; she had a daughter called Cleis; she had a lover called Cleis; she was a poet who performed all the standard roles of a poet in the period, producing wedding songs, drinking songs, little squibs and searing lyrics; she was a poet who created a new feminine aesthetic, away from the masculine spheres of war and violence, in a new luxurious space of sensuality and sensitivity, celebrating personal relationships between women. The standard judgement of ancient readers was that Sappho was the greatest of lyric writers, the 'tenth muse', and was admired with a passion throughout antiquity. Her work, whatever the gender dynamics of its love-stories, was sung by men at symposiums for centuries, though it is hard to imagine exactly how it felt for a man in that patriarchal society, even in the playtime of the symposium, to perform her lyrics.

Sappho shows more than any other figure how modern sexuality has used ancient Greece as a mirror in which to find itself. She is a model of how the West uses ancient Greece to think about desire. Since so little is actually known about the real Sappho, she is a wonderful canvas on to which to project an image of desire. Three Victorian paintings will help make this process of projection visible. They are three images from hundreds which could have been chosen. Sappho has constantly been used to express female longing in a man's world.

Figure 24 is a brooding, full-length portrait of Sappho painted by Charles-Auguste Mengin in 1877, and presented to the Manchester City Art Gallery seven years later. Mengin is an undistinguished Parisian painter, but this is a memorable picture. Sappho, 'dark' as Ovid describes her, though not perhaps so short or so ugly, appears as a passionately moody young Romantic artist. Her left arm is languorously draped over a shadowy pillar, her right holds the lyre, her instrument and symbol of her authority. She stares with an inward gaze, her face shadowed by her hair and robe which run into each other, her eyes hooded by her brows. Her black tunic also flows into the shadows around her. She emerges into and from the darkness. This is not the Greece of light and purity, sunshine and rationality. This is the embodiment of a burning and dangerous passion. Since Byron, himself the archetypal hero of dangerous romantic passion, wrote 'the isles of Greece, the isles of Greece / where burning Sappho loved and sung', Sappho has indeed burnt and smouldered.

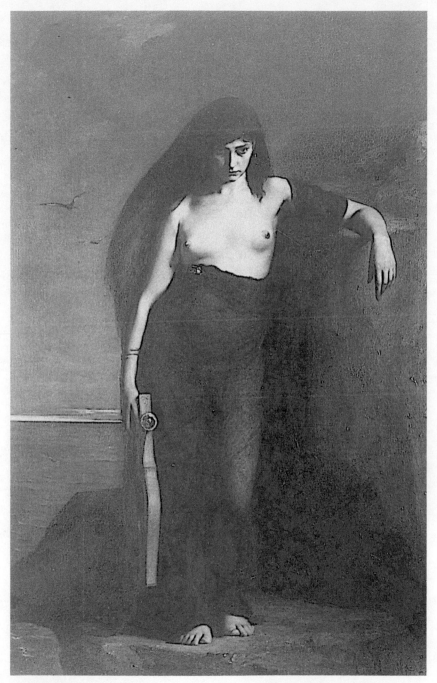

24. Sappho *by Mengin*

But in a powerfully erotic gesture Mengin has bared Sappho's breasts and shoulders, and allowed these parts of her body to be as brightly illuminated as the rest of her is shaded. It's not clear where the light could come from to irradiate her body in just this way and leave such deep shadows elsewhere in the picture. It seems as if the light from her breasts reveals what we can see of her face. This is a totally bizarre dress code, as if we are meant to think that this is how poets wandered about in archaic Lesbos. Mengin's dream of the Greek world and of Sappho's life lets the viewer gaze at the young girl's exposed body. The painting could be intellectualized as a metaphor for the passion of artistic creativity: the burning love in her breast is a passion which flares out, and puts light in her face, the mirror of the soul. But the viewer is actually caught in a more obvious erotic stare at the girl's fleshy breasts, and takes pleasure in the looking. This is a very sexy painting about a poet of love.

The second picture (Figure 25), drawn in 1841, presents a very different image of Sappho's passion. Here is Sappho on the top of the cliff, presumably preparing for her leap into suicide; the sun is setting into a no doubt wine-dark sea, and the poet stares upwards towards heaven out across the waters. Her hair has a neatly tied-back bun in mid-nineteenth-century style, from which a few strands have escaped in the most refined distress. She is kneeling in the familiar position of a penitent. Her hands are joined, not in simple prayer, but perhaps to indicate a degree of emotional turmoil or inward reflection to match her gaze heavenwards. Her dress is standard Greek issue, uncovered arms and shoulders, with the barest hint of bodily form underneath. What makes this picture peculiarly fascinating is that it is drawn by Queen Victoria herself, when a young woman. It's signed, dated and labelled 'Sappho'. This is a picture of the young queen's imagination.

Queen Victoria's Sappho is *really* Victorian. The image may hint towards contemporary fascination with the 'fallen woman', the archetypal seduced female who sank in society because of her moral flaws, embodied in her sexual error, until she has no option

25. Sappho *by*
Queen Victoria

but to kill herself. But this is a rather more chaste picture, a forlorn woman battling with love. The etching may have been intended as a private moment for the young queen, but it was also published in 1900 towards the end of Victoria's long reign. 'It will be hard to refine upon the poetic beauty and romantic intensity of Sappho as etched by Her Majesty the Queen,' declares the accompanying article. 'It is simple and impassioned.' It's hard not to hear a courtier's over-heated flattery in this art criticism, but it insists that this sketch is viewed as an intense and passionate embodiment of female desire. Like Mengin's brooding lover, the queen's image shows not the object of desire, but the desiring woman herself. Mengin's more lurid imagination contrasts all too clearly with the social regulation embodied in Victoria's Sappho.

In contrast with Victoria's etching, the glorious canvas in Figure 26 is by one of the great popularizers of a vision of Greece for Victorian society, Lawrence Alma-Tadema. Alma-Tadema painted a string of lush and often louche images of the ancient world whose decorousness and archaeological accuracy scarcely conceal the titillating fascination with corruption, decadence and

26. Sappho *by Alma-Tadema*

voyeuristic pleasure. In this painting of 1881 entitled *Sappho*, the Mediterranean darkly glistens in the background, beneath a brightly lit sky glimpsed through a canopy of pines. The scene is an outside marble terrace, called an *exedra*, set up as a small recital area with a curve of banked seats in two tiers. This area is decorated with small statues and a grey marble pillar (*stele*), and individual seating places are marked out on the benches with raised stone ribs. This sort of scene is typical of several of Alma-Tadema's luxuriant landscapes. He painted many a canvas in which an archetypal and dreamy love scene is enacted by a young man and a woman in Greek clothes on a Greek stage of shiny white marble and brilliant blue skies and sea. In *Sappho*, then, both poetry and erotics are cued by the scenery as well as the title.

The performing poet here, lyre in his arms, is Alcaeus, a man who is said in some stories to be Sappho's lover. He is depicted as young and beautiful and, as he plays, he stares intently across the performance space at Sappho, who sits resting her head on her arm against a lectern. She returns his stare with a dreamy intensity. On the lectern, between the listening female poet and performing male poet is a laurel wreath, a victor's crown awaiting a head. Behind Sappho, arranged on the marble benches, are three girls in various states of concentration, rapture and critical observation. A fourth stands behind Sappho. She is crowned with daisies, and, while she too looks at Alcaeus, her arm is draped across Sappho's shoulders in an affectionate and protective manner. The stone benches are scratched with graffiti, which spell out in Greek the names of girls who were said to be the lovers of Sappho – Anaktoria, Atthis, Gongyla. One of the few criticisms when this painting was exhibited was that the letter forms are inaccurate for the Greek of Sappho's time and place!

The sexual tensions of this painting are carefully calibrated. Sappho is transfixed in her shared gaze with Alcaeus. Is this erotic? Or is this a poetic rivalry? The laurel wreath is set between them, and the two poets are linked also by the wood of the lectern, Sappho's reading stand, and the wood of Alcaeus' chair and lyre, his performance space. This is poet face to face with poet. At the same time, the discarded golden drinking cup beneath Alcaeus' chair suggests a certain decadent ease. Sappho, however, is placed among her girls. The graffiti listing her lovers' names, set like plaques for each seat, spell out a history of poetical love affairs. The blazoned names and the protective hand of the beautiful standing girl suggest that, if there is an erotic tension here, it might be between the tradition which has Sappho dally with girls and the tradition which has her dally with boys. Is Sappho to cross the line between her band of girls and Alcaeus? The picture asks the viewer to read desire in this painting. Who wants whom and on what terms?

This is a quite remarkable painting, particularly for the Victorian period, precisely because of its rare ability to suggest – thanks to its classical veils – a tension between a woman's sexual love for women and her love for a man. There is nothing quite like it in Victorian culture. There are a few, self-conscious, elegant poems written by women who use Sappho to encode their desire, and these in turn look back to a longer, often concealed history of 'Sapphic' writing. But Alma-Tadema is a man at the height of his public fame. Other men who made Sappho's desire too explicit suffered greatly for their artistic freedom. The poet Swinburne lost his reputation for ever when he published the heady, sensuous words of *his* Sappho, desperate to put her lips to Anactoria's body:

> Ah that my lips were tuneless lips, but pressed
> To the bruised blossom of thy scourged white breast!
> Ah that my mouth for Muses' milk were fed
> On the sweet blood thy sweet small wounds had bled!
> That with my tongue I felt them, and could taste
> The faint flakes from thy bosom to thy waist!

Swinburne became ostracized for such erotic explicitness. (His taste for flagellation is as obvious in 'Anactoria' as his homosexuality.) He had once been the intimate friend of the classicist Benjamin Jowett at Oxford, but he died a lonely and broken man.

The only other picture I know which shows Sappho being touched by a woman is Simeon Solomon's small watercolour *Sappho and Erinna in the Garden of Mytilene*, now in the Tate Gallery collection in London, in which two archetypal Pre-Raphaelite girls, with long flowing locks and lush mouths, nearly brush lips in a kiss. But this scandalous picture was not for public viewing. Solomon was a renegade Jew, one of the most outrageous of the flamboyant group of aesthetes around Walter Pater and Oscar Wilde. He cavorted naked with Swinburne; like Swinburne, he was cut off by his family and 'all good society' because of his perversely homosexual behaviour and his risqué publications. While it was fashionable among the self-elected aesthetic elite to have a picture by Solomon on the wall, few outside that clique knew his work. It had none of the public status of a painting like Alma-Tadema's *Sappho*, and this emphasizes how extraordinary Alma-Tadema's painting is. In the heart of Victorian high culture, something is articulated on canvas that cannot be named. Through Sappho and her Greek landscape, silenced desire finds a voice.

Sappho shows brilliantly how Greece inhabits the modern sexual imagination. She is a figure through whom to talk about desire, to paint desire, to fantasize desire. The perfect male body of Greece provides a canonical image which shapes our vision of masculinity. Sappho has no one physical form – but the idea of Sappho provides the shifting mirrors on which a kaleidoscopic range of expressions of desire is produced. Sappho lets the modern world articulate and feel desire.

8

Doing What Comes Naturally?

In this ancient Greek love-story, two fundamental claims have been pulling in opposite directions. On the one hand, our inheritance from Greece is pervasive. The Greek body fills our mind's eye with images of how to be male. The history of sexuality repeatedly finds its roots in ancient Greece. On the other hand, the differences between ancient and modern worlds are strikingly evident, whether the British censorship laws are contrasted with the culture of display in ancient Athens, or ancient expectations of sexual behaviour are contrasted with modern practices.

This tension between finding ourselves as the descendants of antiquity and seeing antiquity as quite alien has often proved highly provocative, both to the policemen and to the baddies of modern Western culture. It's not simply that classical Athens looks different. Modern Western culture is always capable of dealing with what looks different: it calls it 'other', 'strange', 'baffling', 'anthropologically interesting', and in that way bolsters its own sense of self. Describing the 'not us' is a fundamental strategy for defining the 'us'. Wearing nothing but a penis-gourd is 'exotic', 'foreign' and instantly recognizable as a cultural sign that does not belong to us – except as a self-defining other world.

The trouble is that ancient Greece cannot be just 'the other'. It's one of those privileged sources from which modern Western culture derives its own values. At Plato's *Symposium*, discussing male love for boys, are a philosopher, a comic poet, a tragic poet, a doctor and a politician. We inherit philosophy, theatre, medicine, political theory and our beloved democracy from ancient

Athens. As Shelley announced: 'We are all Greeks.' Classics is foundational.

This tension was nowhere more strongly felt than in Europe of the nineteenth century. For the Victorians who wanted their Greeks to be pure and white, and who wanted to criminalize homosexuality at any age, the tensions between the idealized image of the past and what that past produced by way of art, philosophy, literature and, simply, behaviour was hard to deal with. At one level, the most common and proper level, the tension was actively and awkwardly silenced. E. M. Forster, whose books loved to probe the brittleness of English propriety, describes with amused horror the English schoolmaster translating Greek with his pupils, and solemnly intoning 'omit: a reference to the unspeakable vice of the Greeks'. The need to speak of the unspeakable always produces odd repressions and revelations. It's quite hard to know how much of Plato's *Symposium* could be translated under that rule.

At another less salubrious level, studying Greek and invoking the beauties of Grecian things became a coded way for a select group of young men to move through aesthetics towards a way of life that flouted society's norms and laws. Oscar Wilde intended to undertake serious research and produce an edition of a Euripidean tragedy before he became the darling and bugbear of London society. Defending himself in court against the notorious charge of gross indecency, Wilde argued that male love was the very noblest of attachments, a love 'such as Plato made the very basis of his philosophy . . . pure . . . perfect . . . intellectual'. That the trial's spectators erupted in a surprising burst of spontaneous applause for Wilde's ringing rhetoric made no difference. He was still finally sent down to languish humiliated in Reading Gaol. With the example of Wilde, the tension between Greek love and the glory that was Greece in the Victorian cultural imagination was forced into glaring limelight.

The provocation of the case of Greece hasn't gone away, however, and is still central to contemporary arguments about the social and moral impact of sexual desire. For those who wish to declare homosexuality unnatural, as it has been termed in so many laws and in so many insults, it is a troublesome fact that in the glorious culture of classical Athens, where many of our most cherished ideas and institutions started, many men took it for granted that desiring boys and having sex with them was a perfectly ordinary thing to do. Without the invented restraint of law and social regulation, it might seem, males will desire males. It makes it harder to call such desire 'unnatural' when it appears to be such a natural part of ancient culture. Even if it is believed that sexual acts between men are simply wrong because, for example, the Book of Leviticus says so, the example of Greece can suggest that the biblical rules are necessary precisely because without such rules there would be nothing to stop males desiring each other and acting upon that desire. As with the biblical laws against eating pork and lobster, we need a rule banning what would otherwise be part of what normal people might ordinarily do.

But, for those who want to call homosexuality 'natural', things are equally awkward. The reason for this isn't only that the institutions of male desire in ancient Athens are so very particular that it is difficult to see ancient Athens as a paradigm for the modern West, let alone as a universal model for the nature of things. The problem actually runs deeper. Perhaps the best way to make the difficulty clear is to ask the rather formal question whether 'homosexual' and 'heterosexual' indicate 'natural kinds'. Have there always been 'homosexuals' and 'heterosexuals' in nature, however different languages and societies function? Or does the fact that different cultures organize the way they think about sexuality so differently mean that 'homosexuals' and 'heterosexuals' exist only when they can be named, thought about, seen and engaged with? In short, are homosexuals and heterosexuals like the continent of Australia waiting to be discovered and named, or are they like football, something that exists only when invented, whatever anyone has done before with feet and balls?

It is possible, of course, to be more precise. The term 'homo-sexual' and its partner 'heterosexual' were first used by Richard Krafft-Ebing in the 1870s in Germany, and some twenty years later in English when Krafft-Ebing's work on sexuality was trans-lated. Krafft-Ebing, along with Havelock Ellis, Freud and many others, worked to produce a new way of thinking about a person's sexuality, which had immense impact on law, medicine and social expectation – which we are still living through. In the nineteenth century for the first time, as medical historians have shown, a pathology called 'homosexuality' was expressed: that is, there was described a psychological state which defined a person according to the gender of the sexual partner of their choice. For the first time you could *be* a homosexual – and could be treated, cured, punished or loved as such. In many places and times previously, sex between males has been recognized, enjoyed and stigmatized. Sodomy has been a crime in many places in the world, and indeed it still is. Men caught in such acts have often been humiliated in psychological and physical terms as 'soft', 'effeminate', 'unnat-ural'. There have also been groups, like the Molly Houses of eighteenth-century London, where men gathered for self-consciously transgressive pleasures. But it is only very recently that the authoritative institutions of law, medicine and philoso-phy have begun to work with the idea that 'homosexuality' is a human condition and a person's nature can be defined by homo-sexuality, or defined simply and absolutely as 'homosexual'.

This is an area of modern social thinking where hope and history, ideology and intellectual argument tend to become deeply muddled. The claim that human nature is constant can be heard every day: 'people are the same the world over', 'there's human nature for you', 'that's what people are like' and so forth. You can hear it on a much grander intellectual scale when Freudian psychoanalytic work finds unchanging patterns of human psychological development in the dim and distant past: the Oedipus complex in Oedipus' home town, as it were. The desire to find 'homosexuality' running through history is a motivation for some gay historians at least: to feel time-honoured provides strength and authority.

Yet it's also easy to show how arguments for an unchanging human nature have to ignore many startling differences over time and place, and also have to assume the presence of all sorts of things for which there is no solid evidence. For a modern audience, it seems obvious that dreaming of having sex with your mother must always indicate a deep-seated psychological worry connected to the Oedipus complex. Yet, for that to be obvious, it is necessary to ignore what ancient dream-books say. Ancient dream-books declare first that it's *how* you sleep with your mother that matters: what position you are both in. And, second, the dream, they deduce, will be about your political career and the motherland. Nothing to do with sexual character at all.

It is also necessary to ignore the fact that ancient Athenian culture had different expectations. When in Sophocles' play *Oedipus the King* Oedipus himself expresses a fear that the oracle might come true and he might sleep with his mother, he is told not to worry: 'Many men sleep with their mothers in dreams: it comes to nothing; they live happily.' It's ironic that these words are spoken by Oedipus' own mother with whom he has already slept and had children. But the utterance is not one that would fit easily into a modern tragedy – where calmly announcing that loads of people dream of having sex with their mothers and that it's no bother would probably produce outrage, bafflement or laughter. Moreover, the argument that human nature is always the same has often been used in a particularly unpleasant way to support a conservative agenda against the threat of change. 'It's because you can't change human nature' that 'women shouldn't be allowed to get an education, play sport, have a job, speak in public' (which are all real examples from the nineteenth-century debate on the so-called 'woman question'). The general recognition that 'people will always be the same' can easily mutate into brutal insistence in the dark alleyways of prejudice and power.

The tension between these two principles – on the one hand,

that human nature is constructed in and by society, and, on the other, that human nature has its essential and unchanging characteristics – is not likely to be resolved, at least to everyone's satisfaction. But what makes the case of classical Athens so stimulating is the way in which it throws down such a challenge to that Victorian idea of 'homosexuality' as a defining pathology of a human being – and to its modern heirs. For in Athens sex between males isn't *one* sort of moral, social or even physical thing, and certainly doesn't imply one sort of psychological condition. There is little doubt that some adult males have sexual relationships with each other. When such relationships were known about, or fantasized about, they were derided, often viciously. It was a model held up to be scorned as not proper and even as unnatural. Worst of all was the *cinaidos*, the man who took pleasure in being used sexually, and the character of a *cinaidos* was in all ways corrupt. But the *cinaidos* is a derided extreme at one far end of the scale of things, who stands to proper love between males as a crack-addict to wine-tasting. And proper love, with all its spinning of the rules of courtship, and all its care for the noble soul of the freeborn youth, was a practice and pleasure fully accepted in society. Acceptability, normality, naturalness are not defined by the fact that it is between males that desire flares into existence. You can't *be* 'a homosexual' or 'gay' in ancient Athens.

This explains why arguments about 'Greek love' tend to be so heated and prompt such strong attachments. Conversations about sexual behaviour don't get very far before 'the natural' or 'the normal' comes up. But the example of Greece provokes a real and disturbing worry. To what degree are our cherished ideas of nature inevitably just one culture's self-defining beliefs? To what degree can any cultural rules be based on a solid principle of 'the natural'? 'Just doing what comes naturally' is a fine line in a song but doesn't make much of a motto for a reflective life. Unless we can start to analyse these ideas of the natural within a history which we are all still living through, we are destined merely to live out a set of inherited but unconsidered myths.

'Greek love' should make you think again about what 'natural' means, where you need to look to find it – and how hard it is to look at such ideas critically. Sexuality and the natural are inevitably part of any notion of identity. The case of Greece will always add a question mark to who you think you are.

II

WHERE DO YOU THINK YOU ARE GOING?

I

The Empire of Religion

Even the most committed atheist must recognize that a huge amount of the art and music which are fundamental to Western culture is fully embedded in the traditions of the Judeo-Christian West. From Bach's *B Minor Mass* to Messiaen's *Quartet for the End of Time*, from the Sistine Chapel to the figure of Christ above Rio de Janeiro, to approach such great works of art without a grounding in the passions and arguments and stories that produced them will inevitably mean that much of their significance and power is lost. To read Milton's *Paradise Lost* without the Bible is obviously crass; but even a novelist like George Eliot who so struggles with her religion, or a playwright such as Ibsen with his obsessive anti-clerical thinking, will be eviscerated for the reader who is cut off from the intellectual fervour that motivates the writing. Without a grounding in the Bible and its religious force, much of the art, music and writing of Western culture will become little more than familiar postcards on a tourist trip of the past.

To approach the great artistic and philosophical tradition of Western culture without understanding its long engagement with Christianity is to be destined to superficiality. Yet to try to understand Christianity without appreciating its long and passionate involvement with Greek and Latin language and society is no less superficial. As T. S. Eliot demanded, 'readers who wish to see a Christian civilisation survive' must acknowledge 'the importance of the study of Latin and Greek'. For Eliot, the continuing existence of Christian civilization depends on a commitment to studying classics.

This is a stark argument. But Christianity came into existence in the culture of classical antiquity, and Eliot saw that its birth and development cannot be understood except in that historical context. For him, the attacks on classical education fashionable in his day had damaging consequences for our ability to comprehend the religion that meant so much to him personally and for what he understood by society. In fact, Eliot's worry has been sufficiently fulfilled that for many people today it may seem surprising to find a discussion of Christianity in a book on why classics matters. Although Christianity, like all religions, places immense weight on a full understanding of its genesis, contemporary education finds it all too easy to forget that Christianity began in classical antiquity, and that the first four centuries of its development, its foundational years, occurred during the Roman Empire. Christianity simply is a classical subject.

Christians have often declared themselves to be wholly different from 'pagans' – and there is now an institutional divide between studying classics and studying the early Church. But a figure such as St Ambrose shows how misleading such a divide will always be. He is one of the four Doctors of the Catholic Church, the saint who baptized St Augustine into the Church. He is a tremendously influential and revered father of the Christian religion. But Ambrose spent many years as an extremely successful Roman administrator and government official. It is something of a shock to modern preconceptions that he converted to Christianity only when he was appointed Bishop of Milan, a position of enormous power. Christians were much harder to tell apart from Romans than some later Christians would have us believe. The Roman Empire became Christian, but Christianity in the process took on the form of the Roman Empire.

Indeed, the vast majority of influential early Christians grew up in Greek and Roman cities, were educated in Greek and Roman culture, and lived their lives in Greek and Roman institutions. They spoke Greek and Latin, read Greek and Latin writers and were surrounded by Greek and Latin architecture – the architecture of the mind as well as of cities. It should be no surprise that early Christianity is fully a part of the classical culture of the Roman Empire.

This is a history which impacts on all of us today, Christian and non-Christian, at the most fundamental level of our lives. But it may not be easy to appreciate at first glance. Because more and more people over the last century throughout the West have turned away from Christianity as a regime of worship and as a dominant moral authority, the formation of early Christianity might seem like an increasingly irrelevant past, even though most modern Western countries are still identified as Christian. (In the case of England, the connection of Church and state makes this formally true; in other European countries and in America, the linkage is not constitutional, but is often even more strongly felt.) The impact of this history is fundamental even in secularized society, however, because the most general values promoted by Christianity have become so fully incorporated into a modern way of life that they have come to seem the familiar and traditional values of society itself. Many of our most basic assumptions derive from this history, and their power over us arises precisely because we take them for granted.

It was Christians, for example, who proposed that marriage was a sacrament that should last for ever. The modern ideal of a happy marriage 'till death us do part', and the consequent stigma of divorce or remarriage is the product of Christianity's influence. The idea that a man should have sex only with his wife, and that any other form of sex constitutes infidelity or adultery or immorality is also not Roman, Greek, Jewish but Christian, and this forms the basis of modern ideas of faithfulness in relationships. All societies find some form of sexual activity unacceptable or disgusting; but the idea that flesh and sex itself are somehow dirty – an idea that underlies so much modern guilt, prurience and prudishness – is also largely a Christian inheritance.

All of us have this Christian, classical history inside us. Even someone who has no intention of getting married in a Christian church will recognize these basic, inherited values as a social norm. Many people, whether Christian or not, still want to get married, to have a marriage that lasts, with a faithful partner, and think that these values matter. Yet it is precisely in these most basic areas of life – marriage, family relationships, sexual morality – where the tensions of social change are most sharply felt in contemporary society. How marriage should function is a pressing social and personal question. These principles by which life is lived have a Christian history – and it's that history which makes them what they are today. The more these principles are challenged in modern society, the more important it is for all of us to understand where they come from and how they have such power. This project is the shared enterprise of any contemporary man or woman who is trying to find their way in the society of today.

Christianity began as a minor, rebellious sect of Judaism in the Roman province of Judaea. At first, all those who thought of themselves as Christian also continued to practise as active Jews. This situation changed in the second half of the first century AD, when Paul began his attempt to convert non-Jews with his 'Mission to the Gentiles'. Small groups of self-appointed Christians started to grow around the Mediterranean, focused often on the larger cities like Rome, where an infrastructure of authority formed. Different writers struggled to express what it meant to be Christian, and, through the second century, argued fiercely among themselves, often with vitriolic accusations of heresy and with equally strong self-righteous statements of piety.

When a few Christians began to cause trouble for the Roman authorities, they were put to death by the usual suspects in the usual way. Some were sent by magistrates to the arena where the gladiators fought; others were crucified, a regular punishment for slaves and other low life. More bizarre punishments, too, were chosen – Romans were excellent at devising unusual tortures. These victims were taken up as martyrs. A martyr is literally a 'witness', and bearing witness to a belief in a Christian God by being prepared to die for that belief became one of the exemplary images of early Christianity. A cause needs its martyrs. In Egypt from the 270s onwards, ascetic groups retreated into the desert to live apart from Roman society. These Desert Fathers are the founders of the Monastic movement, and St Anthony, who retreated to a desert in 270, is their founder and leading light. A cause needs its heroes and saints, too.

Gradually, through the third and fourth centuries Christianity became a more and more publicly evident religion – there was a growing number of people involved and they expressed themselves in a more organized way. This was a crucial turning point. To the local authorities, Christians became increasingly worrying because of their disturbing and disruptive obstreperousness. In the second century, only a tiny percentage of the Roman Empire had been Christian. It was beneath the notice of the authorities. At the end of the third century, they were numerous enough to deserve at least the violent attention of the Roman government, in what Christians call the 'persecutions'. Like the earlier martyrdoms, the persecutions increased the Church's sense of embattled heroism, and strengthened their self-identity as a group. The most significant of these persecutions ('The Great Persecution') began in 303, when the emperor called for the destruction of churches, the burning of holy books and the removal of Christians from positions of rank and privilege.

Yet, in an astounding turnaround by 312, the Emperor Constantine himself had converted to Christianity, and the Empire became formally Christian. Like Paul on the road to Damascus, it's an iconic story of seeing the light. Constantine was said to have seen a flaming cross in the sky before a battle, with the words 'in hoc signo vincas' ('under this sign/banner you will triumph'), and he converted on the spot. The politics on the ground are likely to have been more complex and pragmatic. There were already a significant number of Christians among the Roman elite, and the continuation of the vast apparatus of Empire meant that it was possible for many officials to live their lives as Christians much as they had lived as traditional Romans. None the less, the conversion of the head of state was crucial to the development of the Christian Empire. The military and political power of Rome now worked to support the new religion, and the emperor's conversion supplied a massive symbolic authority for Christians within the system and beyond.

The emperor may have declared the Empire Christian, but there was still plenty of time for backsliding. Julian the Apostate, when he became sole emperor in 361, reverted to pagan religion and re-established many cults; many Romans had been slow to follow Constantine, and remained so. There were still huge and violent debates over what the beliefs and practices of orthodox Christianity should be. Christians killed each other out of principle and there is a stirring list of destroyed alternatives, made heretical by the victory of what became orthodoxy – Pelagians, Gnostics, Arians, Montanists, Marcionists. From the end of the fourth century onwards, the Roman Empire was fully a Christian empire, and its administrative organization was staffed by Christians. The lonely ascetics of the desert had become the administrators of a vast civic system. From now on the embattled arguments about how to be Christian take place from within the power structures of a great institution.

The history of early Christianity has always been a history to argue over – and sometimes to kill for, and much more could be added to this brief account to give a more developed picture. But what is clear is that Christianity at each twist and turn of this complicated narrative developed in and against classical culture. It first found its force by deliberately turning upside down the classical culture in which it was born. The radical, aggressive surprise of infant Christianity can be appreciated properly only in that framework. It demanded recognition for itself as an anti-classical religion. But as it spread it became more and more embroiled with Roman power structures and Roman systems of thought.

When the Empire became Christian, Christianity became Roman – the origin of the Holy Roman Empire.

Modern culture has repeatedly downplayed or forgotten the strange and extreme roots of Christianity: the self-image of Christianity today in particular resists its difficult and aggressive ancestors. But both for the practising Christian and for everyone else – non-Christians, atheists, agnostics – it is important to see how the dominant religious tradition of the West took shape within the classical world. It is nothing less than the story of the formation of Western culture. To forget Christianity's long and passionate involvement with the Greek and Latin language and society, or to forget the birth of Christianity in that culture of antiquity, threatens us with being mere tourists in Western culture. And I for one would rather *live* in Western culture than be a tourist in it.

2

Superstars of the Flesh

Simeon Stylites stood on a pillar. On the mountain ridge of Telnesin in Syria, north of Antioch, he stood for thirty years, night and day, in continuous vigil on a column sixty feet high, a living image of the crucified Christ. This was not his first act of suffering for God. 'In hunger and thirst, in heat and cold, continually, unceasingly, in supplication, without interruption, and standing at all times, he gave no sleep to his eyes, nor repose to his body for 56 years, night and day,' as his biographer insists. He had spent nine years in a monastery fasting 'in wonderful discipline and severe practices'; he had then spent ten years standing in a corner of the small monastery near Telnesin, sometimes in a cell. He next stood on a small pillar for seven years. Finally, he moved to the sixty-foot pillar, on which he lived until his death in 459.

This was a suffering his biographer revels in: 'He publicly fastened his feet upon a pillar, clothed mysteriously with heavenly power. The fleshly body of his feet burst open from standing, but his whole mind was kindled for the Lord. The joints of his vertebrae were dislocated from continuous supplication, but he strengthened his mind with love of Christ the Helper.' His action is a public demonstration of his love for the Lord, like a martyr. His fleshly body is racked and destroyed – his feet split open, his vertebrae dislocate; but his spiritual love is fired, and his mind full of religious joy. 'He was not afraid of his physical sufferings,' explains the *Life*, 'and gave no enjoyment to his body for even one hour.' A good Christian should be fearless in his service of God, and the devil's weapon is enjoyment or pleasure – that sign of the Fall and dread temptation to sin. The biographer continues with a lengthy itemization of Simeon's pains. His bones were visible from the standing; his stomach burst open; he lost his eyesight for forty days at a time; his left foot, filled with ulcers, emitted a foul odour and was alive with maggots. The smell was so bad that his disciples could not get halfway up the ladder to reach him. Even the ruler of the country begged him to come down. But for forty days and nights, a skeleton, unable to speak, he fought with the devil. As everyone thought he was dead, he emerged triumphant, cured, to continue his ascetic life. Simeon is a hero of suffering, a victorious athlete in the competition of pain – a *saint*.

Even his loving biographer imagines that someone might ask why Simeon did all this to himself. The instant answer is a standard theological one: so that 'by the distress of his servant, the Lord might arouse the world from the heaviness of its lethargy of sleep, and so that the name of his divine glory might be proved through the instrument of his believer'. Simeon is an example of the power of belief, who is to make everyone wake up to God's message.

But a saint was important in other ways, too. He also played a role in village society of the eastern Mediterranean, as a Holy Man. A monastery of disciples flourished around the base of Simeon's pillar; and local public meetings took place there, as well as visits from pilgrims. Simeon, when not in anguish or bursting open, acted as a kind of special magistrate to solve disputes. His status as Holy Man depended on the crowd of villagers from round about, who were transfixed by the sight of him, and used him as a resolver of conflicts because of his special holiness. Like a powerful landlord – but without the hassle, misappropriation of funds or potential brutality – the Holy Man could act as a mediator in village life. He was a focus for a sense of community. He advised on ritual; he decided on law suits; he sanctioned water rationing. He could instruct the priests and local bigwigs to cancel debts, to lend money at low interest and to observe neighbours' boundary markers. High up on his pillar, above the chaos of ordinary life, close to God, Simeon Stylites embodied a connection between the human world and the divine; and he used this authority. He was good for the community.

Simeon Stylites died in 459. He was a superstar in the roll-call of Holy Men, great sufferers all, for which Syria was particularly famous. These saints stood at the pinnacle of the new Christian attitude to the body. These ascetics, as they are known, were devoted to a disciplining (*askesis*) of the flesh. Through fasting, sleeplessness, prayer and abstinence from sex, they hoped to 'mortify' the flesh, to make the flesh *dead*, by destroying its fleshly warmth and moisture and vigour. In this way, a woman could *dry* her flesh to hardness, stop herself from menstruating, refuse pregnancy and become desexed. (The nun's only marriage is to God.) Origen, the greatest theologian of the early third century, found his own extreme answer. He was so desperate to maintain his celibacy and to conquer his fleshly desires that he castrated himself. It was the only way to subdue the erection, the physical sign of man's inability to control desire and to conquer the flesh. Like Simeon Stylites, Origen lived out the consequences of his theology in his body.

The Christianity which Simeon Stylites embodies was set aggressively against the ideals of classical culture. In the social contexts of the gymnasium, market place, bathhouse, army, theatre, the Greek beauty was a free citizen of a certain age, surrounded by his admirers, fully active in a social space. He was a youth who would grow into a man, and whose behaviour was always governed by that expectation of change. So Socrates could criticize his companion Epigenes because he had 'the body of someone who just isn't properly engaged in public affairs'. The body of the classical citizen *should* show how he performs his public duty as a soldier, an orator, a good man. Each man's body acts and is seen to act in this social sphere.

Simeon Stylites undoubtedly makes his body public: his

cracked and weeping form is a visible sign of holiness to the disciples at the foot of the pillar. But this is a new Christian body on display.

For the Christian and his body, struggling against Satan and his temptations, holiness is crucially an act of separation. The monk in the desert prays on his own. The word 'monastery' is derived from the Greek word *monos*, which means 'alone', 'on one's own'. The monastery is a paradoxical community of men 'on their own'. Christians admired the 'anchorite' who lives as a hermit, completely on his own, in a cell or cave, removed from human society. Sexual abstinence, a vow of silence, turning eyes to heaven, a regime of prayer, a commitment to fasting, are all ways of destroying the social links between humans. Even Socrates, the most self-controlled Greek philosopher, hangs out at the gym, drinks at the symposium and lies under the blanket with Alcibiades. The Christian Holy Man is exemplary by refusing these social bonds, those shared pleasures.

This gesture of separation was evident at every level. The most basic form of Greek and Roman religious activity was the sacrifice, a communal activity that led to a communal meal. The ritual of sacrifice defined the social group. It divided the insiders, the 'us', who participate in it, from the outsiders, the 'them', who are excluded. It might be a family event or a state ceremony or a guild of workers or an army of soldiers. But it linked that group together in a shared, participatory practice. If murder or some form of sacrilege had been committed, the punishment often specified 'exclusion from sacrifices'. That made the criminal a social pariah. One way in which early Christians publicly demonstrated their difference was by refusing to join in sacrifices. They willingly – and wilfully – excluded themselves from the community. Many stories of martyrdom turn on this refusal to participate in a sacrifice. It was not just a theological gesture against Greek or Roman religion. It was a public and shockingly aggressive statement of a radical separation from all that made a social group a community.

Christians did constitute their own communities, of course. They formed cells and sects and meeting-houses to pray together. They feasted together – and came together to fast. They praised 'brotherhood' and they formed partnerships by circulating letters and texts between different groups and individual intellectuals. Over the centuries, their institutions formed the dominant social structures of Europe. Yet from its beginnings Christianity also made saints out of men and women who rejected the bonds of human society in a passionate attempt to forge a singular relationship with God. This construction of the holiness of separation, based on an intense inwardness, remains integral to Christian theology. Christianity is founded on the inversion of what were the essential signs of Graeco-Roman culture.

The Christian also made himself or herself separate by deprivation. At the beginning of Lent, the disciples of Simeon Stylites sent him a pot of lentils up the ladder. At the end of Lent, they retrieved it, unopened. Simeon Stylites had gone forty days without eating. The ascetic's willing embrace of the ache of fasting is perhaps the most extraordinary of his many self-chosen deprivations, especially in the ancient context of this choice. The ancient world was always a subsistence society where most people lived with a permanent and genuine threat of starvation. To eat well was the triumph of civilization, a combination of a farmer's hard work and the blessing of the gods. A glutton is condemned precisely because of his disgusting and greedy appropriation of scant resources. Someone else must suffer to make the glutton fat. The connection between agriculture and culture was deeply ingrained in the ancient world. The farmer's land is the basis of what makes human life human.

The Christians who retreated to the desert presented a remarkable and difficult challenge to this way of thinking, this necessity of civilization. The desert is by definition the opposite of agricultural soil: it produces nothing. And the ascetics fled to this inhuman zone to struggle against their own bellies, by fasting with a competitive obsessiveness. The calendar for ordinary

Christians might alternate fast and feast, Lent and Easter. But the ascetic followed an unbroken pattern of deprivation. As he strove and starved for spirituality, the body became 'purified', purged of its own fleshliness. By fasting, he hoped, in the words of St Anthony, to 'receive a portion of that *spiritual body* which it is to assume in the resurrection of the just'.

For a thousand years or more, a Christian couldn't, shouldn't be fat. Fat might be a political issue for the classical Athenian: for the Christian it was a religious issue that imperilled your immortal soul. Today if you give up chocolate for Lent or eat fish on Fridays, or even if you just get the joke of Robin Hood's Friar Tuck with his big belly and love of food, you are imitating these distant but foundational models of sainthood, however feebly. Here's how one fourth-century theologian summed up the good of fasting – rather like a salesman extolling the powers of a wonder drug: 'fasting ... cures diseases, dries up bodily humours, puts demons to flight, gets rid of impure thoughts, makes the mind clearer and the heart purer, the body sanctified, and raises man to the throne of God'. With such amazing benefits from fasting, it is perhaps not so surprising that Gregory of Nyssa declared that the sense of *taste* is 'the mother of all sins'. The difference with the classical world couldn't be more vividly marked. Greeks and Romans loved their fish, their pickles, their cheese, an eel, some oil, well-kept wine. Terence, the Roman comic playwright, wrote 'sine Cerere et Libero friget Venus' ('without Food and Wine, sex gets cold'). He was recommending a nice dinner and a few drinks to help seduction and sexy pleasure. The same words are quoted with humourless approval by the Christian Jerome – but to show why fasting helps damp down sexual urges.

Sexuality was the other key battleground where the ascetic's deprivation aimed to bind his fleshly desires. The struggle for purity of heart in the desert produces extraordinary stories of temptation and will power. Greek philosophers had praised self-control – and Alcibiades could rise untouched from the bed of Socrates. But abstinence, the total denial of pleasure, was a dangerous and unpleasant extreme in their eyes. As the goddess Thetis says to her son Achilles in the *Iliad*: 'it's *good* to sleep with a woman'. But, for the Christian ascetics, total repression of sexual urges was the aim.

The difficulty was the inevitable inability of men to control fantasy, dreams or even the responses of the body. The erection, the wet dream, the unbidden memory, humiliated the godly. That difficulty proved the need for increased vigilance and effort. And still the godly were humiliated. Those dreams, those tempting fantasies, showed up each man's innermost state of purity. However much a thin body and holy look could signal purity, sexuality was a barometer of the most intimate, secret and telling fight with sin and impurity. Even if sexual behaviour could be curbed and sexual longings dulled, what rose up in the night was a constant reminder of a battle not yet won.

'I pity you if you are not thinking about sex,' writes one ascetic, 'because you must be doing it.' There's not much room for spiritual calm or grandeur there (or much of a choice). Stories of the failure of sexual control abound, from nocturnal emissions and lingering dreams to the more consequential slips of siring children, or of sexually harassing the novices. 'Purity of heart' moves easily into fear of temptation, and from there to misogyny. This misogyny can be expressed in brutally physical form. One monk is described as dipping his robes into the putrefying body of a dead woman, so that her smell would prevent any thoughts of women that did not reek of flesh and death. The chastity of a monk was a fragile possession, threatened on all sides, and most of all from within. Conquering Satan is a full-time job.

It is striking how radical this attempt to curb sexuality is in the context of Graeco-Roman culture, and it produces some extraordinary juxtapositions. Plato's *Symposium* collects together a group of intellectual men to talk about sex and desire in as flirty and funny a manner as philosophy can allow. Methodius, a second-century Syrian Christian, also wrote a *Symposium*, but his version is about a table of female virgins who praise the merits of permanent virginity. They discourse in a sober if keen manner, and intersperse their denials of the flesh only with the occasional hymn to chastity. We are not in Athens any more.

The Christians' attitude to pain also articulates their distance from the classical world. An ability to withstand heat and cold, hard work and danger is one of the qualities which the Greek citizen–soldier held up as an ideal. The Roman soldier, too, celebrated his hardness in the face of the enemy. But it could scarcely be said that pain was a willed choice, or that the destruction of the body was a desirable aim. Yet the Christian, in imitation of Jesus on the cross, willed not merely a body purified by deprivation, but also a body that needed and wanted suffering. As God made the suffering of Simeon Stylites an example for all humans, whose lot *is* suffering, so the martyrs in particular embraced pain to demonstrate their transcendence of it. 'Violent punishment is a pleasure' to the martyr, because to laugh at pain is to signal the triumph of the inner spirit over the body of this world.

The martyr's triumphant pain is adopted by the ascetic's discipline of pain and becomes fully part of the language of Christianity. As with all ideals, this early-Christian logic of separation and deprivation and pain was negotiated in a complex variety of ways. For some, the martyrs and ascetics were the elite soldiers of the army of Christ. They were the models which all should aspire to fulfil and reach towards. For others, the existence of such extreme figures made it easier to muddle along in their own lives without any such over-burdened expectations. For others still, they were figures of fascination or revulsion, curiosity or regret. In practice, disappointment, failure, guilt and simple avoidance played a powerful role in such negotiations – though, as ever, it's hard to trace the record of such intricate, shifting and often private religious feelings. The martyrs and ascetics remained fully part of Christianity's own history and self-assertion – however Christian institutions and communities developed. Every history needs its heroes, and for early Christianity it is the ascetics and martyrs.

The saints of suffering like Simeon Stylites are wilfully

extreme. But the most general and ordinary ideals of bodily deportment also shift from the classical world to the Christian Empire. Christianity invented Christian man by reversing the most cherished ideas of self-representation in Greece and Rome. It took the deliberately humiliating and painful punishment of a non-citizen – crucifixion – and made of it a symbol of the triumph of the new order. In ancient Athens and in ancient Rome, the citizen's body should be inviolate. It should not be penetrated; it could not, by law, be tortured, although a slave's body was open both to torture and to penetration. A citizen could not be flogged. A slave's standard punishment was the whip. The dividing line between slave and free was given this vivid physical embodiment. The Christian glorified the martyr's torture; and he so revelled in the body's violation that one martyr, as he is repeatedly stabbed, thanks his torturers, since now he has 'so many more orifices through which to praise God'. Far from avoiding the slave's whipping, some Christians demanded self-flogging – flagellation – as a sign of servitude to God.

The ancient orator is told to stand tall, to strike a pose that displays his own dignity, honour, status, position. The Christian is ordered to be humble. This does not just mean avoiding unpleasant arrogance. It means a self-humiliating, physical submissiveness. The Christian is encouraged to abase himself before the shrines of martyrs, to lie on the floor, weeping and murmuring prayer. The ancient citizen strides in the gaze of his fellow citizens, aiming for the splendour of success in the public sphere: 'Look at me,' bellows Achilles, 'do you not see how big and beautiful I am!' The Christian is ordered: 'Accustom your eyes never to look at the body of any person, nor even, if possible, at your own.' Exercising naked in the gym, relaxing at the baths, displaying the body – all of these standard and privileged signs of Greekness and Romanness were made impossible for a Christian community. The Christian should carry himself in exactly the opposite way from the striding, self-promoting Greek hero. This new body language – the value of modesty, the dignity of suffering, the shame of the body – has had a long inheritance in the West, and still affects every one of us. As the hymn still demands: 'All Christian children should be meek and mild.'

The culture heroes who became the saints of Christianity took the image of the classical body and redrafted it in the most shocking way. The biblical idea of the 'service of God' was crystallized into a notion of human slavery that brought with it the slave's abasement, suffering, humiliation and torture – but as positive qualities. Christianity does not simply spring up from Jesus or from Paul. Its radical newness stems from a precise overturning of traditional classical values. This is the beginning of Christianity's long and turbulent engagement with Greece and Rome. During its foundational centuries, Christianity means living out an *anti-classical* logic of separation, deprivation and pain to prove a love of God to a wondering world.

3

Sex and the City

Flesh and the Word

The haggard, anguished and longing body of the saint was one of Christianity's most potent images. But as the Empire became Christian, and the saint's ideals of solitary deprivation had to be accommodated to the state's requirements of maintaining and reproducing society, then marriage and attitudes to the sexual body inevitably became a particular arena of conflict. This is a history which casts a long shadow over contemporary life: the modern institution of marriage starts here. The way in which Christians reinterpreted the classical norms of family life has resulted in the 'traditional', 'conventional', 'expected' values of contemporary Western society, for Christians and non-Christians alike. Understanding how these assumptions developed explains many of the tensions and family troubles of modern society. It's a history from the Roman Empire that still dominates the choices and dynamics of modern life.

It would be hard to imagine an institution which has had a more profound impact on the social life of the West than Christian marriage. Not only does it construct the family relationships in which most people have lived over the centuries, but also it brings with it a set of attitudes about how sexuality functions in society, and how individuals should interrelate. Marriage is the cornerstone of society, which is why it is so often used as a barometer for 'the state of society today'. In the modern Western world, it is often declared that marriage is under threat because of the divorce rate, alternative styles of living and different versions of self-fulfilment. How we think of marriage is a telling sign of how we view our place in society. Now is an especially important time to try to understand why marriage developed the way it has – and what is at stake for us in its formation.

Christian marriage, now the most traditional of choices, itself began as a radical, alternative lifestyle. It brought with it a strange and threatening set of attitudes to how life should be lived and what self-fulfilment should mean. Its institutional formation took shape in and against Graeco-Roman culture, and within the political organization of the Roman Empire. The invention of Christian marriage is fully part of the first four centuries of the current era, classical history; but its effects are fully part of modern history.

The Anglican wedding service reveals this buried history vividly. It is a familiar, weepy occasion – from novels and films, as much as from life. The congregation is welcomed 'to join together this man and this woman in holy matrimony, which is an honourable estate, instituted of God in the time of man's inno-cency, signifying with us the mystical union that is between Christ and his Church'. We are reminded shortly after that matrimony 'is commended of St Paul to be honourable among all men', though the common twentieth-century rewrite of this original 1662 version replaces the name 'Paul' with 'Holy Writ', and drops the reference to 'man's innocency'. There are usually so many things to celebrate – or worry about – at that particular moment that those words are rarely attended to too closely by the congregation or by the bride and groom. (Although it's hard, because novels and films so love it when marriage ceremonies stall on the brink, *not* to anticipate a disaster at even the best run of weddings.) But the words of the ceremony actually indicate a nasty and contentious history. The modern marriage ceremony itself forms an excellent route into this bizarre story of radical social revolution from classical antiquity.

Paul is the authority, the Holy Writ, which commends mar-riage as 'honourable among all men'. Indeed, he does commend matrimony. In the Letter to the Corinthians, he says, 'Let every man have his own wife, and let every woman have her own husband' – which sounds unequivocal. Everyone should get married and be monogamous. And he develops throughout his writings a set of laws to enable patriarchal marriage to continue in a way which Greeks and Romans and Jews would recognize: the woman is to be subordinate to her husband, not just in marriage but throughout society. 'The woman is the glory of the man. For the man is not of the woman, but the woman of the man.' This patriarchal control goes right down to dress. Typically Paul demands that women cover their hair, while men can go bareheaded. At one important level at least – namely, his negative attitude to women – this religious revolutionary follows the most conservative social agenda. But – and this is where generations of intense arguments and considerable physical violence have been spawned – he introduces his advice to get married with this equally unequivocal and more worrying statement: 'it is good for a man not to touch a woman'. He wishes that 'all men were even as I myself', and committed to absolute celibacy. 'The unmarried woman careth for things of the Lord that she may be holy both in body and in spirit; but she that is married careth for the things of the world how she may please her husband.'

There is a clear league table here, and marriage is a poor second to virginity. A father may marry his daughter off, but it is better that he should have her kept as a virgin. Paul speaks to the authority of the father when it comes to a girl's choice. The father is expected to dispose of her. A man may himself marry, if he is incapable of controlling his desires, but it is better he should remain apart and, as Paul says, make his 'body a temple'.

It is unlikely that when most people hear St Paul and his Holy Writ mentioned in the marriage service they realize quite how selective his support for the honourable estate of marriage is. Paul does commend marriage, but he does so only in order that those who can't bear celibacy can avoid burning in hell from the sin of fornication. That's what makes it 'honourable'.

The Acts of Paul and Thecla, the story of St Thecla, shows what happens when girls do listen to Paul's advice. Thecla's life, unlike the life of St Simeon Stylites, might belong in a novel, and it shows Christianity's connection with the Greek world in a fascinating way. Written down at some time between the second and fourth centuries, many years after Paul had died, it is a tale firmly located in the Greek-speaking eastern Mediterranean, the world in which the Greek novels were actually written. Thecla wanders over the same territory around Antioch where Simeon Stylites' pillar was to stand, but it looks like a very different time and place in this story.

Thecla is a beautiful young woman of good family who is already engaged to a man called Thamyris. Paul is preaching in a house that belongs to Onesiphoros, a neighbour of Thecla's. She is seated at her window and hears Paul's words drift up to her. She is hooked by his talk of piety and chastity, and for three days and nights she sits in vigil by her window. The family see that, despite the fact that she is 'a maiden of such modesty', she is 'dominated by a new desire and passion'. A family row breaks out. While Thecla sits transfixed, everyone bursts into tears; her mother begs her; her slaves mourn her; her fiancé Thamyris is desperate at the loss of his bride. He goes with the magistrates and a crowd of citizens armed with clubs round to Onesiphoros' house and demands entrance. 'You have corrupted the city of the Iconians and in addition my fiancée, so that she refuses me.' And the crowd chants, 'Carry off the magician! He has corrupted all our wives!' Paul, here, is seen as the leader of some weird and sexy cult, leading women astray and disturbing the marital bliss of families throughout the city. That is enough to get him hauled before the proconsul and thrown into prison.

This is where the novelistic tone becomes decidedly more racy. Thecla bribes the guards, enters Paul's cell and goes for some private preaching. 'Her faith increased as she kissed his . . . fetters.' That dot-dot-dot is an attempt to convey something of the barely repressed erotic charge of a woman alone in a cell at night with a man, especially a woman who kisses chains. The generic expectations of Greek or modern novels, or modern opera, prepare an audience to think the worst. Indeed it is no surprise that a full-scale public row breaks out when Thecla is found there the next morning by her angry family 'as if bound with him in affection'. The 'as if' in that sentence is a necessary and hardworking defensive phrase. It shows we know the erotic potential of the scenario, but it really wants us to see such innuendo as the sort of mistake that would be made only by someone as wrong and foolish as Thecla's angry family.

Thecla is questioned by the proconsul, but she refuses even to answer, and just stands in silence staring intently at Paul. Here begins the miracle and martyrdom story. The court condemns her to death. Yet each time she is saved by divine miracle. The fire on which she is to be burnt is put out by rain and hail; the lions and bears lick her feet (and so forth). Paul is exiled and she escapes and follows him, like a lover who has lost her man. In Antioch, she is condemned to death again for refusing to marry, this time by being thrown into a pool full of sea-lions, but she is saved by a miraculous flash of light. She chases the apostle across Asia Minor. He seems studiously unimpressed by her, until, finally, in a somewhat anti-climactic close to the tale, he allows her to preach the Word of God, which she does until her death in her mountain retreat aged ninety-one. In view of Paul's highly aggressive opposition to women preaching, this might seem something of a remarkable event. But the story treats her mission as a reasonable and decent ending to a tale whose real excitement lies elsewhere – that is, in the highly charged story of marriage denied.

Like the heroine of a novel, Thecla travels far and wide to find her beloved, experiencing adventures and challenges on the way. Like a heroine, she survives them all; but she doesn't end up winning the 'crown of martyrdom', and certainly doesn't get her man. In fiction – whether Greek novels or Jane Austen – marriage between hero and heroine is reserved for the last page. It's what makes the plots tick, but is also at the very heart of the ideology of the society depicted in the novels. The household of the Greek world, like the 'family' in Jane Austen, depends on marriage as its cornerstone. This is what makes Thecla so shocking. She is *in* a novel, as it were, but the Christian narrative makes her deny the very principles on which the novel is based. By refusing marriage, she deserves to be put to death, in the eyes of the Greeks, because she threatens the whole basis of society: the family, children, inheritance, property. Thecla is, in Greek terms, profoundly anti-social – and that is what makes her a candidate for sainthood in Christian life. In terms of Paul's Letter to the Corinthians, she wants to be the virgin who cares for God, not the wife who cares for Thamyris. The sexiness of the scene in the prison may strike a false note, but it shouldn't detract from this Christian rewriting of the story of 'woman meets man'.

Thecla became a popular saint for Christian adoration, a model for virgins who avoid marriage. She appears as a heroine and an inspiration in many a girl's life-story. But what should a Christian woman do if she is already married when she sees the light of chastity? The Acts of Andrew, written at about the same period as the Acts of Paul and Thecla, give one memorable answer to that question. Neither work is accepted these days into the canon of holy scripture, but both were immensely popular for centuries. They are stories which changed lives.

St Andrew is summoned by the Roman proconsul Aegeates because his wife Maximilla is ill, and Andrew has a reputation as a healer. Aegeates, the husband, really loves his wife. He 'stands by the bed weeping, and wielding a sword in his hand, so that as soon as she dies, he can stab himself with the blade'. As a good husband, he is prepared to die for love. Maximilla is duly cured by Andrew; but when Andrew is offered a fee for his services he refuses money and retorts instead, 'Offer yourself to God, if you can.' This sentence begins Maximilla's change of life. Aegeates is summoned to Rome on imperial business, and Andrew becomes increasingly friendly with Maximilla and her brother Stratocles, who is something of a philosopher. Andrew succeeds in converting them both to Christianity and to celibacy.

Here the story becomes more like a comedy. Aegeates comes home and hears Maximilla praying, and catches his own name on her lips. He is delighted because he assumes he knows what the prayer must be about, and he lavishes praise on his beloved wife for her devotion. Actually, Maximilla had been praying, 'Rescue me at last from filthy intercourse with Aegeates, and keep me pure and chaste, giving service only to you, my God.' The reader – the faithful reader – is invited to enjoy the joke at the husband's expense. And the jokes and farce mount up. First, Maximilla refuses his kiss, because 'a praying woman's mouth should never touch a man's'. Then – and here we really are in a world touched by the strange excesses of the erotic novel – she trains a wanton slave to impersonate her, and for eight months, the husband fails to recognize with whom he is having 'filthy intercourse'. The slave seems happy enough. Eventually, of course, he finds out, and is devastated that the woman he has 'always revered as a goddess' has so misled him. 'I am in love,' she confesses, 'I am in love, and the object of my love is not of this world . . . night and day it kindles and inflames me with love for it . . . let me have inter-course and take my rest with it alone.' Again, love of God is expressed in a highly sexualized language, as marriage becomes the battleground of religious piety. It will come as little surprise that Andrew is imprisoned by the proconsul – and eventually Maximilla leaves her husband for a life of piety.

As with Thecla, the outcome of this story is the destruction of the family. Christianity promotes social collapse, in the name of what is 'not of this world'. Giving away property undermines the economic security of the household, and sexual purity blocks the aim of a family's continuity across generations. The family's normal commitment to the future is its own continuation through children and property. Christianity demands instead an individual's commitment 'to the world to come' – a radically other sense of the future. The story of Maximilla tricking her husband with a loose servant may seem funny, but the stakes are seriously high for Greek and Roman society.

Maximilla had been married for twelve years when her desire for purity led to her departure. She was leaving an established and wealthy Roman house. However miraculous Maximilla's and Thecla's stories may seem, they offered powerful models for women in real situations. These are inspirational stories to live by. Married women did leave their houses to become nuns – sometimes with chaotic results for the family – just as married men left home to become monks. Girls did choose virginity. In some cases, men and women agreed to live together in spiritual marriages where sexual activity would not be accepted – a solution Maximilla's husband resolutely refuses. Others remained married and strove to find piety despite, or through, the procreation of children. Each of these routes towards piety can be seen as a response to that double message of Paul – marry but only if you can't be a virgin. Every Christian, it seems, needed a place on this map of choices – even those who tried to muddle along as before, even the ones who tried to shut their eyes to the extremism and passions around them. Maximilla and Thecla are heroines in stories. Real life was both more messy and sometimes more shrill and violent than these tales of triumph.

Virginity, Celibacy or Marriage?

For a Christian woman, to make one of those life choices was a hugely significant decision. The 'virgins of God' or 'brides of Christ' were dedicated in the formal sense to a life of permanent virginity. Where Greek doctors saw marriage as the cure to a virgin's condition, Christians wrote a staggering number of treatises praising permanent virginity as the only source of good health – spiritual and physical – and attacking the sickness of desire and sexuality. These can make for quite rough reading. The flesh is 'raw meat' which is 'salted' by chastity. Salting meat is a process to remove blood – and blood is always a sign of corruption in the female. As the purity of a virgin's flesh will give the

Lord pleasure and her nose will take in His sweet perfume, so you can smell from a woman's clothes if she has fallen from the ideals of virginity. A touch, a glance, a chaste kiss from a relative, could reverberate through the person just as the touch of a snake caused the whole body to shiver.

So seclusion was necessary. Fasting and constant prayer were buttresses for weakness. One virgin had never taken a bath without draping her whole body in a large black robe. By the fourth century, chanting choruses of virgins were a normal part of a bishop's pomp and circumstance. A woman could demonstrate her faith and piety by a dedicated virginity in the church or the private home, and the virgins brought glory and religious fervour to Christian communities. In the form of the nun, this tradition remains perhaps the most familiar stereotype of Christian asceticism in the modern West. A girl who was dedicated to God in this way opted out of the traditional life cycle of ancient society, and was honoured by the Church for her choice.

Macrina was the sister of Basil, and she was born around 327. Basil is the founder of monastic life in the East – that is the founder of all male communities of ascetics living according to shared rules and established authority. Macrina and Basil were from one of the very richest families in the area, Greek-speaking and heavily involved no doubt in the civic life of the Empire. They were related to all the most important Christians in that region at that time. Macrina was given an exceptionally good education for a woman in that period, including a fair training in classical literature, though nothing as disturbing as Greek tragedy or as dubious as the myths of Homer. At the age of twelve, she was engaged to a young man of promise. But while they were waiting for the legal age of marriage to be reached – fourteen – he died. Macrina, contrary to contemporary expectations of someone of her class and wealth, made a decision to live now 'by herself'. She dedicated herself to God as a consecrated virgin, and took up the social and legal status of 'widow'. This new and unusual role – a virgin widow, as it were – led her to increased levels of prayer, to

taking up the sort of menial work which only slaves would normally do, and finally she retreated to the family estate at Annesi.

This was not the desert. It was a fine house, on a grand estate,
in beautiful countryside, on the far side of the river from a small
village. It was comfortably off, supported by bequests as well as
by family money. Here Macrina began to gather other women to
join her, along with her mother and her sister, in a pleasing life of
prayer and seclusion. She was joined by her friend Vetiana,
another woman of class and background, who had been married
into the highest echelons of imperial military administration, like
Maximilla. She – a widow – also joined the community as a 'dedicated virgin', though not a physical virgin, of course. Widows and
virgins came to Macrina to be part of an ascetic community, with
Macrina as their 'guardian and teacher'. Macrina was constructed
by her biographers as an ideal of Christian womanhood, and her
community as a model of women's religion.

The 'dedicated virgins', even those who had been married,
follow Paul's injunction to think of God and not their husbands.
But many other Christians continued to observe the need for
marriage, even at the highest level of the Church. Synesius, who
became bishop of the important town of Cyrene in North Africa
in 410, was quite clear. He wrote a public letter when he took up
the post, in which he laid down his terms: 'God, the Law, and the
holy hand of Theophilos gave me my wife. I declare before all and
bear witness that I will not be separated from her at all, nor will I
visit her in secret like an adulterer. The one is impious and the
other wholly illegal. I will desire and I will pray to have many
excellent children.' Synesius couldn't be more direct. He had
been married in a holy way: it was spiritually upright, and hence
he appeals to God as his witness. It was within the rules of the
Church, and hence he cites the Law. The person who had married
them was Theophilos, one of the most fire-and-brimstone of
bishops, a real power-player of the African Church – Synesius had
political support for his marriage too. But as he declares his decision not to divorce, which he calls illegal, he also raises a solution

that others may have taken. It was possible to divorce your wife in formal terms, but continue to 'visit her'. This – the behaviour of a secret adulterer, or lover, as in a novel – he dismisses as 'impious'. Instead, he will do what all good Greek men do. He prays for good children to continue his family line.

If we want to see the full symbolic weight of Synesius' blunt commitment to marriage, we could look for comparison to perhaps the greatest writer and thinker of Latin Christianity of the period, St Augustine. It was Augustine who famously prayed to be chaste, but not yet. Before he converted to orthodox Christianity, he lived for thirteen years with his mistress, a woman whom he loved and with whom he had a son. When he came into the Church and saw a career in it for himself, he sent his mistress and his child away, never to be seen again. But he still found it necessary to take another lover, such were the temptations of the flesh for him. Synesius can't really be called a happy family man. His hoped-for children died young, and he writes movingly of his own despair. But his publicly stated willingness to maintain his traditional household contrasts strikingly with the vacillation and difficulties of the saint, Augustine, on his route towards his life of piety, which he attained late in his career, only after many years of angst.

Augustine, once he had become a priest of the Catholic Church, imposed a strict code of sexual celibacy on himself and his clergy. He no longer visited any woman without a chaperone, and forbade even his own female relatives from entering his bishop's palace. He wrote some of the most detailed and impressive arguments to bring *both* marriage *and* virginity into the structure of the religious life of the Church – and through his extraordinary work the *Confessions* he remains the most profound explorer of the human frailties which sexual desire exposes. Yet when he writes that if a married man were to be suddenly ordained, then God would give him the grace required to give up sleeping with his wife, it is hard not to think of Synesius, who was suddenly ordained when married, but who just said no to the call to destroy his marriage in the name of chastity. Synesius, too, is an honoured father of the Church.

Such debates about sex and holiness, virginity and marriage, were always potentially explosive. The rise of Christian beliefs threatened the most secure and cherished values of Greek and Roman society and it is not surprising that so many stories of the growth of Christianity are told as stories of militant battles, violent persecution and martyrdom. The debates were also violent and passionate between Christians, and the infighting around sex and body in the fourth-century Empire was particularly intense. What could marriage be? Could a good Christian get married? Was it always only second best? Was only a life of virginity the true option? How should a virgin live? Could virginity be lost 'even by a thought' – as St Jerome declared in one rather overheated passage? Could a priest or a bishop have a wife? Should a priest or a bishop be chaste, celibate or a virgin, in order to be truly holy? These questions were not merely theological issues but changed lives. They made up the hard and fraught life choices of Christians for hundreds of years.

Nor have these questions gone away. The issues of the celibacy of priests, the role of sex in marriage, the intimacy of clergy and congregants, the sexual purity of a true Christian, are still with us. Regarding divorce and remarriage as a sin that society should not tolerate, the demand that men as well as women should have sex only with a spouse, and only after marriage, the very associations of sex with guilt and dirtiness, are the commitments of a radical Christianity aggressively opposed to standard Roman behaviour and expectations. The less such commitments are observed in Western society, the more confused becomes the relation between Church and state, between the life of citizens and the pronouncements of moral authorities. So many uncertainties of modern sexual life stem from this confusion, as the commitment to traditional values fails to appreciate its own history.

In many ways the model of modern Christian marriage, like modern Christian attitudes to deprivation, seclusion and pain, has moved much closer to secular, bourgeois ideals. Few today would find Jerome or Thecla the inspiration or monument which they proved for so many Christians over the centuries. It is because of this modern shift of understanding, this systematic silencing of early Christianity in contemporary religion, that the Anglican wedding service is so easy *not* to hear in its full and majestic statement of principle. It declares that, whatever has been said and thought over the first 1,500 years of Christian theology, whatever ideals motivated the founding fathers and mothers of Christianity, whatever extremes of celibacy have been celebrated by the saints of Christianity, none the less we are there as a congregation to bear witness that marriage *is* an honourable estate. And that we should read St Paul as confirming that assertion. The Anglican marriage service is taking a strong position on marriage and shouting about it. It demands that marriage must be a modern institution and not what it was imagined to be by the founding fathers of Christianity.

This is true of the rest of the first sentence of the service, too. The 1662 version also declares that God established marriage 'in the time of man's innocency', as though Adam and Eve were married. But were they? For Christians, the story of Adam and Eve is the tale of the horrific eruption of desire into the world which results in the Fall of Man. Before such desire came into things, was marriage necessary? Virginity and fasting were precisely the desperate attempt to regain man's innocency. Marriage was at best a second-rate attempt to control fornication. The modern service normally shies away from this controversial phrase and simply drops it. The service also claims that the marriage signifies 'the mystical union that is between Christ and his Church'. For the 'brides of Christ' *the* mystical union is between the virgin and God – truly a match made in heaven, a real virgin bride. This union too may be hinted at, but it's not really to be mentioned at the wedding ceremony. Marriage is to become just a positive symbol for the Church, without any of that sense of second choice to virginity which Paul and Jerome so strongly give it.

There are good reasons why the words of the wedding service

do not receive close attention from most people at the ceremony. It might be anti-social or disruptive to hear what is being silenced, or aggressively forgotten, when we put on our best clothes and agree politely that marriage is an honourable estate. After all, the white wedding is meant to sum up tradition and conventionality; and the radical politics of the family that is fundamental to Christianity is perhaps not a story to raise too pointedly at such an occasion.

Contemporary Christianity has obvious ambivalences about sexuality in modern society, and displays rather public difficulties about what the Church should teach and practise when it comes to sexual behaviour. Marriage, a white wedding in church, might seem the place where things are clearest and easiest. But the service is actually testimony to the long-running crisis in thinking about sexuality, which stems from Christianity's first attempts to distinguish itself from classical culture. Seeing Christianity's struggle to emerge from within classical antiquity explains the genesis of this still unresolved crisis in how modern life is to be lived.

It is a crisis that is still broadly shared, and goes well beyond those who are married in Christian churches. Everyone in today's society participates in the questions of how marriage should work, whether it should last for ever, whether having sex outside marriage is a wrongdoing, how having sex with many partners is to be viewed, what faithfulness means, even whether there is one model of sexual relations that society should encourage. These are not easy questions, especially for society as a whole to formulate a response. But it is clear that, without a historical understanding of how these have come to be the issues which now so concern the modern West, any answers we give to these questions will be superficial. If we want to understand the tensions with which modern marriage struggles, we need to understand that 'tradition' is a long story of revolution, conflict and change, a story which produces those tensions.

4

What's Athens to Jerusalem?

Where Angels Come From

The superstars of the flesh may have made their religion by radically overturning classical values, but classics was much harder to kick out of the minds and hearts of the citizens of the Roman Empire than they had hoped. Christians continued to live within classical culture as much as they were fighting against it, and they were constantly absorbing ideas and arguments from the Graeco-Roman world around them. The art and philosophy of Christianity, which so dominates European galleries and minds, owe a huge amount to their origins in the Roman Empire. Classics remained the history inside Christians.

One night, Jerome had a nightmare about this. He dreamt that he was taken before the tribunal of heaven, where the grim figure of Christ the Judge asked him to identify himself. 'I am a Christian,' he said humbly. 'You lie,' thundered the Judge, 'you are a Ciceronian not a Christian.' And so Jerome was flogged, while the flames of his conscience tormented him painfully. Finally, he declared tearfully, 'Lord, if ever I again possess secular books or read them, I have denied you.'

Jerome was an astounding scholar, who had studied the classical traditions of Greece and Rome profoundly. He is so ashamed – or so he tells us – because he has spent so much time in this sort of study that flogging is the only suitable penance. He tries hard to deny his own love of the great writers of Latin – though every page Jerome actually wrote shows how deeply he loved and had fully absorbed them. There is no simple, pure, original Christianity, especially for a Jerome.

This ambivalent relation to the culture of Greece and Rome courses through early Christianity. Its extremism stems from its willingness to turn the rules of Greek and Roman society upside down and inside out: rejecting marriage, the cornerstone of society; preferring the emaciated, pale and punished body to the buffed athlete; willingly striving for an anti-social world that could make a culture-hero out of a man who stands on a pillar for thirty years. This radical strangeness of Christianity provided the shocking, inspiring and difficult images and stories on which the religion fed and flourished.

But Christianity also had another way of talking. In the cities in particular, Christian men and women needed to be able to maintain a dialogue with the Greeks and Romans they lived among – and Christian men and women could scarcely avoid being influenced by the culture around them, even if they set out to reject it. They were after all still Greeks and Romans, citizens of the Empire. Christianity forged deep-rooted links with Greek and Roman society, in thought and in practice. When Roman citizens became Christian, they did not forget their education, shut their eyes or lose all their bearings. The Christians who took over the administration of the Roman Empire – or the Roman administrators who became Christian – happily dressed in the same uniform as their predecessors, and followed much the same course of political infighting, secular ambition and pursuit of earthly pleasures as earlier generations of powerful Roman bureaucrats. They sat at desks and did not stand on pillars. Not everyone can share in a constant assault on the comfort zone of self-satisfaction. It is this tradition of Christianity that most modern religion finds easier to deal with.

Christian accommodation to the Roman Empire functioned at all levels of cultural activity. Ancient cities were decorated with glorious statues, which caused Christians to react with consternation. According to the Hebrew Bible, 'you shall not make any graven image', and in general Jewish tradition has followed that law to the letter. In the synagogue of Dura Europos, excavated in 1932 in Syria, floors have been found with mosaics, including signs of the zodiac and other images. But this seems to be a rarity. It is also the case that when the Israelites were instructed to build the Ark of the Covenant, it was to have on it 'Cherubim with their wings folded over the cover'; but this is the description of a work which ancient Israelites couldn't see, any more than we can (and ancient Jewish commentators also found this a very vexing passage). Early Christians found the artwork of Greece and Rome deeply troubling. The early theologians were vitriolic in their attempt to keep Christians from looking at such things. As far as Clement of Alexandria was concerned, having a picture of Aphrodite on the wall was as sinful as committing a terrible sexual crime: 'We declare that the sight of such things is to be forbidden . . . Your eyes have whored; your sight has committed adultery.' At various points in Christianity's later history, strong puritan movements have demanded the destruction of all deceptive and corrupting images from churches. Following the Bible strictly, art should be banned.

However, as early as the fourth century at least, although they used the same Bible, Christians were beginning to produce art themselves and to borrow images from the so-called pagan world and reuse them. Angels, for example, take their form – tall, chastely robed figures with wings – not just because of that one passage in Exodus where the wings of Cherubim are mentioned. Equally influential are the figures of *Nike*, 'Victory' – tall, chastely robed figures with wings – which were so common on the monuments of the Greek cities. As is evident from Figure 27, when Christians came to paint the Annunciation, for example, they had ready models to hand. The putti of Roman art – Cupid, the boy god of desire – also easily folded into Christian representation.

This process of absorption was certainly not without argument and even violence – little of early Christianity was. In 382, when the Roman Empire was officially Christian, there was a major

27. Nike – Victory

debate about what should be done with the Altar of Victory that stood in the Senate House in Rome. The emperor, Gratian, ordered it to be removed, but traditionally minded senators were outraged, and organized a protest, sending a delegation to him in Milan with his pontifical robes – the traditional costume of the head pagan priest, which was the emperor's role. It took more than Constantine's conversion to change the Roman sense of tradition.

But in the fourth and fifth centuries, there was a surprising complicity between pagan and Christian art. Prudentius, a Latin Christian poet of the fourth century, sums up the principle in a remarkable way. He gives the following speech to the good Christian emperor Theodosius:

Wash the marble stained with rotten splattering,
O nobles. Let the statues, works of great artists
Stand clean. These are to be the fairest ornaments
Of our Fatherland.

Pagan art can be cleaned to make Christian monuments. Far
from rejecting pagan art outright, here Theodosius reveals a
more welcoming accommodation at work.

It's not always easy to see what makes art Christian at all. The
beautiful silver casket in Figure 28, designed for a woman's

28. Projecta Casket

makeup, is from Rome in the fourth century. It is a luxury item of
the most expensive and lavish kind. On the top of the box, the
bride and groom to whom it was presented are depicted together.
They are framed with a laurel wreath held up by a pair of naked
Cupids. On the front there is Venus sitting on a shell, rising from
the sea – an image of the type which leads directly towards
Botticelli's *Birth of Venus*. She is looking at herself in the mirror,
as Venus often does. She is surrounded by a chorus of nereids,
marine creatures who celebrate her, with little Cupids riding on

their backs. Venus is doing her toilet – ever since Homer, the goddess of sex and desire is especially associated with makeup, unguents, oils and beautifying baths. Figure 29 shows the casket

29. *Projecta Casket*

from another angle. On the bottom frieze a woman is seated, well dressed with elegant hair and jewellery – presumably the wife herself. From left and right she is being brought a casket like this one and a mirror like Venus' for her to do her own beautification. There is a neat and flattering parallel between the beauteous wife and the goddess of love herself, seated immediately above her. The inscription on the casket reads in Latin 'Secundus and Projecta, may you live in Christ'. These words are all that indicate that Projecta, the wife who owned this casket, and her husband Secundus were Christian.

This is certainly not the relic of an ascetic. Secundus and Projecta must have been very affluent Romans who had few Christian worries about such luxury items, or about dedicating time and money to beautifying oneself with makeup. Even so, it's difficult to know exactly how the image of Venus, the pagan goddess of sex, should be viewed. Should it be reduced to just an ornament, despite the strong connection in theme and position between wife and goddess? This would suggest a continuity of imagery to set against the new religious fervour, and a willing if not entirely consistent reuse of pagan art. Or could it be seen – in a more creative way – to symbolize Christian love in marriage, as the inscription might suggest? In either interpretation, the very active intertwining of Christian and pagan artistic imagery is striking: the naked Venus seems more at home in one of those awful dreams of the monk in the desert than as a symbol to celebrate a Christian marriage.

Dressed in a toga, silver cosmetics box in hand, it was difficult to appear a good Christian; nor was it easy for a Christian to view the tempting wonders of classical art properly. In the ornate ancient city, to look like a Christian needed constant care.

Philosophers and Holy Men

This two-way conversation between Christianity and Graeco-Roman culture can be seen across all aspects of social interaction. One of the ways that Greeks and Romans tried to comprehend the saints and preachers of Christianity was through the lens of their own holy men and culture heroes. When it came to martyrs, for example, what more striking figure is there than Socrates, the philosopher who always fearlessly pursued the truth and had been put to death by the Athenians for his troublemaking? He had been offered the chance to escape from prison and thus live on – but rejected it on the ground that there were stronger principles at stake. Moreover, on his deathbed Socrates had led a highly emotive discussion on the immortality of the soul. When Socrates claimed that he was fearless before death because the philosopher's soul would be freed from the shackles of the body and would reach a finer place for its immortal life, Christians readily heard a precursor of the Christian martyr. Justin Martyr, the second-century Christian apologist, epitomizes the pull of this image: 'Those who have lived reasonably are Christians . . . such as, among the Greeks, Socrates.' Indeed, 'Christ was partially known even by Socrates.' For Justin, who was to die for his faith, Socrates is so important a model that he has to appear as a Christian.

The philosopher Diogenes the Cynic lived in a barrel. He discarded all superfluous material things, and kept only a loincloth and a drinking bowl – and when he saw a shepherd boy drink from a river with his hands, he threw away the bowl too. The word 'Cynic' means literally 'like a dog', which refers at one level to the way of life of a Cynic – on the street, scavenging, without regard for social norms. In another sense it refers to their 'biting' wit. Cynics were famous for their sharp put-downs and general disregard for status. Many a story of a Christian martyr's wit in the face of a torturer sounds strikingly like one of these Cynics – as the hermits in the cave no doubt reminded Greeks of those Cynics in a barrel. Diogenes, for all his asceticism and anti-materialism, was not a Christian athlete of the soul when it came to sex. He was spotted masturbating in the market place. He merely commented: 'I wish the hunger in my belly could be so easily reduced.'

The connection between Cynics and Christians was explicitly made by Greek writers. Lucian, the second-century satirist, was put on the Index of banned books by the Catholic Church because of his brief dismissive comments about Christians. His sneer was that they had been duped into thinking a second-rate Cynic, a charlatan called Peregrinus, was their 'prophet, cult-leader, church warden' – a 'new Socrates'. For Lucian, Christians appeared as yet another weird, philosophically influenced cult.

The figure of Jesus himself, however foundational and unique for Christians, was also assimilated to the stereotypes of Greek and Roman society. There were many holy men and sages who made their living in the eastern Mediterranean. Apollonius, who came from Tyana in Asia Minor, was one of the most successful. His life-story was written by the Greek intellectual Philostratus – at the request, he tells us, of Julia Domna, the wife of the Roman emperor, because she was fascinated by the sage. Apollonius was a man of supernatural powers. He performed miracles, including curing people. His wisdom was profound, and often expressed in profound sayings. Accompanied by a disciple, Apollonius travelled to India and Persia, where he met the fabled wise men of the East, the Gymnosophists and the Brahmans, with whom he swapped wisdom and learnt the gift of foretelling from them. People came to honour Apollonius as a more than mortal figure. Shrines grew up – and statues of him still survive.

These holy men gave a narrative context in which to understand the holy men of Christianity. The often strange folklorish stories which circulated around such magicians and prophets fed readily into the stories of the saints, as they were constructed with such gusto and miraculous magic into holy texts like the Acts of Paul and Thecla. Greek novels too often include a young female heroine, like Thecla, who is threatened in her sexual purity by pirates, or lecherous landowners, or officials. These girls fight for their virginity. One of them, faced by a would-be rapist, screams: 'Set out your tortures, bring in the wheel! Behold my hands – let them be stretched! Bring in your whips too: behold my back – let it be beaten! Let fire be brought: behold my body – let it be burnt! Bring the sword too: behold my neck . . .' and so on. These words might be spoken by a Christian martyr, but they are spoken by a figure in a funny and sexy novel, who has already been all too happy to climb into bed with her lover (when her virginity was preserved only by her mother's interruption rather than by a passion for purity). Christians and non-Christians could read the novel and the female-martyr tales in the light of each other. Narrative techniques slid from classical culture into Christian writing.

But the single most important area where Christianity absorbed classical culture, and had its most difficult and perhaps productive encounter, is with Greek philosophy. Philosophy, which started with Plato in the fourth century BC, had become a fully institutionalized profession by the second century BC. There were well-established branches, each with its own professors, and a huge array of technical writing. Above all, philosophy was a fully integrated part of the educational system. Every Greek and Roman of a certain class and background studied philosophy, and it helped inform the intelligence of all properly educated men. Cicero was typical in spending a couple of years as a young man in Athens, the home of philosophy, where he honed both his deep regard for Greek thought and his sniffy attitudes towards Greeks. Even if you didn't study philosophy seriously, you should at least be able to nod with recognition if it came up as a subject of conversation at dinner. Educated Christians could not bypass Greek philosophy. Christianity demanded an obsession with the inner life, and philosophy for generations of Greeks and Romans had provided the authoritative guide to spirituality and self-reflection.

Philosophy was a psychological as much as an intellectual resource for the citizen of antiquity. Ancient philosophers, hawking for business, took their cue from Socrates on his deathbed: philosophy, they say, offers a preparation for a fearless death. It was necessary to recognize how irrational it was to fear death. And a crucial step in this process was evaluating what life was really worth. One of the standard images of the philosopher is the man who can dismiss the cares of the world as trivial and superficial. Cynics, laughing and scorning, mocked those who cared about money, status, fine possessions, positions of power. The Stoics taught how to be stoical – not to be moved by such temporary and unimportant pleasures. A good Stoic would rather die than accept a corrupt life – and would die happily. So Seneca, the philosopher and tutor of Nero, sat in his bath and opened his veins to bleed to death. The historian Tacitus describes how, as he lay there, he realized he had forgotten to write a letter. So he bound up his veins, got out of his bath, wrote the letter, then calmly got back in the bath, undid the bandages, and bled to death. Seneca, a master of self-representation, was fully aware that he was constructing a brilliant image of how a philosopher should die, and he made sure that the manner of his death was witnessed and recorded for posterity.

The power of this image of the ancient philosopher is still vividly felt today. A calm evaluation and rejection of the hurly-burly of ambition and lust and avarice is like a photographic negative of the picture of modern society provided by newspapers, film and television. It was a way of life that easily fed into the Christian desire for a better existence, a counter-life to the Empire of this world. That is a fundamental reason why philosophy was so attractive and so worrying for a Christian. It was rather too like Christian ideals, despite being the acme of pagan culture.

The pagan philosopher, moreover, promoted philosophy as a 'therapy of the passions'. Philosophy gave you the techniques by which you could control the anger, lust and avarice that twist and distort your soul. It gave you the arguments and the inner strength to reach emotional calm. Epicurean philosophy made this state of calm – *ataraxia* – its highest goal. Stoics learnt to rise above all the blows of life. Cynics laughed to scorn the seductions of materialism. Each of these schools of philosophy encouraged the 'care of the self' – introspection, reflection, a search for self-control and the practice of self-possession. True happiness comes not from the fulfilled needs of pleasure but from lack of want.

Philosophy offers the inner resources to deal with the complexities and disappointments of a brutal and confusing world. Greek and Roman literature loved to portray the meeting of the philosopher and the ruler. The ruler embodies the arbitrary exercise of power, the lusts of ambition, the pursuit of worldly success; the philosopher represents the control of calm, the power of inward authority. So Alexander the Great visits Diogenes the Cynic in his barrel. 'What do you want?' asks the man who longs to conquer the whole world. 'For you to move. You're blocking the sun,' replies the relaxing philosopher. Less pithily, but with the same autonomy of spirit, when the Emperor Nero banishes the philosopher Musonius to an obscure island, Musonius responds with a treatise on how exile means nothing to a true citizen of the world. Seneca's magnificent calm in the blood-filled bath is his answer to the death-sentence passed on him by his former pupil

Nero. Nero had not learnt his master's lesson that a philosopher could not be humiliated by such a punishment.

Philosophy's power to explore the inner life of the emotions and to teach control, self-control, still puts the *Meditations* of Marcus Aurelius in the bestseller lists. Unlike Nero, this Roman emperor had fully studied the lessons of Greek philosophy and absorbed them. He exhibits a wonderfully cultivated self-portrait to demonstrate how with true philosophy inside us even a position of absolute power will not corrupt our inner being. Marcus Aurelius' *Meditations* represents his struggle to transcend his position as emperor by nourishing and training his truly philosophical self.

Philosophy also offered an immediate lure for the searching religious soul. The Christian who sought inner strength, control of the emotions and the ability to rise above the dangers and the materialism of society's ambitions would have found many of his own ideals reflected in Greek philosophy. Indeed, he would have found his concerns discussed in a highly intelligent and productive way, and there were schools and social support for such study. A Christian could easily have a real and significant dialogue with an educated Greek, based on their shared interest in training the body and the mind, and conquering the emotional seductions of a pressing social world. Precisely for these reasons, early Christianity was also deeply suspicious of philosophy: it offered an intense inner life, but without the worship and the strictures of the Christian God.

One Christian who exemplifies this dialogue with philosophy is Clement of Alexandria. He lived in Alexandria in the second century and, in as much as there was an institution of the Church in Alexandria at that time, he was an authority in it. He writes elegant and sophisticated Greek, full of echoes of Plato and other philosophers. He knows his way round Homer and tragedy. He writes not just for the converted, but for an educated Greek audience, some of whom were no doubt committed Christians, some of whom may have been less committed – but all of them needed to integrate their Christianity into their Greek lifestyle. So he quotes Plato, 'It is impossible to describe God to all, when you have found him'; he agrees with Plato's explanation that this is 'because God cannot be described', and then adds his own comment: 'Well done, Plato, you have hit the truth! But don't give up . . .' He then proceeds to give Plato a fully Christian spin. Philosophy, for an intellectual like Clement, formed a bridge between the city Christians and their neighbours.

Other Christians reacted very differently to the attractions of philosophy. Tertullian was a hot-head and separatist, who lived further round the African coast in Carthage a few years after Clement. As a bishop, he was eventually excommunicated for heresy. It is typical of his extremism that he wanted all women to be veiled because of the double threat that women might look sexy to men and thus be corrupting, or that women might look sexily at men and thus be equally corrupting. (The Islamic burkah has a history in Christianity too.) Tertullian may have had a Roman training in rhetoric, but he wanted nothing to do with Greek and Roman intellectual culture. 'What's Athens to Jerusalem?' he rants. 'Away with all efforts to produce a mottled Stoic–Platonic–Dialectic Christianity!' It sounds as though he is fulminating against someone like the sly intellectual Clement. 'Where', he explodes, 'where is there any likeness between a Christian and a Philosopher?!' Unfortunately for Tertullian – and his outraged rhetoric suggests that he knows this himself already – the likenesses between a philosopher and a Christian were all too evident to most people, and all too tempting. Tertullian's rage, like Clement's slyness, show Christianity struggling to deal with philosophy's authority over the inner life.

Even when Christianity became the official religion of the Empire, and could have banned pagan philosophy and pagan rhetoric from its schools (as it did occasionally try to do), philosophy continued to maintain its authority. It could also prepare the ground for becoming Christian. In the last years of the fourth century, Synesius, also from Africa, became Bishop of Cyrene. He had previously spent years studying philosophy, loved hunting and refused to give up his wife or become celibate. His life, he announces sweetly, was just 'books and hunting'. As a philosopher, he had severe doubts about some of the basic tenets of Christianity. He could not accept the end of the world, for example, because it was a philosophical principle that matter can only be transformed not destroyed. And he found the resurrection in a literal sense hard to fathom. But, he tells us disarmingly, as a bishop, 'at home I do philosophy, in public I do myth' – 'not', he adds quickly, 'that my teaching will change anyone's standard assumptions'. That a bishop could dare to call his public teaching 'myth' seems astounding. Synesius is a Christian whose secular philosophy appears to determine how much Christian dogma he can accept!

Such arguments about how much secular learning should affect religious principles and thought have always been part of the Church from the beginning. When the Bishop of Durham in England declared in the 1980s that the resurrection in its literal sense wasn't a crucial part of his theology, his words were leapt on by the press as a sign of his horrifically trendy modern thought. The fact that such arguments come from a fourth-century father of the Church played no part in the manufactured outrage.

It is at the highest levels of theology, however, that philosophy presented the greatest challenge and influence. The great masters of theology– Origen, Jerome, Augustine – all studied and engaged deeply with philosophy. Augustine's *City of God* remains a philosophical masterpiece that has had a massive influence well beyond the limits of Christian theology. This extraordinarily complex and layered depiction of the universe and man's place in it is a Christian response to Plato's *Republic*, the founding text of idealist political philosophy. In this way, Augustine is absolutely typical of the dynamic tension between Christianity and pagan or secular philosophy. In the *Confessions*, Augustine describes his love-affair with pagan philosophy, and especially with Cicero, which started him on the road to serious intellectual activity. At that point, he still found 'the Bible unworthy in comparison with the dignity of Cicero'. Augustine was led only gradually towards orthodox Christianity, as he tried out other systems of thought in his search for spiritual and intellectual satisfaction. The *City of God* aims to replace Plato's *Republic* with a new vision – and cannot but echo continually with the saint's engagement with the tradition of pagan thought he is trying to overcome. Augustine shows all too clearly how hopeless it was for men such as Tertullian to fight to keep Christianity free of philosophy. As men and women in the Roman Empire searched for an authoritative guide for their perplexed inner lives, philosophy and religion overlapped in their promise of emotional and spiritual fulfilment.

Augustine is a high point of intellectual, philosophical Christianity. But the authority of philosophy is already being evoked in the apparently simple narrative world of the Gospels. The Gospel of John begins – in the King James version – 'In the beginning was the Word; and the Word was with God and the Word was God.' These words are now so familiar, it's difficult to appreciate just how odd and baffling they are. What can it mean to say 'In the beginning was the Word'? In Greek, the language in which the Gospels were written, the expression sounds much more normal. The term translated as 'word' is *logos*. In Greek, *logos* does not mean 'word' in any usual sense of the term. It has a wide range of meanings including 'rational order', 'argument', 'logic', 'system', 'reason'. To say that 'rational order' is the first principle of things, and that 'reason' is possessed by God and defines God, is theologically consistent and grammatically comprehensible. It is a standard form of expression hallowed by centuries of Greek philosophy. John may be rewriting Genesis, which opens 'In the beginning God created the heaven and earth,' but he is doing so in Greek philosophical terms. This is one indication of John's expected audience. The Gospel may talk of the poor, the weak, the ignorant, but John is reaching out to an educated Greek reader through his philosophically loaded vocabulary.

From the earliest days, Christianity *both* created a violent divide between itself and what it called pagan culture, *and* made all sorts of accommodating moves towards it. It put Simeon Stylites on a pillar and took over the administration of the Empire. It declared its message to be a new understanding of the world, and at the same time engaged in a long dialogue with Greek philosophy. To understand Christianity it is essential to see this complex dialogue of difference and similarity, extremism and accommodation, at work. Christianity develops in classical antiquity; it is part of the ancient world; and it develops by both rejecting and negotiating the culture of Greece and Rome.

Modern Western culture is formed from this melting-pot of tradition. Christianity has continued to find it difficult to deal with classics and the classical ideal, whether it is nudity and sexuality, or philosophy and art. Those fig-leaves decorously added to lavishly displayed classical sculptures nicely capture the constant mixture of longing and shame. But there is one moment in our European history when the passion for classics contributed to a rupture that threatened to set Christianity uncontrollably at war with itself. That moment is the establishment of Protestantism in the Renaissance. The Reformation and the Counter-Reformation constructed the modern map of Christianity, with all the bitterness that still infects Ireland and other countries where Catholics and Protestants struggle together. This is a further story of how classics matters profoundly for Christianity, not in the ancient world but in the sixteenth century.

5
Greek is Heresy!

The Renaissance marks the rebirth of ancient Greek and Roman culture in the West. This era of artistic, intellectual, religious and social turmoil was fuelled by a passionate rediscovery of the classics. The story of the Renaissance has been told many times in many registers. The turn to classical art, the excitement of newly rediscovered classical science and medicine, the invigorating power of classical authors, all helped to change how the world was seen, understood and represented.

But the Renaissance was not just the light of a new dawn triumphantly sweeping away the shadows of medieval Europe. It was a hard-fought battle about the deepest values of culture. One of the oddest but most significant turning points in the history of this war hangs on the translation of that first sentence of the Gospel of John. 'In the beginning was the Word.' The birth of Protestantism is intricately linked with how much Greek you know, and whether Greek philosophy should have a place in Christianity, ancient or modern. At this fundamental juncture, studying classics proved central to the whole sweep of Western history.

Every battle story needs a hero, and here it is Erasmus. Erasmus is one of the most influential men in the history of western Europe, which makes it all the more surprising that his life and works are not more fully part of the standard cultural repertoire of today. More than Shakespeare, Leonardo da Vinci, Michelangelo – to take three giants of the Renaissance – Erasmus changed lives, filled minds and became one of the most important catalysts in what might be called the biggest change in Christianity since its inception: the invention of Protestantism and its split from the Catholic Church.

The bare facts of Erasmus' career more than justify these impressive claims. Erasmus was instrumental in the complete overhaul of the English education system, and wrote the textbooks used by every schoolboy for more than two centuries. He composed explanatory paraphrases of the Gospels, which every single cleric in the country below the exalted level of Doctor of Divinity was required by law to own. It was law, too, that every parish church should put a copy of these paraphrases next to its Bible. He translated many Greek texts (including Lucian, which he did with Thomas More) and they became runaway bestsellers, spreading the Renaissance love of Greek into many a household. He wrote and published thousands of letters, which invented what we now recognize as the stereotype of the humanist scholar among his books: these published letters let the eager and curious world eavesdrop on the exchanges of the stars of the Renaissance. His letters were so well known in his own lifetime that a would-be intellectual could be trashed by the question 'So where's his letter from Erasmus?' But, above all, it is Erasmus' biblical scholarship that made him one of the most famous men in Europe.

St Jerome, letter-writer, pious scholar and translator of the Bible, was an obsession of Erasmus, who published an edition of Jerome's letters in 1516. It was a work he had been planning for years. 'I had worked myself to death that Jerome might live,' he wrote to the pope, Leo X. 'It cost Jerome less to write his works than it has cost me to restore them and explain them.' Jerome was for Erasmus the epitome of what a saint should be – for a humanist scholar. The smelly, painful and lonely sufferings of a Simeon Stylites are not what Erasmus looks for. He praises Jerome to the pope in these terms: 'What skill in languages, what a knowledge of antiquity and history, what a retentive memory, what a perfect familiarity with mystic literature, and, above all, what zeal, what a wonderful inspiration of divine breath.' Erasmus is delighted that Jerome took his library to the desert with him. He'd have done the same.

What is especially extraordinary is how Erasmus rewrites the medieval image of Jerome that he had inherited. In the Middle Ages, Jerome had become a man so holy that he remained a virgin till his death at ninety-six. He drank no wine and ate neither fish nor meat. He could hardly even say the word 'meat'. He wore a hair-shirt, slept on the ground and whipped himself three times a day till the blood flowed. There was even a sect called the Hieronymites, named after Jerome (whose name in Latin is Hieronymus), who were ascetic hermits, particularly taken up with flagellation and starving. Erasmus had a different model in mind. 'Whoever achieved such familiarity with history, geography and antiquities? Whoever became so equally and completely at home in all literatures, both sacred and profane? If you look to his memory, never was there an author, ancient or modern, who was not at his immediate disposal.' As Erasmus tries to paint a correct portrait of his hero, his hero starts to look increasingly like himself. Saints are like Renaissance scholarly gentlemen, because Renaissance scholarly gentlemen want to be saintly. Memory and language skills are not part of the life of Simeon Stylites.

In Figure 30 we can see the most famous portrait of Erasmus, painted by Quentin Metsys, one of his friends, and sent to Thomas More, friend to both of them. This portrait of the pious scholar in his study, a faint smile on his thin face, intently writing, surrounded by his books, has become the most familiar image of Erasmus today. He is well dressed, though without any gaudy ostentation. He has a pouch on his lap – which indicates the financial interest and mobility of a merchant perhaps, a world of business quite alien to Jerome at least. The book facing the viewer, lit up so that the title can easily be seen, is *Hieronymus* – Erasmus' edition of Jerome's writings. This reminds the viewer of Erasmus' famous book, of course, but it also gives a different sort of visual cue. For the portrait has been carefully constructed to remind us

30. Erasmus
by Quintin Metsys

of another image – St Jerome in his own study. In the fifteenth century, Van Eyck had painted Jerome in his library, and other painters from the Low Countries seem to have imitated in particular Van Eyck's loving representation of the physicality of the saint's books and his comfort among them (Figure 31). Like Erasmus, Jerome is intent on a book. He is dressed in the bright-red robes and hat of an authority of the Catholic Church. The tame lion beneath his desk is a symbol of the taming of the bestial in man. (There is also a story which had him, like Androcles, removing a thorn from a lion's paw, and earning the lion's gratitude and service.) The image of Jerome as a scholar in his study, rather than as a penitent or an ascetic in the desert, was a particular invention of the Renaissance. The construction of the image of Erasmus has a powerful message: here is the pious scholar in the pose of his hero – Erasmus *as* Jerome.

Erasmus first learnt Greek in order to rescue Jerome. 'I would rather be mad with Jerome than as wise as you like with a crowd of modern theologians,' he wrote to a friend back in 1501. Because modern Christian scholars did not know Greek or study

147

31. St Jerome
by Van Eyck

antiquity, they had mangled all sorts of things in Jerome and in the other founding fathers of Christianity. Erasmus recognized that, for a proper understanding of the authorities of Christianity and Christianity's founding moment, it was absolutely necessary to master the study of classics.

Ironically, this started Erasmus on a journey that led him to be vilified as the heretical attacker of Jerome himself. For Jerome was said to have written the Vulgate, the Latin translation of the Greek New Testament and the Hebrew Bible. The Vulgate was the Bible which had been used for hundreds of years in every church in Europe. It was what the people knew and trusted. It was authorized not just by use but by the full weight of the explicit stamp of the Church's approval. It is clear enough to any scholar, even then, that Jerome could not actually have been the author, certainly not of all of it. But he was the saint of the head of that tradition. This was the Holy Book. It was to this Erasmus turned next – and it was here that all the trouble started.

Erasmus' Greek studies, his work on Jerome and his own deep religious feelings led him inevitably back to the Gospels, written, of course, in Greek. He found that the Greek was inelegant, unsophisticated and weakly constructed in syntax and grammar, at least in comparison with the classical models available. He also found that there were different manuscript traditions of the Holy Writ, which posed tricky problems of choosing between alternatives to determine what the real text should be. So he decided to produce a 'critical edition' of the Greek, with a facing Latin translation, in order to get the Greek and Latin right. The result was a Latin Bible that was outrageously different from the Vulgate, and a Greek text that in places threatened to provoke a social crisis. His first version was rushed through the press in 1516. It was lousy with misprints and errors, and the notes in which he explained what he was doing were rather perfunctory. In 1519, he went to Basel to see the second edition through the press himself. Here he pulled no punches. It was full of new and radical suggestions, defended with stridently aggressive scholarship. This was a book that looked as if it was designed to change the world.

It is difficult to overstate how much was at stake here for the Renaissance world. Catholicism, centred on Rome, was the dominant religious and social power in Europe – and the only institutional focus of religion. During the Middle Ages all theological discussions, from which law and practice derived, were conducted in Latin and were based on the Latin text of the Vulgate. All religious services were conducted in Latin. The Bible, for all intents and purposes, was a Latin text. The social order and the authority of the Church in the medieval world depended on the status of the Vulgate. It was Jerome's Vulgate that Erasmus was changing. If the text on which all this was based could be changed, what price the authority of the Church? If the Holy Book could be altered, what happened to God's Word? The social and moral outrage that Erasmus unleashed was not just an issue of translation or wording. The very order of society itself was at stake. Erasmus' opponents feared that, by changing the Vulgate, the institution of the Church itself would be threatened – although Erasmus himself remained a committed Catholic throughout his life. Even from the historical perspective of the seventeenth century, it would seem that Erasmus' opponents were quite right. In the space of a hundred years, England had become a Protestant country with a Church that denied Rome. Germany had followed Martin Luther into his version of Protestantism. Switzerland and most of the Low Countries too were fully Protestant. The Church was indeed violently dismembered by this new intellectual movement.

One simple story exemplifies the shocking power of Erasmus' scholarship. When Erasmus found that none of the ancient manuscripts of the letters of St John included a particular sentence that was to be found in modern editions, he reasoned that it must have been added later by another, unknown person, at some point well after the letter had been written. So he left that sentence out of his version. The sentence comes in the Letter of John I and reads, 'There are three that bear record in heaven, the Father, the Word and the Holy Spirit, and these three are one.' It's a sentence that declares how the Trinity – ever a difficult notion – should be understood. Here was a moment where Erasmus' reliable scholarship caused havoc. A sentence on which religious arguments had been built for years was suddenly no longer the Word of God.

In June 1569, fifty years after the publication of Erasmus' New Testament, an Anabaptist called Hermann Van Flekwyk was burnt to death at the stake. The inquisitor, a Franciscan friar called Cornelius Adrian, declares, 'You have sucked at the poisonous breast of Erasmus . . . but St John says "There are three that bear record in heaven, the Father, the Word and the Holy Spirit, and these three are one."' Van Flekwyk replies, 'I have heard that

Erasmus in his *Adnotationes* upon that phrase shows that this text is not in the Greek original.' Erasmus' scholarship is here literally a life-and-death matter – a martyr's credo as he is burnt alive. In the Reformation and Counter-Reformation, hundreds were questioned, tortured and burnt to death for their take on the wording of God's Word. Dying for the Word was again the martyr's credo, as Europe was convulsed in civil war.

The single phrase which became the lightning rod of all the anger and hostility was Erasmus' translation of the first sentence of the Gospel of John. For centuries, the Gospel had begun 'In principio erat verbum' ('In the beginning was the Word'). Erasmus printed instead, 'In principio erat sermo' ('In the beginning was the conversation/discourse'). It was the most pugnacious and arresting opening, designed to shock the reader into attention. And shock it did. There were hundreds of pages written about it at the time, and many a vitriolic row.

In scholarly terms Erasmus has a good case. Augustine and other Church fathers were aware of this translation with *sermo* and some preferred it; so it has ancient authority. As a translation of *logos* in its casual or more philosophical sense, *sermo* is more effective than *verbum*, though neither quite catches the range. *Ratio*, 'reason', 'order', might have been better still, suggested Erasmus in a note. *In principio erat verbum* would have sounded very strange to an intelligent non-Christian Latin reader of the first century, despite the fact that the two words *logos* and *verbum* had some overlap in sense, especially in the plural. The very strangeness of the expression, however, played a role in the attractively mystical and opaque effect of the opening of this new take on the order of things. But it was not the scholarship itself that dismayed people. It was the mere fact of change. St Jerome, when he wrote the preface to his own edition of the Bible, had worried that everyone would 'burst into cry and call me heretic and sacrilegious because I dare to add, change, correct something in the old text'. Ironically, it was Erasmus who suffered exactly what his master had predicted.

The battle lines were now drawn up. Erasmus was an intellectual star linked to the greatest scholars around Europe. He had been instrumental in promoting Greek studies for twenty years. He now wrote letter after letter, trying to wheel out all his potential support from the pope downwards. He published book after book defending his scholarship. By one criterion at least, Erasmus could be said to have been triumphant. For Greek did become central to university education, and classics did become a mainstay of learning and culture: that is a success of the Renaissance.

But in religious terms, despite all the furore, he was sidelined within twenty-five years. In 1546, the Council of Trent, one of the largest collections of cardinals ever gathered for such debate, made the dizzying but binding declaration that the Vulgate was 'authentic'. Not the best translation, nor the text that is authorized for use by the Church – but authentic. That a translation could be called the true and original Word of God sets the stakes very high indeed. The cardinals also demanded that 'nobody dare or presume to reject it under any pretext' – even though they themselves recognized that it contained some errors of translation. Until the late twentieth century, the Vulgate was the only allowable text for the Catholic Church and its ritual. Protestant religion eventually turned to the vernacular – ordinary people's language – and Tyndale's English version of the Latin became the norm for most English people's inner life. The compulsive rows over Erasmus' version were forgotten.

Erasmus was resisted with an extraordinary fervour. One Cambridge college passed a formal resolution that no copy of Erasmus' book could be brought on to college property 'by horse, boat, wagon, or porter'. Erasmus wasn't sure 'whether to laugh or cry' when he was told that. But he was more angered by John Standish, who preached publicly in London against him. 'Keep your children from Greek. That's where heresies are borne,' was the theme of this tirade. Standish was not the only senior cleric to preach against him. Across Europe, religious authorities stood up to persuade their congregants to have nothing to do with

Erasmus. One especially hurtful attack was written by Edward Lee, the future Archbishop of York. He wrote a detailed and scholarly rebuttal of Erasmus' working methods and aims – based largely on the first edition of 1516, which did indeed have many misprints. Erasmus put many of Lee's corrections into his next edition, and also wrote a vicious rejection of him, which he published too.

This particular fight produced some strange responses. A whole book of poems was published by Erasmus' supporters, each of which made fun of Lee and his name. But the oddest reaction of all took place in a library. A copy of Lee's book was put on display in the public reading room. A couple of days later, readers started to complain of a horrid smell in the library. It was traced to Lee's book. It was discovered that someone had smeared it with human shit. The humanists loved this story, and a couple of poems in praise of the smearer were promptly penned. Thomas More, a few years later, in one of his less than saintly modes, wrote of Martin Luther: 'Luther has nothing in his mouth but privies, filth and dung . . . mad friarlet and privy-minded rascal with his ragings and ravings, with his filth and dung, shitting and beshitted.' This sort of abusive lavatorial language indicates the strength of feeling on all sides, but one of Erasmus' supporters seems to have literalized it in a gross gesture of theological disgust.

Erasmus had a more testing time with a colleague called John Maier, who was professor of theology at Ingelstadt. Maier was polite, learned and highly critical. He shows how the Church worried more about the maintenance of authority than about the niceties of getting just the right word. 'Listen, dear Erasmus,' he wrote, 'do you really think that any Christian will patiently endure being told that the Evangelists in the Gospels made mistakes? If the authority of the Holy Scriptures at this point is shaky, can any other passage be free of the suspicion of error?' Maier lays out the problem as clearly as possible. If the Greek is shown to be mistaken at *any* point, then at any *other* point suspicion could fall, and the foundations of all that matters start to shake. How could the Evangelists make mistakes? Meier appeals to the story of the Apostles speaking in tongues to give divine authority for his views. 'It was not from Greeks but from the Holy Spirit that they learnt their Greek.' Would Erasmus really correct Greek from God?

Erasmus took this argument on full face. He turns on it all his weapons of sarcasm and strident self-justification. 'If you maintain that the Greek which we see in the Apostolic Fathers is a gift from heaven,' he writes, 'from where comes all the clumsiness of language, not to say barbarisms, which we cannot attempt to conceal?' Why should God teach *bad* Greek? As he writes with studied casualness in his own defence, 'it is known that the Apostles wrote Greek, but not very correctly . . .' And he reminded anyone who would listen that Jerome himself is 'not afraid to charge Paul with imperfect knowledge of Greek'. The authorities of the Church themselves had questioned how much Greek each knew and had confessed weaknesses in their knowledge. Erasmus' argument was fundamentally a historic one: 'All philosophy and all theology in those days belonged to the Greeks.' The foundations of the Church could not be challenged by learning Greek, because the foundations of the Church *are* Greek. Erasmus' appeals to truth and scholarship, and Meier's appeals to the value of tradition and authority, rehearse the archetypal conflict between reformers and conservatives.

Less sophisticated opponents of Erasmus than John Meier took matters into their own hands. There was an extraordinary club in Oxford called the Trojans. Who better to fight against 'the Greeks'? Here is a contemporary description:

Their senior sage christened himself Priam; others called themselves Hector, Paris and so forth. The idea, whether as a joke or a piece of anti-Greek polemic, is to pour ridicule on those dedicated to the study of Greek. And I hear that things have come to such a pass that no one can admit in public or in private that he enjoys Greek without being subjected to the jeers of those ridiculous 'Trojans' who think Greek is a joke for the simple reason they don't know what good literature is . . .

This is a fascinating snapshot of a spot of local bother in a hot-headed university community. It would be no more than that, except for the fact that it is written by Thomas More, the most influential politician of Henry VIII's court. He published it as a public letter to Oxford academics. He complained that these Trojans called Greek scholars 'heretics' and tried to ban classical learning. And he threatened them with the full weight of royal power. More writes from the side of the king, and he points out with barely concealed menace that royal patronage could not be relied on if 'these stupid factions' are not stopped. Henry VIII had dissolved the monasteries, confiscated their land and thereby destroyed centuries-old institutions. The universities might go the same way. The row over Greek embroiled the very highest powers in England. More here uses that power to support the cause of his good friend Erasmus. Greek was a national interest.

It turned out to be a national interest in a way that Erasmus could never have predicted, and would have found dismaying. England became officially a Protestant country in 1559 with the religious settlement under Elizabeth I. Elizabeth I and Edward VI were taught by John Cheke and Roger Ascham, both Cambridge academics who had been profoundly influenced by Erasmus and the humanist cause, and who were both avid reform-ers. Ascham was obsessed with Greek learning, and both the young king and the young queen were taken through a rigorous education in Greek – and reform. (Edward VI's translations into Greek are still among his papers.) These royal tutors were crucial in helping to form the opinions and attitudes of these first Protestant monarchs. The political negotiations that led up to the religious settlement involved almost entirely Cambridge-educated men – a small group of interconnected politicians. They were linked by the common passion for Greek studies and Protestant doctrine. It was a clique of like-minded men, educated in the new and trendy study of Greek, passionate about that study, which led England to Protestantism.

Thomas More had himself been put to death long before the settlement. He, like Erasmus, would have resisted such a split from the Catholic Church. He had actively pursued a campaign to crush any attempt to have the Bible put into English. This was not an unthinking conservatism, but a precise and intense worry about translation, and how misleading an English version would have to be. If, for example, the Latin word *caritas* is translated as 'love', as it is in Tyndale's version, rather than 'charity', this choice of terms has massive implications. It would imply that 'faith' rather than 'good deeds' counted most. It valued faith ('love') over ritual ('charity') – and *that* is a Protestant idea. It's a rather unpleasant irony that men were killed and books burnt over the issue of whether 'love' or 'charity' is the better word to choose. The English Bible is often celebrated as a return of Holy Scripture to the People out of the misty obscurity of a foreign tongue. But the use of English actually began as a radical and aggressive gesture of support for the Reformation.

The birth of Protestantism was a bloody business, as the passions of the Reformation and Counter-Reformation ran their course. These violent disagreements still flare up in the modern West. Central to the progress of the Reformation and Counter-Reformation was the issue of classical antiquity. Christianity came from antiquity – but how much Greek should a Christian know? What would – what *did* – happen to Church authority if the language of the Bible, its Greek and Latin, were looked at critically? How tradition is to be valued is an absolutely central issue for the differences between the Protestant and Catholic Churches. Exploring that sense of tradition means tracing steps back towards the Gospels and their Greek, and the fathers and their Latin. In part at least, this is what T. S. Eliot meant when he said the study of Greek and Latin is necessary for those 'who wish to see a Christian civilisation survive'. He knew how much classics matters to understanding Western tradition.

6

Knowing the Answer

Sarah, the sixteen-year-old daughter of a friend of mine, was being prepared at school for a public exam in Religious Studies. For homework, she was asked the question 'Why does Jesus tell parables?' She was encouraged by her father, a pleasingly troublesome man, to read the Gospel of Mark, and especially chapter 4 verses 12–14, where Jesus explains his teaching technique. She dutifully did so, and quoted Mark in her answer: 'I tell parables so that outsiders will not understand.' Sarah's teacher corrected her and said, 'No, Jesus tells parables so that he could make his message available to all. Parables are a good way to get through to the ordinary, simple folk whom Jesus loved.' Sarah pointed out that the Gospel said the exact opposite. Parables are to exclude and baffle people. Her teacher underlined that 'The *answer* is "so that everyone can get the message".' What's a Gospel compared to a standard exam answer?

A parable should be a fictional tale and it shouldn't usually be funny. But this story, despite being true and funny, looks very much like a parable itself. The first message is not always to trust fathers, especially those who are happily troublesome. After all, a good shepherd would have directed his charge also to Matthew 13, where Matthew does a notable job of rewriting Mark. The version of Mark, the earliest Gospel, is direct enough. The disciples have asked Jesus why he uses parables, and with some exasperation he replies, 'To you has been given the secret of the Kingdom of God, but for those outside, everything is in parables *so that* they may see and not perceive, and may hear but not understand, *lest* they should turn again and be forgiven.' This statement was called 'repellent' by Albert Schweitzer, and it's easy to see why. Not only does Jesus tell parables to exclude the outsiders from the secret of heaven, but he does so because he doesn't want people to repent and be forgiven. This harsh doctrine just does not chime with most people's ideals of Christianity or Jesus.

Matthew is less bleak. He tells the story in a similar way, but with significant differences. Jesus is once again asked why he uses parables, and explains that it is because the disciples but not the people have been given the secret of the Kingdom of God. But he continues: 'I speak to them in parables because seeing they do not see and hearing they do not hear nor do they understand.' That is at least closer to the answer Sarah's teacher wanted. Because the crowd can't understand the secret, they need parables. They do not understand, but at least here they have a chance. Matthew goes on to explain that using parables also fulfils a prophecy in Isaiah, and he takes the disciples inside for some further private instruction into the secrets – for which, as readers, we are encouraged to see ourselves as potential heirs. In Matthew, unlike in Mark, there is less sense that the damned are damned are damned.

Faced by such different versions, biblical scholars have had to make difficult choices. Often, with a sigh of relief, Matthew is taken to be the true version, because it is less repellent – despite the fact that Mark is the earlier text. It is assumed that Mark somehow misunderstood or got it wrong. But it is a drastic step – as Erasmus showed – if it becomes necessary to argue that the Gospels are faulty. What price the Word of God? It could equally well be claimed that Mark's uncompromising message has been toned down by Matthew for his own persuasive purposes. Defending Mark, like defending Matthew, has the same troubling consequences. Centuries of scholarship, hunting for a third line of compromise, have failed to reconcile the stories into a neat package.

But my parable about Sarah and her teacher and her father is concerned with how thinned down and blanched out is the version of Christianity which the modern education system and modern society feel capable of dealing with. To look at Christianity without its classical roots and classical wars is to look at religion like a tourist – with its seriousness, its radical provocation, its *passion* lost to blandness. Why should cultural history, let alone religious history, be satisfied with such triviality and superficiality? Why should Christianity want to forget where it comes from – and how difficult that birth and growth were?

Christianity came into existence in antiquity. It is first formulated in the authoritative languages of the Roman Empire – Greek and Latin. The Gospels are written in Greek and then translated into Latin. The founding fathers of the Church wrote and thought in Latin and Greek. Jesus may have spoken Aramaic as his first language, as did at least some of the Gospel writers. But it is through Greek and Latin that Christianity made itself the religion of Empire. Christianity was formulated in antiquity and constantly walked between a radical and hostile rejection of Roman and Greek culture, and a more sly accommodation and negotiation of its values. Early Christianity is by turns baffling in its extreme and self-willed violence, and recognizable for its family stories. Christianity must find its roots in its founding and foundational moments, but those moments can seem extraordinarily alienating. To appreciate the history of Christianity – where Western culture comes from – we need the full *difficulty* of this picture. We just cannot understand how Christianity came to be what it is without the culture of antiquity. And without making that journey of understanding we cannot appreciate the genesis of the most basic values that all of us in the society of the West follow and struggle with.

III

WHAT DO YOU THINK
SHOULD HAPPEN?

I

Does Politics Need History?

Everyone knows that democracy began in ancient Greece. The 2,500th anniversary of the invention of democracy was celebrated during the 1990s. It allowed politicians and editors to mouth the usual platitudes about history and our values, and Greece held some rather more nationalistic festivities than the rest of Europe (and again asked for the Elgin Marbles back). America began the decade, as it began the next millennium, by going to war in the name of democracy.

The juxtaposition of convivial celebration and the still raw violence of the Gulf War poses as starkly as possible the questions of this chapter. Democracy started in Greece, but does it matter – except in the most self-serving rhetoric – that democracy was invented in that place and at that time? In the face of modern multinational corporations, global media systems and weapons of mass destruction, how relevant can the politics of a small community from so long ago be today? If a week is a long time in politics, what price 2,500 years?

Politics can be a grim and nasty business, and it is all too clear that the pursuit of power and dominance over others doesn't need Aristotle. The politician who seeks to win and to hold on to power might, I suppose, learn a trick or two from Machiavelli (or from a life of Stalin). But the cut and thrust of self-interest requires no more motivation than greed, personal ambition and a will to dominate. It would be crass to underestimate the force of such motivation at all levels of political activity. Power loves to hide – but the bare, ugly pursuit of power is never far below the surface of politics in action. It may seem that the gap between Plato and the dirty business of economic, military and legal force is just too wide to be bridged. It might even seem cynical or insulting to the victims of the last hundred years of political violence to turn our eyes towards so distant a past.

But I think it is a fundamental mistake to cut politics off from history, and to sever democratic politics from the history of democracy. There is more to politics than the exercise of power, and the motivations which lead men and women to fight for social change, or to struggle to maintain the values of a community, go far beyond the attractions of personal ambition. It is here that history and theory – the power of ideas – play a formative role in politics. As Nietzsche prophesied, the most violent and destructive conflicts in the modern world are 'wars between ideas'. It is the power of the idea of democracy that dominates this chapter.

Two hundred and fifty years ago the words 'democracy' or 'democrat' were used primarily as an insult. It was not easy to call yourself a democrat without careful apology, explanation or self-deprecation. When the poet Wordsworth wrote privately to a friend in 1794, 'I am of that odious class of men called "democrats",' he wrote as a defiant young man inspired by the French revolution, but 'democrat' nevertheless is a difficult word for him to use. Even the intellectuals in France before the revolution rarely used the term 'democracy' in a positive way.

The inspiration – and fear – caused by the American and French revolutions initiated a debate which fundamentally changed the political language. Whatever the republican ideals of the founding fathers of the American constitution or of the leaders of the French revolution, 'democracy' has become an unimpeachable term in popular political discourse for us. All rich societies in the West care to call themselves democracies. There is near unanimity about the goodness of democracy. Dismissing or reviling democracy is simply not an option for any contemporary Western politician or political commentator. The Communist Party of

China, the dictators of Arab countries and the military juntas in South America are all depicted as the corrupt rulers of other worlds, which lack and desperately need democracy. The democratic ideal is the banner under which the West lives and fights.

This ubiquitous and often unreflective celebratory brandishing of the word 'democracy' makes it all the more necessary to reflect critically on what it can and should mean. Such critical reflection is especially pressing today, when 'fighting for democracy' has become such a regular battle-cry. At the same time, a self-critical gaze at the political principles of democracy has always been the hallmark of democracy's greatest thinkers and politicians.

'Democracy is the worst form of government,' declared Winston Churchill, 'except all the others.' That may sound wilfully paradoxical, but it is not glib. Churchill knew democratic procedure from the inside and under the most intense pressure. As head of a government of National Unity during the Second World War, when democracy fought fascism, he oversaw the process whereby many of the normal practices of democracy were halted in Britain. There were no general elections. If a member of Parliament died, the traditional politics of opposition was sidelined. When a Conservative member died, the Labour Party did not contest the subsequent by-election, and likewise the Conservative Party did not put up a candidate in a Labour-held constituency. Free speech, freedom of movement and many other basic rights of citizenship were suspended. To win the war, democracy voted itself into a drastically reduced form. To fight for democracy, it seems, the very principles of democracy could be put on hold. After the war, Churchill, the victorious leader, was unceremoniously voted out of office. He had every reason to understand the strengths and weaknesses of the democratic system – what was worth fighting for, and what were its limitations.

But Churchill's knowing comment isn't just a wry retrospect of his own experience. Rather, it succinctly captures an essential aspect of democracy, and why its history matters. Churchill, unlike so many less aware politicians, does not slip into an easy idealism or Utopianism: he doesn't say 'Democracy is perfect,' 'Democracy is morally right,' or even 'Democracy is the best form of government.' He puts his view the way he does for two good reasons.

First, it is impossible to think about democracy as a form of government except in terms of conflict. Conflict is integral to democracy. Democracy depends on people having different and competing views within society and about society. It expects argument, disagreement, compromise. It assumes that there are at least two sides to any question, which need discussion and a vote – and that something would be seriously missing if there was no debate or collective decision. After all, if there were only one true and certain way – as some religious or totalitarian states might hold – who needs democracy? To argue on behalf of democracy requires the recognition that there will be other, competing views. That's one reason why Churchill expresses himself the way he does. He knows he's in an argument.

Second, from its very beginnings in ancient Athens, there is no democracy without criticism of democracy. Democracy necessarily sees itself in opposition to other systems – whether it's Sparta, the traditional enemy of ancient Athens, or the communism of the Soviet Union set against Cold War America, or the fascism that Churchill fought. But it has also always allowed – and provoked – criticism of itself. It prides itself on enshrining the freedom to criticize ('Here at least you can say you disagree . . .'). And it often sees this freedom as a reward for the frustration and annoyance that must come from a system in which any vote is likely to leave some citizens as disgruntled losers. The constant criticism of democracy – even by committed democrats – means that it has always been difficult to promote democracy as a Utopian system. As Churchill knew, democracy sells itself most successfully as the form of government that has fewer disastrous consequences than other systems. 'Two cheers for democracy' – but not the full three – was how E. M. Forster celebrated the

English system against Nazi Germany. Churchill understood that a good democrat has to recognize the problems of democracy even as he chooses it. He is *being* democratic as much as he is describing democracy.

The power of ideas motivates political activity, and critical disagreement is basic to democracy, in principle and in practice. As a result, any discussion of democracy will find itself turning to questions of history and theory. Democrats need to ask what form their government should take, and how it compares to other possible forms of authority, now and in the past. Democracy must bring its citizens or its representatives together to debate its policies, its laws, its institutional practices – what sort of society the citizens wish to make for themselves. This sense of potential – what could be called the 'what if?' question – is where history and theory enter politics. To ask 'How should things be?', 'Must things be like this?', is to begin a historical and theoretical discussion. In this debate, classics has a major function.

Democracy is an unfinished journey, started in ancient Athens; an experiment that is still being refined and tested. Our questions and history of democracy begin in Athens. The lasting power of those questions provides a lens for viewing modern politics with startling clarity – a clarity that is sorely needed. Ancient democracy still provides the grounding for the 'what if' of modern political thinking.

2

Athenian Democracy – Changing the Map

Around 508 BC, Cleisthenes persuaded his fellow Athenians to adopt a new political system, which began the long development of Western democracy. The emergence and establishment of democracy constitute a foundational moment in the history of society, all the more extraordinary in the context in which it occurred.

Athens was a strange city-state. It had a bustling centre, a town growing around the fortified acropolis (where the Parthenon would eventually stand). But its harbour, the Piraeus, was some miles distant from the town. The whole of Attica, a network of villages and small communities, some as far as twenty-five miles from the city, was also 'Athens'. This conglomeration included the most outlying and isolated farms, and major religious centres such as Eleusis, where all of Greece came to celebrate the cult of the Mysteries (Figure 32). Athens was an agricultural community, and many town-dwellers also had rural property, which they worked. The Athenians held that this odd and sprawling collection had been consolidated and unified into the city-state of Athens by Theseus, the city's first king. Theseus had fought the Amazons, as the Parthenon depicted, and had killed the Minotaur; his father was Poseidon, the god of the sea. The Athenians happily recounted this story of their city's political foundation.

Cleisthenes lived at the end of a century of rapid social and economic change. The sixth century was a period of repeated internal crisis for Athens as economic and political inequality led to

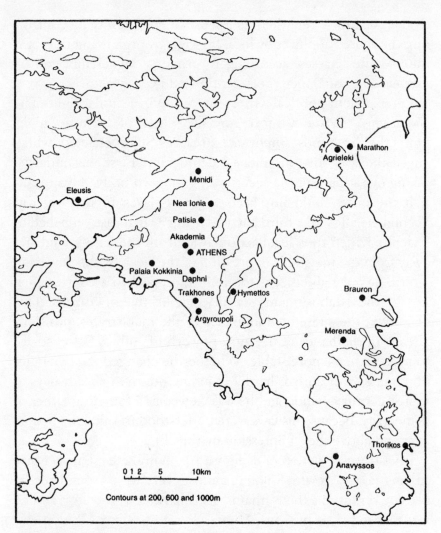

32. Map of Attica

major social unrest and repeated civic violence. Two exceptional men dominate the history of the century, and each is fundamental to later democratic ideology, one as an icon and the other as anathema. The first is Solon, from the 590s. He rose to become leader of an Athens riven by competition between elite families and by a lack of centralized regulation. In the poems he wrote about his own political activity, he depicts himself as a negotiator who argued for strengthening a sense of community by controlling the abuses of power by local bigwigs, by organizing the community into 'classes' according to property ownership, and by establishing a stronger, more centralized legal system.

Later ancient political writers saw Solon in a similar light. The *Constitution of Athens*, a text from the school of Aristotle, highlights the three most important measures Solon enacted, which paved the way for Cleisthenes' democracy. First, he outlawed taking out a loan on the security of your own body. This meant that the poor could not become bond-slaves to the wealthy. Second, he allowed a third party to bring a legal case on behalf of a victim, which took legal action away from the family feud and away from the inevitable oppression of the weak by the powerful. Third, he gave all citizens the right of appeal to a court, which implies the establishment of a jury, a collective of citizens. This countered the supreme dominance of the magistrates, positions already in the hands of the most powerful families. Solon strove to make Athens more stable. Whether he changed the dynamics of power significantly is harder to judge. But in the heady days of fourth-century democracy, he was viewed as a founding father of democracy, because his laws were understood to value the people over and above their oppression by the elite.

Peisistratus, the second figure to dominate sixth-century Athens, contrasts with Solon in almost every way. Around 560 he became tyrant of Athens, that is, its sole ruler or dictator, and he was succeeded by his sons, Hipparchus and Hippias. Solon evidently did not stop competition between elite families for power and status, nor did he succeed in creating a stable constitution for Athens. According to the ancient sources, there were three main groupings in Athens, the men of the plain, the men of the shore and the men of the hills, these last led by Peisistratus. The tyranny was the triumph of this third grouping – though it is hard to know how much these groupings were merely territorial and familial, or linked by some broader political concern. When in power, Peisistratus built huge temples, initiated major building projects, developed new festivals (probably including the Great Dionysia, where the tragedies and comedies were produced) and expanded Athens' major festival, the Panathenaia, into a Panhellenic event to rival the Olympic Games. But, for later democrats, the tyrant was simply the despised and feared anathema of democracy.

In Athens, the tyrants were ousted in an act of murder that became the paradigmatic image of democratic heroism. There was even a ritual cult of the Tyrannicides with honoured statues of the two men who were said to have assassinated Hipparchus (Figure 33). Several of Athens' favourite drinking songs celebrated the killers: 'I'll carry my sword in a myrtle spray,' runs one, 'like Aristogeiton and Harmodius, when they killed the tyrant, and brought equality before the law to Athens.' Like the Marseillaise or the Star-Spangled Banner, it is not so much the zippiness of the lyrics as the emotional force of the song that counts – an emotional force that encapsulates a political ideal.

Cleisthenes' political agenda responded to the crises embodied in the careers of Solon and Peisistratus. After the fall of the tyrants, one might expect the elite families to struggle to fill the power vacuum. But what makes Cleisthenes' actions momentous, as well as surprising, is the fact – the sources tell us – that he first won over 'the people'. Although he himself came from an aristocratic family background in Athens, as did most democratic politicians over the next two centuries, he established himself as the leader of a collective of the peasants – the small landowners and workers in the town. What is more remarkable still is that he used this popular support not merely to establish his own power base, but to set in place a whole series of institutions and systems of decision-making that fundamentally changed Athens – and the possibilities of Western politics – for ever, by making 'the people' their own governors.

The first of Cleisthenes' radical moves was wholly to reorganize the spatial politics of Athens, and with it the sense of belonging, of citizenship. He required each and every citizen – enfranchised males over the age of eighteen – to register in a

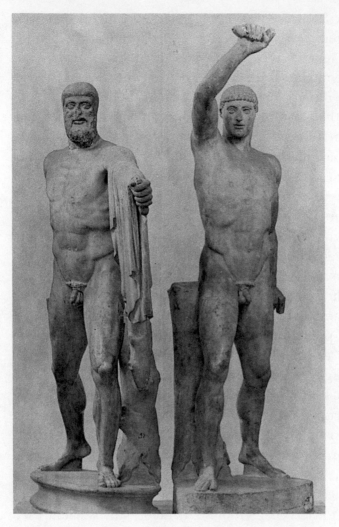

*33. The
Tyrannicides*

'deme'. The 139 demes were not simply parishes or districts
where one happened to live. They were communities whose
members identified themselves as 'demesmen', because, for
reasons of family history, this deme was where they felt at home.
You could not move deme (as you can change parish or district),
and you joined your father's deme as a matter of course. From
Cleisthenes' time onwards, an Athenian would identify himself by
his name, his father's name and his deme. The deme became a

sign of basic social and political identity. The demes had their own cult centres for religious worship, their own finances, their own associations such as theatres and burial societies, and they appointed a 'demarch', a leader of the deme. It was through the deme that a great deal of civic bureaucracy functioned. The important political impact of such foundations was to establish a structure of self-determination in each of the communities, and to give the community a sense of responsibility for all that happened in the community. This was a truly local politics.

The second level of structure was the tribe. The whole of Athens was now divided into ten tribes. Each tribe had a hero after whom it was named, with its own cults. But, most importantly, tribes formed the framework for elections to all the major political institutions and the numerous boards of magistrates and other officials. The army was organized into ten regiments, one for each tribe. Dead soldiers of the state were carried to the grave on wagons, one for each tribe. Competitions at the major festivals were often arranged on a tribal basis. The Panathenaia festival included tribal boat-races and tribal beauty competitions (men only). These tribes were made up of groups of the demes. They were designed to be roughly equal in number of citizens, and roughly balanced in regional and political affiliations. So the tribes were made up of *trittyes*, 'thirds'. Each *trittys* was made up of demes from the town, from the inland and from the coastal regions (hence 'thirds'). In this way, the tribes worked to reduce the old factionalisms with new collective affiliations. One hundred and thirty-nine demes, from the three regions, were structured into ten tribes, to make the one city, Athens.

This new spatial organization was a stunning political revolution, designed – successfully – to produce interlocking communities of local and national ties and obligations. Citizenship and local affiliation remain the basic building-blocks of modern democracy.

This organization of space was matched by the new institutions of the state. Some sort of Assembly had already existed, but the new Assembly (*ekklêsia*) was the sovereign collective of the people, ruled by the principle of one man, one vote. It is difficult to recapture the radical oddness of this. A king, an emperor, a priest, a small council – these are almost universally the dominant structures of authority in the ancient world, as in most of Europe for most subsequent centuries. That each man should be equal in power to decide matters of state policy or the distribution of resources is a fundamental and shocking innovation. Its implications are still being explored.

The Council of 500 was established to prepare the business for the Assembly, to execute the decisions of the Assembly, and for day-to-day administration. The Council was made up of ten groups of fifty men, each over the age of thirty, selected by lot from each of the ten tribes. They were selected from the demes and by the demes, so that each deme had a direct link into the central administration of the state. Each councillor was appointed for a year, and no-one could be a councillor in successive years or more than twice in his life. This meant that every citizen who reached the age of thirty had a very good chance of having to sit on the central administrative body of government at some point in his life. For day-to-day business, the calendar year was divided into ten periods, and each tribe's councillors took control of the business for one period. A chairman was appointed daily. In this organization of things, the level of required political engagement is strikingly high. The Council became the political school of the citizens.

The popular courts, founded by Solon and extended by Cleisthenes, became the emblem of democratic rule. Cleisthenes established new courts, which continued to expand in number and business after him. There were large juries of citizens, up to 501 men, who were chosen by lot from a roster of 6,000 available citizens over the age of thirty. Jurors came to be paid to attend court, so that even the poor citizen could fulfil his civic duty in court. Unlike modern courts, there were no professional lawyers or judges (although there were officials to keep the business on track or to read out official documents). Each prosecutor and defender had to speak for himself, and was judged by his peers. Unlike the justice handed down by a king or priest, this was open business, debated and recorded publicly, regulated by the rule of published law. The random selection of jurors prevented bribery and *parti pris* political decisions, much as the lack of a caste of professional lawyers kept technical, elite learning out of the business of conflict resolution. It also led to the development of professional trainers in rhetoric, and the growth of a group of professional speech-writers: our first media experts and spin-doctors. The courts dramatized social conflict, but set it within the frame of the people's political authority.

Certain areas of state business were under the jurisdiction of the magistrates, or 'archons'. It was the job of one of the archons, for example, to choose which playwrights would be supported to present plays in the tragedy and comedy competitions; it was the job of an archon to oversee religious festivals. Under Cleisthenes' reforms, the magistrates were elected from the most aristocratic families. After you had served as an archon you automatically progressed to sit on the Areopagus, the highest court of the land, which dealt, for example, with first-degree murder trials. This court was of the highest prestige, and the archons had undeniable influence in their respective domains. To this degree, the elite remained active in their traditional areas of authority.

The archons, however, remained strictly under the authority of the Assembly, and could not direct or instruct the Assembly or the Council. What's more, apart from the position of general, each magistracy could be held for only one year, which reduced the potential to build up power in any particular sphere. Even this ability of the elite families to seek power through official position was drastically altered in 486 – twenty years or so after Cleisthenes' initial reforms – when the Athenians decided that in future the archons would also be chosen by lot from a shortlist, rather than elected. The only position now through which an aristocrat could actively seek power in the state was that of general, and this was a position full of political and military risks.

Such moves towards limiting aristocratic authority continued throughout the fifth century. In 462, the reforming politician Ephialtes passed a measure to limit the role of the Areopagus court. Under the slogan 'Back to Basics', Ephialtes stripped the Areopagus of all business except judging certain limited cases of sacrilege, and of first-degree murder. Although the archons had been appointed by lot for the last twenty years or more, this was seen as a 'democratising' proposal, not least because the Areopagus' other business reverted to the popular courts. Ephialtes was assassinated shortly afterwards. Democracy means 'rule by the people', and fear of tyranny or counter-democratic coups led to careful restriction of the powers of any individual and of the aristocratic elite in particular. Again, the restriction of the power of an inherited elite by accountable citizens designing and running the state's institutions is a mainstay of all later democratic systems.

The most novel and uniquely democratic institutional device to restrict individual power was 'ostracism'. The Assembly had the power to vote that any one particular man should be forced to leave the territory of Attica for ten years. There was a quorum of 6,000 citizens for such a vote – a very high number indeed. Unlike most votes, the balloting was secret. Each citizen had to write the name of the citizen he wished to see ostracized on a broken piece of pot (an *ostrakon* in Greek, hence the name). The most famous story is of Aristeides the Just. He was asked by an illiterate farmer, who did not recognize him, to write his own name on a potsherd. He did so, but asked the farmer why he wanted to ostracize Aristeides. "Because I am sick of hearing him called "the just",' replied the farmer. Archaeologists have found a cache of 191 *ostraka*, dumped in an ancient well, with the same name of Themistocles written on them in fourteen different hands – which suggests some organized vote-rigging. Ostracism was not actually utilized until 487/6 (which makes some historians wonder if it were really available in the Cleisthenic reforms), and it was not used again after 417, but in the political turmoil and paranoia around the Persian Wars it was used with some frequency. The *ostrakon* illustrated in Figure 34 has the words

34. An ostrakon

'*Kallias Kratio[u]*', ('Kallias, son of Kratios'), clearly etched on one side. On the reverse is a scratched cartoon of a Persian bowman. It seems that Kallias is being set up as an enemy of the people and a friend of Persia. The people's fear here is not just of the power of one man, but of one man helping all Athens become a slave to a foreign king.

The one major position in the new state which was not time-limited or appointed by lot was the position of general. There were ten generals appointed each year, and by the 470s they included the commanders of the military forces. Pericles was appointed general for many consecutive years, and had such authority that the historian Thucydides, ever sharply cynical, describes it as '*de facto* rule by one man, for all that it was called democracy'. Even the generals, however, were directly subject to the authority of the Assembly. After the battle of Arginousae in 406, when the defeated Athenians failed to recover the bodies of their dead, the generals were sentenced to death by the Assembly. It's not by chance, though, that Pericles himself comes from one of the grandest aristocratic families of Athens. The position of general remained the one political office through which the elite could reach the desired pinnacle of prestige and authority within the new politics of democracy.

The institutions, festivals and rituals of this new constitution continued to develop over the next century and more, but the fundamental structure was outlined by Cleisthenes. It is an extraordinary and unparalleled experiment in structural thinking, and a quite astounding act of political will and imagination. For the first time, the people of a state were committed to self-determination, autonomy and responsibility for decision-making – the business of government. Cleisthenes established the structural principles by which democracy still functions: citizenship based on local and national affiliation, institutions run for and by citizens, agreed and accountable structures of power, with checks and balances. Even in a modern cynical and corrupt political environment, this remains an idea and an ideal with the power to inspire and astonish.

3

The Good Citizen

This institutional organization provided a structure for government, but the principles and attitudes to make it work also had to be developed. The Athenians needed to think themselves into being democratic citizens. The experiment of living in a democracy meant manufacturing and maintaining the bonds to hold together these different people and different interests as a community. For modern citizens, the Athenian discovery of politics produces a compelling insight into the differences, as well as the similarities, between ancient political motivations and the driving spirit of modern democracy.

The first and most basic concept that linked Athenians was the idea of citizenship itself. In democracy, a man is not subject to a king or lord, but is a citizen of the state. Citizenship brought many benefits – the festivals to celebrate, the status of being an insider in what rapidly became the leading city of the Mediterranean, the financial fruits of Athens' imperial policies. The law defined who was entitled to be a citizen, and the Athenians worried constantly about such definitions. Hotly argued trials about cases of disputed citizenship reveal Athenian anxiety and conflict about who had the right to citizenship (especially as Athens became more prosperous and more populous). But it is the sense of self projected by the idea of the citizen which provides the most telling contrast with modern democracies. 'Participation' is the watchword. The Athenian citizen was expected to attend the Assembly, to serve on the Council at some point, to act as a juror on occasion, to vote, to do the business of the deme, to take part in festivals and to fight in the state's army or navy. Modern democracies talk obsessively about rights. Ancient democracy thought of citizenship more as an issue of duties and activities.

In Thucydides' famous account of Pericles' address to the assembled citizens, the city's leader declares: 'We do not say that a man who takes no interest in politics minds his own business; we say he has no business here at all.' In democracy, to be unengaged is to be 'useless'. The standard word for a private citizen is *idiôtes*, from which we get the English word 'idiot', a fool who lives in his own world. No doubt the poorer citizen who had less leisure time, or who lived in a distant village, could engage less in the regular meetings in the town than the men who lived in the urban centre – the Assembly met forty times a year. And there certainly were citizens who consciously chose a minimalist engagement with the messier and more time-consuming aspects of the political process. None the less, it is striking that in any decade between a fifth and a tenth of all citizens would serve on the Council. There were frequent law cases in the many courts which required large juries. Athens had more festivals than any other Greek state. The opportunity to discuss war by the men who might be called upon to fight it could dominate the business of the Assembly. Each citizen could be directly and individually involved in passing laws, in setting budgets, in deciding state policy, in declaring war.

This last element is particularly important. Throughout the fifth century Athenians were involved in war. The Persian Wars culminated in the great battles of Marathon, Salamis and Plataea, by which the Persian invaders were defeated. In the continuing campaign of the next thirty years, Athens was involved in expeditions as far afield as Egypt; and they were also locked in combat against the Spartans for more than twenty-five years in the Peloponnesian War. Throughout this period, Athens had almost no mercenary forces; it mobilized a citizen army and navy (though it did sometimes hire rowers for the fleet). Indeed, to be a citizen meant to fight for the state, and to be prepared to die for it. 'Fighting for democracy' was a personal commitment for all the citizens. There was no standing army of largely working-class, professional soldiers; no draft of disaffected young men, sent off by a council of elders to fight abroad. As Thucydides' Pericles again sums up: 'Each of us is willing to fight and die.'

When the Athenians in the Assembly voted for war, they voted themselves and their own children into war. So it is extremely telling that the Athenians did vote the city into war almost every year of the fifth century (and there were no two years in succession without fighting). War was a norm for the Athenian citizens. It was a crucial way in which citizens participated and were evaluated as citizens. When Plato emphasizes what a noble and brave soldier Socrates was, he is responding to this military ideal. Modern political obsessions – the draft, national service, whether the people want war – are irrelevant to Athenian democracy: war is a shared, necessary enterprise for all citizens, and voted on by the citizens as such.

In Athens, direct democracy requires participation, and a direct relation between decision-making and action. This could scarcely be further from the structure of representational democracy as it takes place in Europe and America. Even at local level – the deme, as it were – a modern electorate appoints a government to take decisions for it, and for many – most – citizens that is the limit of political engagement. Decisions are often taken without reference to those most affected. Because of party politics – something wholly absent from ancient democracy – elections are often fought on slates of policies, and with an eye on national and international agendas. It is extremely hard for a voter to use a vote to indicate support for one aspect of party policy but to reject another. Individual laws or proposals may, rather rarely, be put to the vote by referendum – but even then there are few forums for sharing public debate, as opposed to opportunities for opinions to be circulated. Indeed, it might be said that nothing frightens modern democracies as much as the spectre of popular participation.

This striking difference between what the classical Athenians and the modern West understand by democracy can be explained in many ways – from the size of modern populations to the history of the development of modern democracies. For contemporary society, there can be no return to Athenian-style institutions. But the difference also depends on a fundamental disjunction in how the 'democratic subject' is understood. 'Democratic subject' means the idea of the person which makes sense of the democratic system, or the idea of the person which is presupposed by the democratic system. Pericles, in Thucydides' famous description of the idealism of democracy, declares, 'We Athenians, in our own persons, take our own decisions.' Aristotle defines the basic idea of the citizen as the person 'entitled to participate in decision-making and authority'. These definitions have far-reaching implications. For Athenian democracy, it means that any decision is best put to a collective, and the sum of individuals together will make a decision which is not merely binding but the best decision available. The members of the Assembly will decide directly on foreign policy or economic matters, just as a jury will evaluate the competing claims of prosecution and defence in the courtroom.

In a modern representational democracy, the citizens are usually asked to make a choice between those who will be asked to take a decision for them. A government (senator, Member of Parliament, congressman, Member of the National Assembly and so forth) is elected, and the government (senator and so on) evaluates the evidence and then comes to a decision. Where ancient democracy starts from an assumption of the equality of citizenship, modern democracy starts from an assumption that some people must be better than the majority at political reasoning, and that the political process should separate these decision-makers from the mass and invest them with authority. The good citizen of modern democracy should *not* be involved in decision-making or policy-formulation. Engagement between the people and the 'servant of the people' is structurally limited. It says something rather pointed about what modern society thinks of the citizen's role in government.

The Athenians took their commitment to the equality of citizens to an extreme degree, in a way which can seem quite baffling to modern society. The principle of appointing officials by lot – that is, by random selection – became by the fourth century the norm for all major positions bar the generals. The assumption is that each and every citizen is capable of performing the necessary duties of democratic authority – of judging well. Random selection is the fairest procedure precisely because all citizens are capable. For some positions, a shortlist was prepared of eligible candidates (which provided some regulation: for the appointment of archons after 486, for example, lists of 500 men were pre-elected by the demes), and for jobs like membership of the Council an age restriction further controlled the selection process. The election of the generals, the most important military and political offices, also shows that for certain tasks, such as leading the army into war, it was perceived as necessary to invest authority in a few, carefully chosen men. None the less, the reliance on lot as a mode of selection for administrative positions of authority would terrify any modern organization.

The procedure was used proudly across every sphere of life. It can be seen in all its eccentric glory in one of democracy's most celebrated institutions, the tragedy competition, a place where the modern world might least expect to see it. There was a good deal of symbolic capital invested in this event. The man who sponsored each production invested not just money but status. The playwrights and actors competed too – winning mattered. The whole competition, as a competition, could cause considerable excitement among the spectators as well. All this puts considerable focus on the business of judging.

Before the festival, the Council drew up lists of citizens selected from each of the ten tribes. We do not know of any special qualification. These lists were sealed in ten urns and kept in the treasury of the Acropolis, the most secure place in the city. At the beginning of the contest, the urns were unsealed, and the archon chose one name randomly from each to get a board of ten judges. At the end of the contest, each judge wrote his order of preference on a tablet. Each tablet was put in a further urn, and the archon chose five of these tablets at random. These determined the winner. At each stage, where we might expect critical judgement, intellectual or artistic acumen or theatrical experience to be relevant criteria for judges and their decision, the system works to randomize. It declares, in Periclean mode, that each Athenian is capable of producing a judgement.

The *pinakion* illustrated in Figure 35 is the token a prospective juror would use when he entered into the selection procedure to

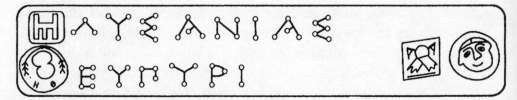

35. A pinakion

sit in the courts. This one has on it the man's name 'Lysanias', and specifies his deme 'Eupuri' ('Eupuridae'). The four symbols probably indicate his eligibility for various offices, including the position of juror. This little token (it is 11cm by 2cm) would be put into the random selection machine (*klêrotêrion*), a pair of pillars with ten vertical slots, which, with a complex system of black and white balls, enabled the random selection of some of the little tablets and the rejection of others. Figure 36 shows a reconstruction of what was the very height of democratic voting technology, based on the principle that every citizen can and should sit in judgement in the courts. The machine randomized which citizens were chosen, and which courts they attended.

The democratic subject in ancient democracy was invested with an extraordinary degree of responsibility and an extraordinary requirement of participation. A citizen was the only thing to

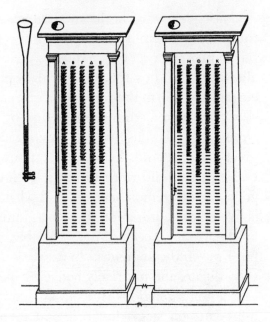

*36. A kleroterion, a random
selection machine*

be in a democracy, and a citizen's life was defined by his participation in the business of the city and evaluated as such. There was
no aspect of a citizen's life that did not have some bearing on the
politics of the city, and the city entered into every aspect of his
life. 'Politics' consequently did not mean a delimited, professional
area of state activity, but meant engaging in the business of the life
of a city: the Greek for 'citizen' is *politês*, and the Greek for the
'city-state' is *polis*: 'politics' is what the *politês* does in the *polis*. It
makes no sense in Greek to say 'My private life is my own and no
business of the state.' When the citizen was in the public eye – and
nowhere more so than in the arenas of the courtroom, assembly,
market place, gym – then his whole life, his whole participation
in the affairs of the city, was open to scrutiny. The men who clash
in the courtroom have no scruple about making sexual allegations
against each other, or mocking their relatives' lifestyles. Going to
the gym, how you walk, how you dress, how you wear your hair,
what you eat and drink, all become signs of what sort of Athenian
you are. Democracy makes public figures of all its citizens.

Consequently, to be in an audience – in the courtroom, the theatre, the Assembly, the gym – is not to be a passive spectator, but to play the role of judging, evaluating citizen. Modest daily allowances, paid by the state, made it possible for even the poor citizen to perform the duties of a citizen: the ideal is that no one should be barred from participation by financial misfortune. So strong was this sense of the importance of judgement that the great orator Demosthenes could mock his opponent Aeschines with this splendid run of insults, each of which stresses what a good citizen Demosthenes is, and what a poor citizen Aeschines is: 'You did the initiation, but I was initiated; you were the clerk, but I gave the speech in the Assembly; you were the third actor, but I was in the audience.' In each case, Aeschines is depicted as subordinate, and not really behaving like a real man – a clerk, an assistant at a religious rite and an actor. For Demosthenes, it is not acting on stage, but being in the audience of the theatre, where the citizen performs his role.

Aristotle, a philosopher who so often takes a carefully articulated, broadly held idea as his starting point, captures this sense of how the city, as an all-embracing political life, defines the citizen. In the *Politics*, his immensely influential theoretical study of political systems, he offers as a basic principle a statement which may seem at first sight completely counter-intuitive: 'the city is in nature prior to households and to each of us individually'. Aristotle knows well that any standard historical account of the development of the city would start with individuals in households and move up towards collections of households, which become eventually a recognizable city. But Aristotle is aiming at a different sort of explanation. For him everything has a potential, a potential which when fulfilled fulfils the end of that thing. It is only when its potential is fulfilled that an object reaches its *telos*, or perfected final form. So an acorn has the potential to grow into an oak tree. The oak tree is the final, perfected form of the acorn. It's what an acorn is for. An acorn while it is still an acorn, or if it remains an acorn, does not fulfil its potential. The perfected, final form is what makes sense of the object in transition, and is always logically prior to it. You need the oak to understand what an acorn is and what its potential is. For Aristotle, therefore, the chicken does logically come before the egg.

In the same way, the city makes sense of households and individuals. It is only when men live together as citizens in a city that men reach their perfected and fulfilled form. Aristotle sums up his ideal in his famous dictum that 'Man is a Political Animal.' He means that man is inherently and properly a creature that lives in a *polis* – a city-state – and is thus *political*. For Aristotle, one of democracy's greatest theorists, man is not fulfilled without a political life.

The contrast with contemporary political life in Western democracies is all too evident. Despite the mantra of 'government of the people, for the people, by the people', or the British tradition of service to king and country, the modern ideological commitment to the sanctity of private life produces an often aggressive tension between the authority of government and the citizen: 'The Englishman's home is his castle.' This approach took its most murderously extreme and crazy form when Timothy McVeigh blew up the government buildings in Oklahoma to protest against intrusive control over an individual's private life. This opposition is matched by a lack of participation by citizens in government – even in voting. Many Americans are not even registered to vote or do not vote, and the low turnout especially for local elections in Britain means that almost no local government and few national governments have the support of even 50 per cent of the electorate. Collective political action is made visible largely in the form of pressure groups, such as the unions, the farmers, the students – except in the remarkable and unexpected revolutionary movements of the sort that brought down the Berlin Wall, where the demonstrators in the street could chant '*We* are the people.' Between modern and ancient democracy, the notion of what a good citizen is seems radically different.

Despite this difference, there are basic principles which link the good citizens of modern and ancient democracy in what looks more like a shared project. First of these is freedom of speech. There are two related ideas here, which Greek makes clearer than English. One is *parrhêsia*, which means 'freedom of speech', or 'frank speaking', a notion which enshrines openness, a spirit of exchange and a lack of violent restriction. Any citizen can address any other. The other is *isêgoria*, which means 'equality of public expression'. Each citizen has an equal right to be heard in the democratic forums of debate. Any citizen can speak at any political event. The Assembly always began with the deeply symbolic announcement of the herald: 'Who wishes to speak?' There is no fixed order or hierarchy in the Assembly: advice can come from any citizen in principle (however restricted it may have become in practice). *Isêgoria* is a narrowly conceived political value, while *parrhêsia* stretches more broadly into any form of social exchange.

In the democratic imagination, the opposite of these guarantees of free speech is the world of the tyrant, where the underling is forced to fawn, and paranoia rather than openness distorts exchange into secrecy and plotting. In Euripides' play *The Phoenician Women*, Oedipus' son Polyneices identifies the very worst hardship of being a refugee in exile as 'the lack of free speech' (*parrhêsia*). His mother immediately agrees: 'That', she declares, 'is the mark of a slave.' A citizen is defined by free speech, and without it he might as well be a slave. Free speech (*isêgoria*), explains Herodotus, makes the soldiers of a democracy stronger than the soldiers of a despotic system, which is why the Greeks defeated the Persians, and remained free men, not slaves.

'Equality before the law' (*isonomia*) is the second unshakeable principle of democracy. Laws must be public and published. Each citizen has an equal standing in law – a right to a fair trial. A person must be judged by the law and according to the law. It is this principle which the Athenian drinking song about the Tyrannicides boasted of: the Tyrannicides were heroes because they 'brought equality before the law to Athens'. The danger of the tyrant is that he rules at his own whim and will.

This love of the law is seen throughout Athens. In his comedy *The Wasps*, Aristophanes makes fun of the Athenian citizens who loved being jurors and stinging their fellow citizens in court. Like Americans, the Athenians could happily mock themselves for constantly being in and out of court. But perhaps the most moving declaration of this power of the law comes from a non-Athenian, Herodotus, writing about non-Athenians. Xerxes, king of Persia, has invaded Greece – and is about to meet the Spartans at Thermopylae. The king cannot believe that so few Spartans would stand and fight against such a huge army. He questions Demaratus, a Spartan who is travelling with him. If there were one supreme king, asks Xerxes, who forced them to obey, perhaps they would act in such a suicidal way, but why would free men – as the Spartans boast themselves to be – act like that? It's incomprehensible. Demaratus is cautious in response. He carefully asks if he can tell the truth even if it is unpalatable, and not face the wrath of the king. This is the inevitable nervousness that comes from facing absolute power, rather than the free speech in a system of law. It acts as a significant introduction to Demaratus' answer. Here is its ringing climax: 'Spartans fighting together are the best soldiers in the world. They are free, yes, but not entirely free. For they have a master, and that master is Law, which they fear much more than your subjects fear you. Whatever this master commands, they do. And his command never varies.'

The Spartans were famous in Greece for the rigour of their social system and for their absolute allegiance to their unchanging laws. The Athenians were – self-consciously – more fickle and willing to propose new laws in the constant search for the best answer to the 'what if?' question. But Herodotus knows that obedience to the law is essential to Greekness and citizenship – a banner for his readers to march under. This allegiance to the law is exactly why Socrates in prison and facing death says that he refuses to escape: 'The laws are the mother and the father' of the citizen, he says, and, even when condemned by them, it would be wholly wrong to go against them. Herodotus, in a brilliant stroke, has the Persian king respond with a light-hearted laugh to Demaratus' eulogy of Greek commitment to law – before he marches his men towards disastrous losses against the brave Spartans. Xerxes' foolish laughter is a great symbol for the incomprehension of the barbarian king, his negation of all that the commitment to the rule of law means.

After Xerxes was defeated at Salamis, he returned to Susa, the capital of the Persian Empire. Aeschylus depicted this bitter homecoming in his tragedy *The Persians*, a play which celebrates the triumph of the Athenian values of democracy over the values of the barbarian East, as much as it lauds a military victory. Xerxes' mother, Queen Atossa, anticipates his arrival in fascinating terms:

> If my son succeeds, he would be an object of awe.
> But if he fails, he is not accountable to the city.
> Assuming he survives, he will rule the land none the less.

These lines show clearly how the defeat of Xerxes – depicted on stage in Athens – has to be seen within the ideological frame of democracy. The audience is asked to reflect on how the king is 'not accountable to the city'.

Accountability is the third great principle of democratic authority. Every man and every official must be accountable to the city – the collective of citizens. This means that each man is responsible for how he votes and acts, and may be held accountable. But most vividly it means that each person in authority is held accountable by and to the people. Unlike the Great King, responsible to no one, in Athens every official at the end of his term of office was required to present 'accounts' (*euthunai*) – a record of his performance, which was open to scrutiny. For the Athenian democrat, accountability was the essential control of authority.

The good citizen of Athenian democracy is a responsible,

accountable, free-speaking, law-abiding – man. The privilege of citizenship depended also on rigorous exclusions. Women and slaves (as well as children) were not only not allowed to vote, but were also not allowed to attend the Assembly, Council or, most surprisingly of all, the law court. A woman, even when being prosecuted, could not appear in person in court, and a slave could provide reported evidence only after physical torture. It was assumed that a slave would follow his master's bidding or would be unreliable anyway, unless the intense pain of torture had tested his truth-telling. Aristotle had no qualm in declaring some races to be naturally servile, and in stipulating that a woman was a deformed man. A woman could not be a citizen in Athens. Where men were proud to be called 'citizens of Athens', women were generally called 'women of Attica': they didn't even have the name 'Athenian'. It was not merely foreigners who were excluded from citizenship; it was the majority of the adult population. It is much easier to promote the equality of citizenship when citizenship is restricted this way to a relatively homogeneous and selective group.

Modern Western democracies pride themselves – rightly – on their achievement of an extremely broad enfranchisement of society and the abolition of slavery. The move towards 'universal suffrage' was, of course, a long and hotly contested progression. The Reform Bill of 1867 in Britain allowed male householders to vote for the first time – a massive increase of the electorate and a radical change of its nature. It was perceived by many as an awful step towards the uncontrolled barbarity of American culture, in language that seems shocking today. 'For England', wrote the Countess of Derby, 'to make a step in the direction of democracy seems to me the strangest and wildest proposition that was ever broached by man.' Robert Lowe, the minister of education, fought against the proposal passionately, ending one famous speech in parliament with 'Surely the heroic work of so many centuries, the matchless achievements of so many wise heads and strong hands, deserves a nobler consummation than to be sacrificed at the shrine of revolutionary passion or the maudlin enthusiasm of humanity . . . History may tell of other acts as signally disastrous, but of none more wanton, none more disgraceful.' The fight against democracy was undertaken as a noble heroic task – one doomed to failure, it turned out. Democracy has become an unimpeachable term of modern political language.

But even Robert Lowe and the Countess of Derby could not imagine that women would ever be included in the franchise. Despite the celebrated protests of the Suffragettes, like Mrs Pankhurst, women did not get the vote in England until 1922, more than fifty years after ordinary men. If, as Hegel argued, a woman was not capable of full moral judgement, or if, as less philosophical commentators suggested, a woman would always vote as her husband directed, why should a woman be given the vote? The argument that it was ridiculous to prefer the opinion of a drunken and reprobate man over the judgement of an intelligent and informed woman cut little ice. The ease with which modern political analysts suggest that 'the female vote' swung the election of Bill Clinton, say, because of his physical attraction or charm is a not too distant echo of the misogynistic arguments that barred women from voting at all. To dismiss women voters as not fully politically responsible is a sneer which the suffrage of women has not stopped.

In contemporary society, however, national or cultural identity dominates the discussion of citizenship itself. What does it mean to be British (English, American, French . . .)? Thus, when citizenship is raised as an issue in contemporary discussion, it usually introduces a debate about 'knowledge' on the one hand, and 'allegiance' on the other. What do you need to know to be a British citizen? Must you speak English? Must you know English or British history? Are there necessary social or moral values without which you can't really be English? Could a list of questions be devised to test a person's Britishness for citizenship? Or if you are a British citizen who also comes from another culture, does that in some way challenge citizenship, or 'belonging'?

'Who do you cheer for in an international sports match?' was how one senior British politician notoriously put it. Finding an American citizen fighting with extremist Islamic forces in Afghanistan posed the difficulty in more pointed form.

The lack of clear argument or public debate about national and cultural identity highlights a fault-line in contemporary political understanding which looks destined to remain a source of intense mistrust and tension in contemporary Western democracy. It is also an area of maximum disjunction between modern and ancient Athenian ideas of citizenship. For a classical Athenian, the idea that a woman who did not speak the language of the state, did not worship the gods of the state and had political allegiances to another state should automatically be a voting citizen of the state would be the wildest comic or tragic fantasy.

In the modern West, democracy as a form of government is remarkably different from its classical Greek model. The historical view reveals not merely superficial differences, or differences that stem from the scale or technological advances of modern states. It reveals fundamental differences in how the citizen is conceptualized. The modern state is right to feel proud of its abolition of slavery, the drive towards universal suffrage and its degree of cultural tolerance (even if current debate about national identity shows how much more serious discussion of the central categories of belonging will be needed in an era of increasing multiculturalism and globalism). This pride finds its roots in a sense of the human being which is not shared by ancient politics – where, paradigmatically, Aristotle is fully willing to see slaves and women as naturally and inherently incapable when it comes to the democratic role of citizen.

Yet, for all the apparent continuity in the principles of free speech, equality before the law and accountability of the officials of government, the modern citizen is not expected or required to engage fully in the political process, and is radically divorced from the decision-making of government. The autonomy of judgement which Pericles celebrated has been replaced by an electoral process which chooses decision-makers. To an Athenian, 'government of the people, for the people, by the people' would seem the hollowest of rhetoric when set against the practice of American democracy. An unelected and unaccountable House of Lords, as in England, not to mention a monarch with a power of veto, is harder still to reconcile in theory or in practice.

Where does this disempowerment of the people come from? How should it be understood? These questions can be answered only by turning to the critics of democracy. So far, this chapter has looked primarily at how democracy describes itself, and, as such, it has inevitably smoothed over some of the contradictions, paradoxes and difficulties of both the theory and practice of democracy. Democrats, like most politicians, find it easy to see their own good sides. From the earliest days, however, there have been critics all too keen to expose such problems. The form of modern democracy is best explained as the paradoxical absorption into practice of the fiercest criticisms of democracy, from those opposed to it. It's from this strange historical mish-mash that much current dissatisfaction with contemporary Western politics stems.

4

The Critics of Democracy –
Experts and Education

Plato is the single most influential critic of democracy in the history of the West. He lived in Athens during the fourth-century BC flourishing of democracy. As a youth, he witnessed a bloody, short-lived, oligarchic coup, in which his uncle was a leading member of the usurpers quickly branded as the Thirty Tyrants. He saw his teacher and idol Socrates put to death by a democratic court, and much of his writing can be seen as a response to the profound anger and despair aroused in him by this event. Plato's *Republic* is the summation of his political philosophy, a massive dialogue where the characters Socrates and his friends outline a blueprint for the perfect society. The criticisms that Plato put into Socrates' mouth in this and other dialogues have dominated Western thinking on democracy ever since. Plato's views have thus influenced the shape of modern democracy. But they have also been instrumental in shaping Hitler's fascist state and the communism of the Soviet Union. Plato has a lot to answer for.

The first and most lasting criticism which Plato constructs is beguilingly simple, and its effect on modern democracy is devastating. The argument is most seductively put in a series of dialogues between Socrates and the citizens he meets. 'If you want advice on how to make shoes,' asks Socrates, 'who would you go for that advice?' 'A shoemaker,' comes the response. The stakes gradually rise. 'If you want advice on who is good at playing music,' continues Socrates, 'would you ask someone who is an expert at playing musical instruments?' 'Of course,' the interlocutor agrees. 'If you want to know who is good at maths, you would ask a mathematician?' 'Certainly.' And so on, until the crunch question. 'If you want advice about politics, would you ask a shoe-maker or a musician, or would you ask an expert on politics?' Backed into this corner, one way or another, with hesitations, counter-cases and further persuasion, it is agreed that in each sphere of expertise there is an expert who is best at the skill in question. Who, then, is the expert in politics? Surely not the shoemakers, or the others who make up the people.

The implications of this argument for democracy are ruthlessly explored in the *Republic*. In the ideal state, the ruling class will be the Philosopher-Kings, men especially selected, especially trained and uniquely prepared for the business of government. An exhaustively detailed education programme will produce the men best designed for rule, and it is to them that ruling should be entrusted. Women may – theoretically at least – be included in this elite class. The military class will be those men best fitted and trained for protecting the state. The others – the workers, the producers, the ordinary men and women – will live happily in the perfect and stable city, enchanted by the Noble Lie, the myths circulated knowingly by the Philosopher-Kings, which offer justification for why the state is as it is.

Plato's first criticism, then, is the claim that experts should judge in their sphere of expertise. The people have not been edu-cated into rule, cannot be expected to make informed judgements and cannot reasonably be asked to evaluate complex arguments. When democracy places authority for decision-making in the hands of the people, it is tantamount to asking a shoemaker for advice on music, or a musician for advice on horse-riding.

This argument was shockingly exploited during the democratic debate of the nineteenth century. Robert Lowe provided the slogan for the opposition to the Reform Bill of 1867. 'It will be absolutely necessary', he declared, 'to compel our future masters to learn their letters.' The brilliance of this slogan, repeatedly quoted ever since, lies in the complex layers of insult. The Oxford-educated minister of education speaks as if he is merely discussing a matter of education policy, but the policy is directed at those he sarcastically and bitterly calls 'our future masters'. The ordinary man, given the vote, becomes the master of those educated men of government. Compulsion, he suggests, will be necessary, because (of course) without compulsion the education process will not take place. The ordinary man is so far below the level now required for 'mastery' that they will even have to 'learn their letters' – gain basic literacy. The franchise is being proposed for the illiterate who will become the wholly unsuited masters of the elite. Lowe's elegant, sneering paradox sums up the lunacy he thinks democracy entails.

Lowe was all too clear about what he thought of the ordinary folk. He dismissed them as 'impulsive, unreflecting and violent people', full of 'ignorance', 'drunkenness' and a 'facility for intimidation'. It was not a view which endeared him to the electorate. But the same argument, in more gentle terms, has become a commonplace of modern democracy. Economics, foreign policy, education policy, transport policy and so on are all complex and difficult areas, overseen by trained professionals. These experts should be entrusted to make informed decisions because of their expertise. Or, more commonly, these experts should be required to give politicians advice, so that they can make the decisions. In modern democracy, the people are debarred from the decision-making of governance in part at least because – the argument runs – they are not competent to make the relevant decisions. The Platonic criticism of democracy has become part of the structure of modern democracy.

Plato would have no difficulty in pointing out the flimsy logic of this apparent acceptance of his criticisms. While expertise is hard won and absolutely necessary, expertise itself needs evaluation by those who govern. It's politicians who decide between experts, and who decide policy. Yet what training or expertise does a politician have? What should a politician know? How does the electorate understand and evaluate such expertise, and hold it accountable? The sarcastic Plato or the mocking Aristophanes would delight in dissecting the 'training' of a modern politician, especially when it comes to the ethics of government.

In a characteristically memorable image in the *Republic*, Plato does offer such a general, theoretical critique of how democratic politicians actually get trained as decision-makers. Being a politician, Socrates declares, is like being a man who is in charge of a fierce and irrational wild beast. The man offers it food, watches the animal's moods and learns what voice to use when he wants to sooth or to annoy it. He cannot tell which of the animal's desires is good for it, or bad, and he cannot give a rational account of what he is doing, even if his experience leads him to a certain familiarity with the beast. 'That man', concludes Socrates, with a shake of the head, 'would be a very strange sort of educator.'

Plato's image vividly suggests that in a democracy a politician cannot be simply committed to truth or justice, but has to follow the whim of a fickle and wilful people, or try and deceive it. 'Public opinion', rather than educated judgement, becomes the rule. The ability to do what is right is constantly compromised by the need to please the people – the untamed beast. Plato's second crushing criticism is that in democracy politicians do not lead but follow the (ill-informed) pleasures of the people.

Modern politics, especially in the democracies of America and Britain, has become obsessed with issues of presentation. Although this is often lamented as the sad collapse of modern politics away from some cleaner and finer past, it was, as Plato shows all too clearly, already a much discussed problem in the classical city. It was debated both at a grand philosophical level and at the practical level of political machination. There was a technical training for sale in strategies of 'spin' and 'self-presentation' from highly paid experts, called 'sophists' or 'rhetoric teachers'.

Democracy depends on the presentation of competing arguments, competing versions of events. It is the job of every speaker in democracy to try to persuade an audience. Persuasion has strategies that can be taught and evaluated. Those who lose a political vote or a case in court are likely to feel themselves the victim of another's persuasive skills. Spin is endemic to democracy: democracy is inconceivable without the recognition of the potential of persuasion, where one man's brilliant argument can always be another's deceptive misrepresentation. Far from being a modern problem, spin is a founding concern of democracy from the beginning.

Plato despaired of democratic politicians' necessary insistence on presentation rather than the bare truth. Yet what for Plato was a sarcastic and biting criticism of democratic politics has become in modern society an industry, a necessary, formalized part of the political process. Every political party has its PR department, its advertising campaign, its media manipulators – all of which are judged by the sole criterion of 'public opinion'. Plato's criticisms once again have been fully institutionalized in the modern system.

In the *Republic*, Plato goes on to dissect 'the democratic subject' with acid wit. He recognizes that the freedom and liberalness of democracy are attractive, 'like gaily coloured things are to women and children'. But the democrat, he argues, can't see that there are good and bad pleasures: 'he shakes his head and says all pleasures are equal and should have equal rights'. So, one day it's wine, women and song; the next, a faddish diet. One day, it's study, the next, physical sports. 'There is no order or restraint in his life, and he reckons his way of life is pleasant, free and happy.' Democracy's freedom means social and psychological lack of control. When 'anything goes', proper order cannot be maintained.

In democracy it is difficult to regulate the pleasures of the citizens, in theory and in practice. But Plato's corresponding passion for 'order and restraint' dominates his political theorizing. For Plato, it was Sparta, of all contemporary Greek states, which revealed the beneficial possibilities of social order. He praised Sparta repeatedly, and the influence of its social system is evident throughout the *Republic*. For Plato, and many other conservative aristocrats, Sparta was an image to set against what they saw as the chaotic liberalism, bordering on anarchy, of democratic Athens.

Sparta was a highly centralized, military state. It had two kings, and a council of elders which advised and directed the kings. Its elite class of 'Spartiates' was produced by the most rigorous physical and mental training. Children deemed at birth to be somehow inadequate were exposed, at the bidding of the state, and left to die. After a youth of repeated exercise and communal control, adolescent Spartans were sent out into the bush to survive by their wits. At their coming of age, they joined a 'mess' where they ate, lived and trained together. Private property and private houses were strictly controlled. The Spartans kept a huge population of 'helots' – a conquered and now enslaved neighbouring people – under control by violent suppression. Their system, the Spartans claimed, had been established by Lycurgus, their law-giver, and nothing about it should change. Under it, they became the most famous and feared fighting unit in the Mediterranean, who defeated Athens in the Peloponnesian War. There was none of the burgeoning of new art, literature and music which distinguished Athens, and which Plato wanted to ban from his *Republic*. Their society was not merely conservative. It aimed at the subordination of the individual at each stage to the collective good. The life of each citizen was organized for the benefit of the state (and thus all), and resisted the blandishments of personal luxury, ease, comfort and change, all in the name of the state.

Plato's praise of Sparta as the embodiment of the order that he wants to establish in his *Republic* has produced his longest and most disturbing critical legacy for the modern political world. Through the eighteenth and especially the nineteenth century, the battle between Athenian democracy and Spartan order was refought by European intellectuals, embroiled as they were in the revolutionary political turmoil of the period. The philosopher and politician John Stuart Mill memorably demonstrates how an image of Greece became a way of debating the present: he bluntly declared that 'The battle of Marathon, even as an event in English history, is more important than the battle of Hastings.' For Mill, there is a continuity between the past and the present, which makes the past worth fighting over for today's politics. In a period of revolution, Sparta could be held up as a model of stability. Even for Rousseau, Sparta could be celebrated because it had not suffered from the political unrest, factionalism and sheer turmoil of Athenian – and, by extension, modern European – political life.

But the mania for Sparta reaches its pinnacle in twentieth-century Germany, where the worst potential of such a commitment to order was fulfilled. The Spartans were the supreme Dorians, who had come from the north. In German nationalist myths, the Germans liked to think of themselves as the New Dorians, and this made Sparta, which seemed to embody the Aryan ideal, immediately attractive. In the 1930s and 1940s, German historians turned to the example of Sparta again and again. The Spartans were exclusive, intellectually and politically – that is, they were free of corrupt Eastern influences. Their constitution depended on a military aristocracy. They were tied to the land, and lived according to the values of truth, honesty and directness, backed up with an intense physical training. Their culling of their own weak children was an enlightened eugenics, based on a strong ideal of racial purity. Spartans did not allow the corrupting poison of modern literature or music. Sparta was a model for the new Germany.

Hitler himself praised the Spartans repeatedly. That a small elite population could control so many thousand helots and other inferior Mediterranean races was testimony to the Spartans' extraordinary strength, based as it was on racial purity and military order. The spirit they showed at Thermopylae was the same as the Germans showed in the First World War, and then at Stalingrad. Sparta was the first *volkisch* state – a state where the purity of the people, the *Volk*, strengthened by obedience and military training, led to a perfection of social order. Most bizarrely, Hitler suggested that the soup of the peasants of Schleswig-Holstein was just like the broth which was the only thing that the hardy Spartans, in their horror of luxury, would regularly eat. From food to eugenics, an image of Sparta fuelled Nazi thinking with classical authority.

The intellectual opponents of Nazism fought on the same ground of Platonic political thinking. As one American educationalist argued: the *Republic* is 'the original philosophical charter of fascism, [and] one of the most dangerous items in the education of the Western world'. Richard Crossman, who would become a leading politician in the post-war British government, wrote his popular volume *Plato Today* in 1937, in which he imagines Plato visiting Nazi Germany (as well as Soviet Russia and other political systems). Although Plato sees much to admire in the Third Reich, he is made to attack a surprised German academic for getting his Platonism wrong and misusing his ideas.

Most influential of all these intellectual projects, however, was Karl Popper's *The Open Society and Its Enemies*, the first volume of which is the most stirring attack on Plato's totalitarian thinking. Popper started his great book in 1938 and finished it in 1943, in exile from his native Austria in New Zealand. Every word is infused with a passionate and brooding sense of the 'darkness of the present world situation'. It begins with the eloquent juxtaposition of two quotations. The first is from Pericles: 'Although only a few may originate a policy, we are all able to judge it.' The second is from Plato. It begins: 'The greatest principle of all is that nobody, whether male or female, should be without a leader. Nor should the mind of anybody be habituated to letting him do anything at all on his own initiative, neither out of zeal, nor even playfully.' It concludes: 'In a word, he should teach his soul, by long habit, never to dream of acting independently, and to become utterly incapable of it.' Politicians who wield the slogan 'law and order' are rarely as explicit as Plato about *how much* law and order is necessary. Or what happens when 'law and order' comes up against the freedom of the individual which democracy demands. After Plato, this has remained a central issue for democracy and political theory.

Plato's criticisms of democracy have been fully absorbed in the development of today's strange and self-contradictory form of democracy; and his opposition to democracy in the name of law and order continues to provide a key intellectual authority for totalitarian government (and for nervous democracies). Plato's questions remain our questions. His arguments continue to structure modern debate and explain modern systems in a profound manner. Fighting with Plato, about Plato and through Plato animates the very idea of democracy – and its political opposition.

5

A Question of Betrayal

If Plato is the most profound critic of democracy, Socrates, Plato's teacher, is democracy's most troublesome citizen.

The intellectual who asks too many challenging questions does not fit easily into democracy's standard gallery of heroes and villains. He is not like the tyrant or the criminal, the exemplary threat to democracy, who must be removed. He is not simply the good citizen, who makes democracy work. The worry is that he may be the enemy rather than the guardian of society: his ideas may distort or destroy the most cherished values of democracy. Socrates fully embodied that worry for Athens.

Socrates was put to death by democratic Athens because of what he stood for. What he taught and how he taught it seemed too dangerous for Athenian society to bear. Yet Socrates has emerged for posterity most often as a hero of democratic free-thinking, who most tellingly interrogates the precarious balance between freedom of speech and the requirements of social order. Today, Socrates bears the symbolic weight of 2,000 years of political argument.

It is impossible to travel back through the images of Socrates to the real man who walked the streets of Athens in the fifth century, arguing with the people he met. Socrates wrote nothing. We know of him through the texts of Plato, the writing of the historian and critic Xenophon, and the comic plays of Aristophanes (as well as a host of fragmentary and indirect sources). The image of Socrates in Plato – the highly ironical, complex, philosophically astute master – is not the same as the more direct and 'useful' figure that Xenophon depicts – and neither matches the charlatan sophist whom Aristophanes mocks. At the same time, there is little which Plato or Xenophon writes that does not have at least half an eye on defending Socrates retrospectively against his attackers. Socrates comes swathed in the veils of apologetic prose.

The relationship between Plato and Socrates, the pupil who writes and the master who leaves no record, is especially difficult to plumb. Socrates may be the leading character of Plato's *Republic*, but it is impossible to imagine that what Socrates says in it represents simply the views of the historic Socrates, or even what Plato thought the views of the historic Socrates were. The *Republic* is a dramatic dialogue, dominated by Socrates, where different characters express their opinion, and where none of them is Plato or speaks simply or consistently for Plato. As a result, there will always be debate about what exactly Plato's own doctrine on any political issue must have been. Plato's readers have always been seduced, fascinated and frustrated by the dialogue form, especially when it stars as a teacher Socrates, who ironically denied knowing anything anyway. It is just impossible to say how much Plato and how much Socrates – and how much irony – there is when Plato has Socrates ask one of his probing questions.

The legal charges that were laid against Socrates were explicit enough. He was prosecuted for 'corrupting the youth' (which does not only have sexual connotations) and 'introducing new gods'. But from the trial onwards it was readily appreciated that the case was political in a broader sense. Socrates was being pursued primarily because he was perceived to be an enemy of the state. Like many a figure who has been branded in this way, however, Socrates soon became an icon of the solitary individual who stands up for the real values of a just and good society.

For innumerable ancient and modern writers, Socrates is a hero and a martyr. His heroism takes the form of his unflinching commitment to asking difficult questions. He is the exemplary dissident, who, in the name of truth, continually and embarrassingly provoked the authorities – and the pompous, the self-assured, the unreflective – into an unwilling recognition that they did not really know what they were talking about. Socrates insisted that the unexamined life isn't worth living. Consequently he demanded to know what truth, justice, virtue, goodness were – and remained dissatisfied with the answers, especially the pat, smug or self-satisfied. Socrates the hero is a disinterested, supremely moral champion of the intellectual values of enquiry and hard thinking. He was, in Matthew Arnold's translation of Plato, 'the only true politician of men now living' because he helped anyone he met towards a true sense of civic life and duty.

Socrates' execution is viewed as a martyrdom, because when sentenced to death in court, he stayed in prison to face execution out of principle. Not only did he die for his convictions, but his convictions also led him to face death with equanimity. One of Plato's greatest triumphs in his defence of Socrates is the picture he creates of him on his deathbed, calmly discussing the immortality of the soul and encouraging his despairing companions. This image has inspired great religious and political art. It is not by chance that the most famous painting of the scene (Figure 37) is by the artist at the heart of the French revolution's passion for classical models, Jacques-Louis David. The contrast between the overwhelmed companions and the calm Socrates is eloquent. Socrates *performs* the benefits of philosophy by his fearless approach to his own death.

This Socrates, the hero and martyr, has been the darling of those political thinkers who celebrate free-thinking, and who resist the tyranny of the majority. It is an image which especially appeals in the era of the Romantic genius, the heroic individual set against the mass of mankind, the lonely prophet of truth questioning the dull conventions of an unthinking society. For this liberal tradition, dissent is seen as necessary to politics and to social progress. This Socrates is often set in passionate opposition to his pupil Plato. 'It is Socrates, not Plato, whom we need,' wrote Richard Crossman in response to the politics of the 1930s. As

37. Death of Socrates *by Jacques-Louis David*

George Grote, one of the greatest political historians of the nineteenth century, provocatively concluded, 'Free-thinking minds who take views of their own become inconvenient and dangerous'; Socrates would not 'be allowed to exist in the Platonic Republic'. For Grote and so many others in a distinguished roll-call of historians, politicians and philosophers, Plato betrayed his teacher. And it is to democracy's eternal shame that it killed Socrates.

Yet there is another, equally long tradition, which is more hostile to Socrates and his questions. Aeschines, the orator, speaking in the same court fifty years or so after it had condemned Socrates, had no doubt: 'Gentlemen of Athens, you executed Socrates the sophist because he was clearly responsible for the education of Critias, one of the Thirty, who destroyed democracy' – that is, the tyrants whose bloody coup, backed by Sparta, overthrew the constitution. Moreover, Alcibiades, whose treason had led Athens to the brink of disaster in the Peloponnesian War, was also an intimate friend and pupil of Socrates. A teacher is judged by his pupils. Socrates' dissent appeared to Aeschines – and to others since – to have created a violent and self-serving oligarchy. The champion of the individual against the state produced individuals who overthrew the state.

The Roman Cato, a conservative if ever there was one, showed equal distaste for Socrates on more general moral grounds. 'Socrates was a constant prattler,' he sniffed, 'who attempted, as best he could, to be his country's tyrant by abolishing its customs and by enticing his fellow citizens into opinions opposed to the law.' Cato, as ever, comes across in this story as blithely and aggressively dismissive of Greek culture. But his jibe that Socrates stood against traditional wisdom isn't simply knee-jerk conservatism. Socrates did question traditional views of things, and this set father against son, citizen against citizen. This social disruptiveness – Socrates as 'gadfly' – stemmed from his oblique, marginal, personal, discordant stance. It is not a stance everyone can take. In this way, Socrates cannot be a model for us all. Socrates was not a stimulus to social cohesion. When democracy killed Socrates, it was defending itself politically and morally from a dangerously destructive force.

These two different traditions of evaluating Socrates arose from the first passionate debates around his trial and have never ceased. He has become one of the most powerful secular images we have. The figure of Socrates has been appropriated, celebrated, manipulated and rejected over the centuries, as his questioning of the collective, traditional values on which any stable society relies still provokes the policemen of political thought and inspires its revolutionaries. Most modern writers find in Socrates the heroic tale of the challenging intellectual put to death despite and because of his championing of the cause of truth and justice. It is a stirring tale, and one that has mattered hugely and movingly for the dissidents in the Soviet Union, in Czechoslovakia, in South Africa and beyond.

But the most pressing problem raised by Socrates the teacher and Plato the pupil is a more disturbing one and will always be hard to answer adequately. How much dissent can a democratic society bear and how much must it cherish? Judging Socrates – again and again – is one way for us to struggle with that impossible boundary between the freedom of the individual and the regulation of the community.

The fate of Socrates and the criticisms of Plato can't be separated from each other. Socrates the teacher and Plato the pupil show that a dynamic tension between individual freedom and community regulation is inevitable in a democratic system. Modern democracies have continued to struggle, repeatedly and inconclusively, with these classical issues. The McCarthy committee on un-American activities is one extreme example where the democratic state's attempted control of dissent led finally to revulsion against such control. The burning of draft cards, however, as an act of individual conscience found theoretical support from one of America's greatest political philosophers of democracy, John Rawls, who argued that civic disobedience was a civic obligation when the laws endangered the essence of democracy. Even Socrates sat obediently in prison, calmly awaiting his punishment by law. The surveillance of citizens by the state and the rights of citizens within the state is now more than ever a daily negotiation. How democracy polices its freedom and how it controls opposition in a democratic manner is the arena where society defines itself and finds itself.

It will always be difficul to deal with Socrates or to respond to Plato. For this reason, democracy has to be messy. It has to keep asking 'what if?' But, for democrats, this risky business is better than the alternatives. It's because democracy cannot pretend to be a Utopia that it can hope to avoid the violent controls and repressions that come from the fantasy of perfection. It is this risk that will always make personal responsibility central to the politics of democracy.

6

The Will of the People

It has never been more necessary to think hard about what exactly we mean by 'democracy' and expect from a democratic system. Ancient Greek democracy, the system from which modern democracy claims in some sense to originate, provides a wonderfully stark and telling contrast with modern governmental organization and modern ideological commitments. It is basic to our critical self-analysis.

There are significant continuities between ancient and contemporary democratic principles, especially the accountability of public officials, equality before the law and freedom of speech (however differently these basic principles are articulated in practice). These principles, none of which obtains under the dictators of Arabic countries in the Middle East, for example, are the basic building-blocks of the social forms which the West values in the celebration of democracy.

The differences between the modern and ancient systems, however, are equally fundamental, and raise far more troubling questions. One of the most intractable problems for democracy in any period is the notion of 'what the people want'. Democracy is said to enact the will of the people. But it is extremely difficult to determine what the will of the people is or how it should be enacted.

Athenian decrees of the Assembly were inscribed on stone pillars, public and fixed. The formula with which they typically begin is 'It seems good to the People of Athens that . . .'. In direct democracy, that inscription is at least the record of a majority vote of the sovereign Assembly – the assembled people – after a collective discussion. But such a record does not indicate whether the decision reflects a particular group of the community winning a vote on what is good for that group; or whether it was a more high-minded decision of the whole community about what was good for the whole community; or whether the vote was actually an attempt to follow some other unstated agenda, which was what the people really wanted. Or some combination of all of these motivations (and more besides). It is hard enough to know what one person really wants. To assume that one could determine easily what a collective of individuals wants can seem an idealist fantasy at best, a self-serving rhetorical gesture at worst.

In direct democracy, a vote can be taken on an issue and recorded. In representational democracy, except for the few cases of a vote taken by referendum on a specific proposal, there are insuperable institutional barriers to finding out the will of the people. It is not possible to record what 'seems good to the People'. The election of a representative is the election of a decision-maker who cannot be mandated by the electorate. In most cases, a representative also represents a political party. The political party will demand allegiance of that representative. The party's collective policies are also being voted on and enacted, but the policies may change without recourse to the electorate and without accountability (except for the prospect of a future election). Governments can make decisions that are deeply unpopular, that go against the apparent wishes of the people.

One assumption that justifies this modern system seems to be the Platonic view that the electorate does not have the expertise or experience to vote directly on complex issues. The threat to good decision-making from ignorance, self-interest and changeability is real, and it is easy to doubt the ability of any large group of people to see clearly what its best long-term interests are, and how to fulfil them. Yet it is far from obvious what qualities or expertise a contemporary electorate seeks to find in a politician, even with regard to the absolutely central areas of economic, military, legal and social policy. Nor is it evident how voters should evaluate or discuss such qualities and expertise. The institutional gap between 'the people' and 'the servants'/'the representatives of the people', seems unbridgeable.

In such a system 'the government' or 'the party' can readily be perceived as a restrictive or unwelcome authority, even when the ideological claim is 'government of the people, for the people, by the people'. The combination of an intense valuing of private life with this disempowerment of the citizen leads inevitably to a tension between governmental regulation and individual freedom or individual dissent. It is a tension which needs constant negotiation, and it is where modern democracy is most insistently articulated.

All too often today the word 'democracy' is bandied about as a badge of Western approval. But it is impossible to understand the trajectory of democracy as an idea and as a form of government without turning to the history and the theory of democracy: the 'what if?' question. Here, Athenian democracy provides not just a historical or rhetorical origin, but also a privileged and revelatory model. The history of democracy as an idea cannot be sensibly broached without the paradigm of Greece, and without its massive influence on the revolutions which have shaped the modern world. Athens still provides the mirror in which our political ideals and institutions are most sharply viewed and anatomized. We need Socrates and Plato to think through democracy.

IV

WHAT DO YOU WANT TO DO?

I

That's Entertainment!

In 1990, a production of Sophocles' *Electra*, starring Fiona Shaw, opened in Derry, Northern Ireland, during a week when eight people had been killed in sectarian violence. The production was brilliantly acted and directed, but when the performance finished something wholly out of the ordinary happened. The audience refused to leave the theatre without a discussion of what they had watched. The play is a brutal exposure of the distorting psychological traumas which a passion for revenge creates, and the drama's shocking dissection of self-inflicted anguish spoke so powerfully to an Irish audience that to leave without the catharsis of debate proved too disturbing. Sophocles hurt in a way few modern dramas could match.

The tragedies of ancient Greece still speak intensely to modern audiences. In London, Berlin, Paris, New York, San Francisco and elsewhere, there has been a remarkable flourishing of Greek tragedy on the modern stage, especially since the 1960s. The narratives and the dramatic resources of tragedy resonate across the generations in a way which takes Greek drama beyond sterile classicism and into real theatre. Although the characters and stories of ancient drama may seem initially distant, this very distance is actually integral to their power to move audiences deeply. Tragedy has an uncanny ability to transcend the specific and thus reach a profound level of emotional engagement in its audience. When Hamlet asks, 'What's Hecuba to him and he to Hecuba that he should weep for her?', he is wondering at tragedy's transcendent hold on its audience's feelings.

Modern drama inevitably looks back to Greece for an origin, and the inspiration of ancient tragedy runs through all strands of the Western cultural tradition from its very beginnings. In the second century BC, a Jew called Ezekiel wrote a tragedy in Greek based on the story of Moses; much later, an anonymous Christian turned the *Bacchae* into a play about Jesus. The very first opera in the sixteenth century was an Italian 'Oedipus the King'; Monteverdi made opera a high art form in the seventeenth century by striving to recreate ancient tragedy's combination of music and theatre. Wagner's Bayreuth festival, the apex of opera, was designed to establish the equivalent of the ancient Athenian drama festival for a new Germany. For Corneille, Molière and Racine, the study of the paradigm of ancient theatre was an integral aspect of the production of the 'classical drama', which dominates the literary culture of seventeenth-century France. Eugene O'Neill and T. S. Eliot, two masters of twentieth-century American theatre, explored the modern world by rewriting Greek plays. The event of ancient tragedy, with its chorus, its masks, its sublime poetry and its audience of deeply moved citizens, is part of the very architecture of modern theatrical imagination.

Like the Parthenon, tragedy has always stood as an icon of ancient Greek culture as a whole, an inspirational symbol of the 'Greek miracle'. Tragic theatre from the beginning was an essential part of how the Athenians thought of their own city. It has remained a key element in how the value of the Greek past has been viewed by subsequent generations. This is no surprise: understanding a society's entertainment goes to the heart of how that society thinks about itself, and how we can understand it. Plato insists on banning theatre and the poets from his ideal city precisely because of the intellectual and psychological impact of tragedy and other such entertainments on the citizens. For him, the formation of a good citizen should not include the experience of theatre. Entertainment is a fundamental activity of self-definition – for individuals, for groups and for a culture itself.

Entertainment is so tied up with society's idea of itself that it has proved a really serious business for politicians, philosophers and social reformers. Over the centuries, the policemen of culture have been sorely provoked by its dangerous pleasures, which threaten the propriety and probity of social order. Consequently, entertainment becomes the battleground of regulation. Theatre has often been singled out for zealous control, from Plato onwards. The Puritans were so successful in banning theatre and all such sinful pleasures that Samuel Pepys did not experience the heady delights of dancing until he was twenty-eight years old, when Charles II was restored. Stalinist attempts to control theatre along with music, art and literature are notorious in their brutality. Modern Islamic states practise similarly aggressive policies of censorship, while importing the technology from the West, which makes such censorship all the more needed and all the more impossible to police. The recognition that entertainment is profoundly dangerous in the eyes of the state or of the religious authorities has produced grim results throughout modern history.

Modern democracies are less murderous than such totalitarian regimes, but they also worry constantly about acceptable public expression. The state censorship of plays in England was finally broken only in the twentieth century by the test-case of *Oedipus the King*. Trying to ban a Greek classic, read by generations of schoolboys, because it was 'about incest' made the lord chamberlain's office look ridiculous, and proved impossible. But contemporary pornography laws still reflect deeply muddled thinking with regard to the state's regulation of images. The 'freedom of expression' guarantee in the American constitution is repeatedly tested in the courts. Constant public expressions of concern about rock 'n' roll, the lyrics of rap, the 'dumbing down' of television, sex and violence in Hollywood and so on testify to the worry but also the confusion about entertainment's role in modern Western society.

The annoyingly disingenuous phrase 'mere entertainment', or 'it's just entertainment', is one sign of this confused thinking. It's a phrase that is meant to prevent any serious reflection on the conflicts of cultural life. When, for example, an especially trite or offensive television show is broadcast, and then criticized, the defence will be 'it's just entertainment'. It is a formulaic response, designed to refuse or to defuse the social implications of the performance. But there are always social implications to any form of entertainment, which is precisely why society gets so vexed by different types of entertainment. So, to defend anything as 'just entertainment' is bound to be naive and self-serving. The phrase has a certain rhetorical effectiveness only because no one likes having their pleasures, their relaxation, their ease, held up to critical scrutiny.

When a man tries it on with a woman, and is rebuffed, and he retorts, 'I was only joking,' what he means is: 'If I were taken completely seriously in my advance, I would now be feeling rejected and even humiliated, but if it is accepted that I was not serious, then the situation can be turned to a shared recognition of the risky and potentially ridiculous games of seduction. I am aware that it will require a comedy of innocence to maintain face in this situation, but that complicity is preferable to exploring the psychological and social discomfort of rejection. So please accept my declaration of non-seriousness.' Or something like that. 'Entertainment' has a similar dynamic. Everyone may know that there are serious social forces at stake in it, but the cover of calling itself not quite serious is always available. So, as with 'I was only joking,' 'it's only entertainment' is a poor attempt to veil social tension. We don't like to look too closely at what our entertainments say about ourselves. They are too tied up with who we think we are.

The following chapters discuss the two most celebrated forms of entertainment of the ancient world, the tragedies of ancient Greece and the gladiatorial games of ancient Rome. In both cases, these emblematic events encapsulate important insights about the societies in which they took place, and, in contemporary popular imagination as in the high cultural tradition, both deservedly hold their place as paradigmatic images of Greece and Rome. But, more importantly and more surprisingly, both forms of activity also hold up a telling mirror to today. These ancient entertainments can help us to be more self-aware about our own pleasures, and what they indicate about modern society. Looking in the mirror of the past will help us see ourselves more clearly.

2

The Question of Tragedy

The sublime plays which survive today as 'Greek tragedy' and which have had such an influence in Western culture were all produced in one Greek city, Athens, in one brief period, the last seventy years of the fifth century BC. This context is crucial for understanding tragedy as a dramatic event: tragedy is fully part of the democratic revolution, an institution formed in the explosion of cultural innovation that made the fifth century such an astounding era.

These plays of Aeschylus, Sophocles and Euripides became remarkably celebrated, and already by the fourth century they were the Classics. They were re-performed in Athens and in other cities across Greece by repertory companies. They became part of the school curriculum. They were learnt by heart. They were read and studied by critics and philosophers like Aristotle in his *Poetics*. But each play was originally written and produced for a single performance in a dramatic competition that dominated the Great Dionysia, a major state religious festival in honour of the god Dionysus, held annually in Athens. It is as though *King Lear* or *Macbeth* were intended to be performed only once. Nor were there other comparable theatres that an Athenian citizen could attend. For the Athenians, going to the theatre meant the festival event, once a year. Watching tragedy in ancient Athens was an astonishingly different experience from any modern trip to the theatre.

Each year, the archon, a leading state bureaucrat appointed by lot, chose three playwrights to enter the competition. It is unclear to us what the criteria would have been, but the fact that Aeschylus, Sophocles and Euripides were selected so often – each was chosen at least twenty times – indicates that reputation probably helped. Each playwright had to compose three tragedies and a satyr play, and his plays were all performed on a single day – making up the three central days of the festival. The farcical satyr play was always last in the sequence. It had a chorus of satyrs, those drunken, lascivious figures, half goat, half man, who were worshippers of Dionysus. The vase illustrated in Figure 38, com-

38. The Pronomos Vase – dressing for a satyr play

memorating a musician of the theatre called Pronomos, shows the actors and the chorus of a satyr play at various stages of costuming – turning a man into a beast through Dionysus' transforming power. Dionysus' realm encompassed wine and release as well as theatre, and it is not by chance that the searing power of tragedy always culminated in the Dionysiac release of these wild, transgressive creatures.

During the Peloponnesian War, each tragic playwright's competition entry was followed by a comedy, a fifth play performed on the same day as the other four. In normal years, however, five comedies rather than three were produced, and all were put on in sequence on the fourth day of the festival, after the tragic competition was over. Athenian comedy, as we can see from Aristophanes' plays, was raucous, bawdy and highly political. The language is as rude as can be imagined, and the characters on stage happily insulted members of the audience by name, all in the context of plots which were often highly politicized satirical fantasies. Its actors had huge phalluses, distorted features and extravagant costumes. Figure 39 demonstrates vividly how comedy inverts the

39. The 'Goose Play' vase – comic actors

physicality of the beautiful body, familiar from so much Greek art. It's a South Italian vase from around 400 BC, and it shows a mind-boggling comic scene (including dialogue coming out of the characters' mouths), involving a grotesque old man, apparently being hung up naked. There's also an old woman gesturing to him, or to the young blade opposite, and a large dead goose. These plays too were fully supported by the state as part of the festival.

Unlike modern sponsorship, the financing of the plays was controlled and directed by the state. Each production was fully funded by a wealthy individual, chosen by the state, in a form of taxation known as a 'liturgy'. The sponsor was called a *chorêgos*, literally, 'the chorus director'. He had to provide the money required for the actors, chorus, costumes and other production costs. The Great Dionysia was a competition between these sponsors as much as it was one between playwrights or actors – a competition for status and success before the citizens. The state festival was an arena in which citizens performed as competitors and audience in the shared, participatory business of democracy.

The festival ran for four days at the end of February, beginning of March. Each day began at dawn. The audience was the biggest collection of citizens in the calendar. By the time that the old wooden seats of the theatre were replaced with stone, between 14,000 and 16,000 people regularly attended. The vast majority of these spectators were citizens: adult males with the right to vote, heads of households. Whereas the Assembly, the most important political body of democracy, regularly had around only 6,000 in attendance and courts fewer still, the Great Dionysia was closer to the Olympic Games in scale. The only other occasion when so many citizens might collect in one place was a major battle. The theatre festival was truly a state occasion.

It cost two obols to attend the theatre, about a day's wages for a manual labourer, and each citizen got a ticket probably via his deme. But there was a fund called the Theoric Fund, which gave a grant of the two obols to any citizen who wanted it. It is not clear exactly when this fund was first established, but it stems from the same ideological commitment that paid citizens to attend jury service and to row in the navy, both duties of the citizens in democracy. Indeed, the Theoric Fund was completely ring-fenced: it was illegal even to propose to change the law which had established it. Even when funding for the army was desperate, during the war against Philip of Macedon, which Athens lost along with its freedom, the state maintained its theatrical grants. In Athens, unlike any modern dramatic event, going to the theatre was a significant activity for citizens as citizens.

Walking into the theatre meant walking into a map of the city. The theatre was divided into blocks of seats (*kerkides*), and each block seems to have been reserved for different groups. It is likely that each tribe (the major socio-political division of the state) sat in its own *kerkis*. One central block of 500 seats was reserved for the Council, the executive body of government. The front row was designated for visiting ambassadors, priests and other dignitaries. Another section was specified for 'ephebes' – young men on the point of joining the armed forces. Another area was reserved for 'metics' (resident aliens) and for foreigners. The seating in the theatre marked out citizens according to socio-political position, age, status. In the theatre, the city represented itself to itself.

Before the plays were performed for this great gathering of citizens, four rituals were celebrated, which turned the theatre into a vivid political spectacle. Each ritual may now seem strange – there is nothing like them in modern theatre – but they were all dramatic displays of the democratic state. The space of theatrical performance was politicized by these rituals, and this ritual frame changed how the plays communicated with their audience.

As with most Greek festivals, there was an opening sacrifice and libation. Piglets were slaughtered and their blood sprinkled around the playing area. Libations of wine were poured to the gods. Who performed this ritual, however, is more surprising. For brought on stage were the ten generals, that is, the ten most important military and political leaders of the state. They came together for such rituals very rarely in the Athenian calendar, and usually for a reason more evidently related to their role, such as a sacrifice for 'peace', or for 'the good fortune of the state'. These were irregular events, which took place only under special circumstances. But every year the generals opened the drama festival. This ceremony sets the whole festival firmly under the authority of the state, as it is embodied in its elected leaders.

Secondly, the names were announced of civic benefactors who had done such exceptional services for the state during the year that they had been awarded an honorific crown. Athens was always a fiercely competitive society, where men struggled for status and honour in the public gaze. Honour, its preservation and loss, is the motivating principle of the plot of the *Iliad*, Homer's defining epic of manhood. Despite democracy's proclamation of the equality of its citizens, there is no doubt that many a citizen wanted desperately to be more equal than the others. So this is a moment of immense personal glory for the citizen whose name was read out before the citizen body – a crowning moment.

But what is most interesting is the way in which this ceremony is viewed by the orators who describe it. Both Demosthenes and Aeschines see it as an occasion when the city itself gives thanks, and thereby encourages all citizens to do their duty. Such rhetoric encapsulates a standard democratic ideal: that every man should act to benefit the collective of the state, and a citizen's actions are evaluated according to how they contribute to the city. The ceremony therefore is not a moment of personal glory so much as a collective expression of the city's values. The orators who debate these issues all have vested interests, not least because Aeschines is attacking the award of a crown to Demosthenes, his bitter personal and political rival. None the less, for all their infighting, they do agree on the ideological import of the ritual. It is a way of projecting and promoting the values of the city.

The third ritual is stranger still. Servants carried in bars of silver bullion and paraded them around the theatre before the huge audience. This is the 'parade of tribute'. All our existing tragedies were written during the era of the Athenian Empire. After the defeat of the Persians, that defining moment of the fifth century, Athens had become the dominant imperialist power of the Mediterranean by virtue of its naval power. It could now compel cities to become 'allies' and demand that they pay tribute to Athens, moneys which were used to support further Athenian military expansion. The allies were required to send their yearly contributions in February, in time to be paraded around the theatre before the assembled citizens. This explains why the foreign ambassadors are there in the front row: to watch their tribute being paraded. And so that the citizens can watch them watching.

It doesn't need great analytical skill to see that this is a spectacle designed to parade the power and prestige of Athens, as dominant military and political force in the Mediterranean. It used the state occasion to glorify the state. Nor should it be a surprise that when Athens had lost the Peloponnesian War and consequently its Empire, in retrospect this ceremony seemed to one orator at least, Isocrates, to be a 'precise way of being hated by everyone'. It was certainly an aggressively forthright symbolic display of the city's status to its citizens and the assembled foreigners.

The fourth ceremonial is also closely tied to the military life of Athens: the 'parade of war orphans'. In Athens, if a boy's father died fighting for the state, the boy was brought up at state expense, educated at state expense, and at the end of this main-tained childhood was presented with armour and weapons by the state, to take up his place in the state's fighting forces. (With the usual gender asymmetry, an orphan is someone whose father has died.) These 'ephebes', or the class of 'young males about to become proper men', were paraded in the theatre in their mili-tary equipment. A herald announced the boy's father's name and made a moving speech which expressed in glowing terms how the fathers had done their duty, and how their boys, now to be men, would also fulfil their military obligations to the state. The boys then took the stirring oath of loyalty to the state. They promised by a long list of the gods of the state to stand by their comrades wherever they were placed in the line, and declared that they were prepared to fight and die for the city as their fathers had done before them. Then they took up their special seats, reserved just for them.

This ceremony vividly reflects the Athenian democratic state's commitment to war. All citizens were expected to participate in the military activities of the city from voting on policy to fighting in the line. Athens was a warrior state, in which each man had to play his role in the fighting. War was to a man what marriage was to a woman – the moment of achieved adult status. A woman only fully became a woman when she was married with a child. A man only fully became a man when he fought as a warrior of the city. Fighting and being prepared to give up one's life for the state was an essential, defining ideal of citizenship. So when the ephebes are paraded in armour before the citizens in the theatre, taking up their places in the army, recalling the death of their fathers, military heroes all, the ceremony displays the full weight of Athenian military ideology. It was a ritual that proclaimed: this is how to be an Athenian citizen.

Four rituals, then, to open the festival of drama. Each one projects and promotes in spectacular form the power of the city of Athens and the values of democratic citizenship. The festival is designed to glorify the state. In the heady days of the expanding Athenian Empire, this grand civic occasion brought the citizens together to celebrate Athens.

Such civic ceremonial makes what follows it all the more extraordinary. Where one might expect state-led propaganda or bland inclusive entertainment, both tragedy and comedy show a world ripped apart, civic foundations shattered and the noble values of citizenship turned against themselves in violence, confusion, despair and horror. There are many state occasions today which could parallel the civic ceremonies of the Great Dionysia. But none follows their ceremonials with performances of tragedy, which depict a society where a man kills his father and sleeps with his mother; where a ruler is ripped apart by his god-maddened mother; where every institution of authority and power collapses. Nor do civic ceremonials today turn into comedy, which mercilessly mocks the city itself for its litigious lunacies, its failing and corrupt leaders, and its citizens led by their penises into farce and humiliation. Ibsen and Brecht were not performed at the Berlin Olympics. Eugene O'Neill is not invited to write plays for Veterans' Day parades. Red Square march-pasts do not stage Chekhov.

The Great Dionysia is an extraordinary occasion, an entertainment that speaks to society about society. But the combination of displays of civic pride with theatrical performances that show the city in pieces raises for us a question of how the social force of this entertainment should be understood.

The tragic festival – the plays and the ceremonies together – can be seen as offering the city a message about what a good city should be like. Nearly all the surviving tragedies are set in cities other than Athens – so the *Bacchae* and the *Oedipus Rex* are located in Thebes, *Medea* in Corinth – and almost all of them are set in times other than the present, indeed often in the heroic era before even the Trojan War – as are, again, *Bacchae* , *Oedipus* and *Medea* – and nearly all concern characters who are other than the citizens in the audience: foreigners, kings, monsters, women. Tragedy is enacted at the scene of the other – other places, other times, other people.

So it is possible to see the entertainment of the Great Dionysia as offering a single message to the citizens. First, we get the pre-play ceremonials which display the positive image of Athens as a city, then there are the grim warnings of the tragedies which show what happens elsewhere to other people, a negative image of how things can go wrong. Together, the plays and the rituals teach the Athenians what the proper values of citizenship are. The festival expresses both the norm and the transgression of those ideological values. In this model, comedy finally provides a safe release. Under comedy's licence, the normal restrictions of law, custom and expectation are loosened and, in a true Dionysiac spirit, the pleasures of the body and the fantasies of self-fulfilment are given free rein. The whole occasion of the Great Dionysia, in this model, is a truly civic occasion, using the full range of spectacle and drama to celebrate and educate the city.

This interpretation, which finds its roots in Aristotle's *Poetics*, is undoubtedly a very strong way of understanding the Great Dionysia. Aristotle saw tragedy as a positive educational experience for the citizen, through its emotional and intellectual impact. By watching the reasoning of tragic heroes, reasoning which leads them into disaster, we can learn better to control our own lives.

The 'pity and fear' aroused by tragedy leads to a cleansed moral awareness of what it means to be a citizen. Aristotle, unlike Plato, thought tragedy made the citizens better men.

But tragedy's message is far more complex and far more interesting than this 'good news, bad news' approach allows. The heart of tragedy is more disturbing, and affects its audiences, ancient and modern, in a more wrenching way. Oedipus is a perfect example. For Oedipus is not merely a negative model, any more than Medea or Pentheus or Orestes are. For all that he kills his father and sleeps with his mother and pollutes his city, it is not the case that Oedipus is just an 'other', who inhabits a different, negative world. Oedipus is also an intelligent, admired and successful figure, who like every member of the audience wants to control his life. He is desperate to avoid the awful fate an oracle predicts for him, and he is desperate to find out who he really is. This search for identity and control makes him a model *for* all of us. As Freud recognized, there is an Oedipus inside everyone. The emotional and intellectual power of tragedy stems from the very difficulty of its examples. The figures of tragedy are not black-and-white villains and heroes, but complex characters locked into double binds of doubt and compulsion, wilfulness and loss. It is the way in which Oedipus turns out to be like us which makes the play so affecting. Tragedy leads to self-questioning through the pain of others.

This questioning has a powerful and disturbing effect on the inherited traditional tales of the city – the myths by which the world is navigated. This is nowhere clearer than in one of the greatest works of Western culture, Aeschylus' *Oresteia*, which takes the paradigmatic tales of Homer and rewrites them for the democratic city.

In Homer, Orestes is the exemplary hero. Whenever Telemachus, Odysseus' son, meets a hero, he is told to 'be like Orestes'. Orestes is the hero's hero. He took control of his own house, exacted revenge against the murderer of his father, and rid the city of the usurper Aegisthus who had seduced his mother,

Clytemnestra. Crucially for Orestes' exemplary story, in Homer there is no mention of how Clytemnestra, his adulterous mother, died. The closest we get is when Telemachus is once again told the story of Orestes by Nestor. 'When Orestes came back,' says Nestor, 'he killed him [Aegisthus, the usurper], and invited the Argives to a funeral feast for his hated mother and cowardly Aegisthus.' 'When *he* killed *him*' turns into a plural funeral. That silence in the narrative is the nearest Homer comes to mentioning a story of Clytemnestra's death.

Aeschylus takes that silence and makes it scream. Centre stage, in the central play of the trilogy, Orestes is faced by his mother who bares her breast and begs for pity. That is when Orestes hesitates and, in the classic expression of tragic doubt, asks, 'What should I do?' Orestes must kill his mother. But he knows he is doing wrong as he does it. 'You did what you ought not, now suffer what you ought not', is his climactic judgement as he leads her to her death.

The rest of the trilogy tries to make sense of Orestes' action, leading up to a courtroom trial in Athens to judge him, where the god Apollo is the defence, the goddess Athene the judge, and the Furies the prosecution. The jury is made up of citizens of Athens. Even with the god of truth, Apollo, arguing his case, Orestes wins only half the votes of the jury. It takes the casting vote of Athene, goddess of the city of Athens, to acquit him. He remains a problem: an example now not of heroism, pure and simple, but of violent, tragic complexity and of the conflicting obligations of human action.

Orestes' story now needs the institution of the courtroom and the structures of the city to find its resolution. The Homeric myth has been rewritten for the new world of the democratic city, but in such a way that no one ever again said, as Homer's characters so often declared, 'Be like Orestes!' Orestes is now the matricide, a figure hard to evaluate and impossible to take as a simple role model. The exemplary hero of Homer has become a problem, for the audience and for himself.

Tragedy again and again takes the ideology of the city and exposes its flaws and contradictions. It sets a man's obligation to his family *against* his obligation to the city. The ephebe can step forward before the plays and promise to 'stand by his comrade': tragedy again and again shows how hard it is to follow through such a principle. The ceremonials before the play can bring the generals on stage, and tragedy will then reveal the misplaced arrogance, disastrous overconfidence and failure of control of those in authority. The ceremonials before the plays may assert the military values of the state – yet drama after drama, set in a time of war, undermines all jingoism and certainty of purpose. Tragedy depicts the hero not as a shining example for men to follow, but as a difficult, self-obsessed and dangerous figure for whom transcendence is bought only at the cost of transgression. The Greeks, as ever, had a word for it: *es meson*, which means put 'into the public domain to be contested'. Democracy prides itself on its openness to questioning. Tragedy is the institution which stages this openness in the most startling fashion.

Comedy is no less provocative – in its own way. Its plays mock the very generals who had opened the festival. It makes heroes out of individuals who scorn the collectivity of democracy, and pursue more sex, more food and more drink, above any political ideal. Comedy turns every institution of democracy upside down in car-nivalesque turmoil. The Assembly is taken over by women in Aristophanes' play *The Women at the Assembly*; the court is hilari-ously ribbed in *The Wasps*; religious festivals are the target in *The Women at the Thesmophoria*; and it is the turn of the military aims of the state in *Lysistrata*. Comedy and tragedy together put the city under the sway of the god of release, transformation and wildness. The Great Dionysia, a state-funded celebration, under the smiling and dangerous authority of Dionysus, sets some of the city's basic principles and most cherished values at risk.

This should make us stop and think.

Despite the lasting and significant legacy in Western culture that the tragedies of ancient Greece have produced, there is one particularly telling way in which the Great Dionysia turns a painfully revealing mirror on the entertainment of the modern world. The Great Dionysia was the biggest collection of citizens in the calendar, the most public of occasions, and the city used that opportunity to explore the emotional and intellectual complexities of life, as well as to laugh and to cry; to reflect on the inherited stories of the city, as well as to join in civic celebration. It enabled and fostered participation and self-reflection on personal, familial, intellectual and political issues of general concern. Where in the public life of Western society could we look for any such equivalent critical and emotional civic engagement?

The Great Dionysia still has the power to pose a stark question about the lack of serious public culture in the institutions of modern democracy. It shows up the poverty of cultural ambition in our society, and reveals how restricted and unchallenging public civic culture is in modern democracy – for all that some few plays, films and television shows do strive to stir their large audiences with intellect and passion. Much as the modern citizen has a deeply restricted role in the decision-making of government, so the opportunities for public culture are severely limited. There is nothing like the Great Dionysia on show today.

What we do is a big part of who we are, and that's why entertainment – how we spend our time – is an integral part of defining ourselves. The contrast between contemporary entertainment and Athenian tragedy at the festival of the Great Dionysia reveals a hole in the centre of our public culture.

3

The Gladiator and the Baying Crowd –
'At My Command, Unleash Hell'

Train-spotting, Sumo wrestling or full-body tattooing may be baffling entertainments to outsiders, but the question 'How could they?' is rarely felt with such shocking insistence as with the Roman gladiatorial games. Part of the thrill that gives films such as *Spartacus* or *Gladiator* their charge is our awareness of just how transgressive such lethal entertainment must seem in Western society. The Roman Empire may be the foundation of Europe's legal system and political geography, but its difference from today seems terrifying when we contemplate the Colosseum. Gladiators are the dark side of the coming of civilization. Rome's technological and bureaucratic expertise – the aqueducts, roads and imperial administration – cannot reduce the sheer otherness of a society that loved to watch wild animals eat humans alive, and thrilled to see men cut each other to pieces.

Gladiators bring for us a strange double frisson: on the one hand, a horror based firmly in our cultural superiority; on the other, a voyeuristic fascination with the laceration of the flesh and with the baying crowd. The modern world may express its squeamishness, moral revulsion and shame at the spectacle of the destroyed human body, but that does not stop gladiators being the image of Rome which the modern world most loves to restage, and most often wants to teach in school. Gladiators ask us to reflect on our own engagement with violence, the human body and the spectacle of power.

And what a spectacle of power the games were! The figures are overwhelming. The Emperor Titus, for example, gave games in

AD 80 in Rome for the dedication of the Colosseum, which lasted one hundred days. They included the slaughter of 9,000 animals in one day, some killed by specially trained female hunters. There were individual superstar gladiator fights. There were mass gladiator fights. There were pitched battles, including one on water with fully manned galleys, which made use of the brilliant technical innovation of an artificially flooded arena. As many as 3,000 men fought on a single day. To keep the populace on the edge of excitement, the emperor had wooden balls thrown into the crowd, which could be exchanged for prizes – food, clothes, money, even slaves.

In the next generation, the Emperor Trajan celebrated a military victory with games that lasted 123 days, when 11,000 animals were killed and 10,000 gladiators fought. It is the equivalent of every current professional American Football player, every current professional American basketball player and every current American professional baseball player all together fighting with lethal weapons in the same event. The thought is staggering.

These imperial extravaganzas were the most extreme cases, of course, but they make even Hollywood epics look positively tame. They were designed to be overwhelming, unique and monumental. They were hugely expensive and constructed to assert the total power of the emperor, a public and aggressive declaration of his control over the material world. Outside Rome, things were less expansive: the opening of a local library was celebrated with twelve pairs of gladiators fighting; one of the grander families in Pompeii, celebrating its own wealth and position, put up thirty pairs of gladiators for a five-day festival. Augustus tried – and failed – to limit regular shows in Rome itself to sixty pairs of gladiators and to two regular shows a year. But even if the games of Titus and Trajan were once-in-a-lifetime occasions, the sheer scale of bloodshed and expense across the Empire over the centuries remains stunning.

The size of the crowd matched the scale of the slaughter. Fully

50,000 could fill the Colosseum at Rome, and did so for the games – men and boys from all levels of society. Women were allowed in the emperor's entourage only (although prostitutes thronged the dark arches on the outside of the Colosseum – the excitement of the games was no doubt good for business). Augustus limited the games to twice a year, though the number crept up over time, and the excitement of anticipation, swelled by advertising, guaranteed an enthusiastic crowd.

The Colosseum's immense structure ordered this mass of people into a socio-political map of the city. The audience was highly stratified (as was all Roman society), with separate seating for the knights, the senators, the soldiers, the citizens and, in the Empire, most importantly, the emperor himself. Each person wore suitable formal attire that marked their rank – senators in their togas with purple borders, citizens in their white togas and so on. If a Roman became a senator, one of the best ways to exhibit this new status was in the change of his seating and clothes at the games. The circular banks of seats, rising to a dizzying height, constructed a space where all could see and be seen, everyone in his proper place.

The games were a stage for the pursuit of status and power by the elite. Rich senators, and the emperors in particular, competed to put on the most lavish and memorable events. Games were advertised, celebrated, discussed. A few philosophers and moralists raised their distaste more against the heated emotion of the crowd than against the spilling of blood. But the games remained wildly successful in Rome and throughout the provinces. Even Greek theatres were adapted for the gladiators. Christianity may have expressed vehement moral objections from the earliest days of religious fervour, but the last recorded gladiator games were held as late as the sixth century. The institution faded out because of lack of money rather than because of lack of support for such entertainment. The games were hugely popular for centuries.

Gladiators fought each other in four standard roles, defined by armour and weapons. Each wore a bulky loin-cloth, and one or two greaves (metal shinguards). Three of these standard types wore heavy helmets, had one arm protected by a metal or leather sleeve and carried a shield. The fourth – the so-called *retiarius*, or 'fisher', 'net-man' – carried a net and a trident, but wore no helmet. Gladiator types were paired to balance their strengths against each other, in particular the speed and mobility of the *retiarius* against the heavier armour of the others. The mosaic in Figure 40 depicts the *retiarius* on the right, with his trident, and his left arm in the characteristic protective sleeve. On the left is

40. Gladiator mosaic from Verona

the *secutor* ('pursuer'), who has a large shield, a helmet, a greave on his lower leg, and armour on his right arm. Strategy for the combat between these types of gladiators was refined, trained and appreciated. Gladiator school was a harsh, intense but highly developed education. The games also celebrated the art of killing and dying.

This standard equipment puts the gladiator's body on display in two particularly telling ways. First, the majority of the gladiators had their heads concealed. The fight was not an occasion for watching individual expressions of anguish or triumph: there were no close-ups to personalize the combat in the way that

Hollywood so loves. That is not what is at stake in the Roman arena. Second, and more importantly, gladiators fought with a bare torso.

The bare torso is not merely the exposure of flesh to the eyes of the spectators and to the edge of the steel. It embodied the positive and valued bravery of the gladiator. Gladiatorial combat, wrote the intellectual and politician Pliny, 'inspires a glory in wounds and a contempt of death, since the love of praise and desire for victory can be seen even in the bodies of slaves and criminals'. Cicero declared that the training of a gladiator turned the lowest form of life, slaves and criminals, into models of Roman virtue:

Look at the gladiators, corrupt men or barbarians, what blows they endure! See how men who have been well trained prefer to receive a blow than basely avoid it! . . . What gladiator of ordinary merit has ever uttered a groan or changed countenance? . . . Who of them has disgraced himself? . . . Who after falling has drawn in his neck when ordered to suffer the fatal stroke? Such is the force of training, practice and habit.

The gladiator was trained both to kill and to die in a way that embodied true Roman virtue. The defeated gladiator had to expose his breast to receive the final blow. He mustn't flinch or hesitate or turn away. He had to take the blow 'with his whole body' (as Cicero puts it). Gladiators may have been low, expendable, publicly displayed creatures, but they were also heroes in the arena that mattered so much to Romans: manliness.

It is crucial for this public display of the brave and lacerated body that gladiators were usually slaves or criminals. Slaves were treated by Romans as a separate category of human life, and, especially in the mines or the vast farm estates, they were close to being used as machines, inhuman sources of labour. A slave's body had none of the protections of a citizen. A slave, unlike a citizen, had no rights, and could not avoid beatings, brandings, torture and forced sex by his or her own master – and all of these were regular features of Roman society in practice. Rape was a punishment for male and female servants, whippings a commonplace. The exposure of the gladiator's flesh and its violent treatment was made possible in Roman eyes because the slave and the criminal were bodies to be used, for punishment, for work – and for entertainment.

Criminals had no choice, and were often viciously destroyed in the arena. But the expensive training, diet and lifestyle of the gladiator has been seen by some modern writers as likely to have been preferable to the nasty, brutish and short life of a slave or even a free but poor man. There were a few volunteers in the gladiatorial schools. Some gladiators did survive their career to retire as celebrated athletes. Others got close, but were killed at the end of a long string of fights. Graffiti and inscriptions record – in different ways – the celebrity status of gladiators, and also the bare bones of a life of triumphs and final loss.

A graffito from Pompeii, for example, records the little history of the victory of a first-timer over an older and much more experienced man: 'Spiculus, of Nero's school, first fight, won; Aptonetus, ex-slave, 16 victories, killed.' The story can only be imagined, but it is easy to tell: an ex-slave might well be a willing gladiator; and he had fought many times successfully. He had a career. But Spiculus, trained in the gladiatorial school of Nero, in his first fight against the old and battle-scarred hand, got lucky or was more skilled. No more is known of either man, or what happened to young Spiculus afterwards. But it is significant that someone took the trouble to write this story on a wall. The gladiator may have been a figure of social disgrace, but he was also a figure of deep fascination for the Roman public.

The gladiator indeed, even before Kirk Douglas or Russell Crowe, was a sex symbol, of a certain rather louche and rough attraction. As Juvenal with his customary sneer puts it: 'What do these women love? The sword. . .' Sex, with gladiators, like sex with gangsters, was never separated from the violence that gave

them their celebrity – and was always tarnished by their paradoxical mix of disgrace and displays of honour (especially in the
minds of upright Roman men, obsessing about their women). But
gladiators, like gangsters, could be sexy even to the noblest
women. Faustina, the wife of the Emperor Marcus Aurelius
Antoninus, saw some gladiators, and fancied one of them. She
made the mistake of confiding in her husband. He promptly had
the gladiator killed, and made Faustina bathe in his blood – before
having sex with her.

This is a story that encapsulates all the Roman ambivalence
about the sexual lure of the gladiator and the corrupting power of
the emperor. The story has an extra charge, however, because the
child of that couple was Commodus, the emperor most tainted by
his attitude to the arena. For, despite his imperial position, he
insisted on fighting in the arena himself. With a spear and bow,
in a two-day extravaganza, he personally slaughtered five hippo-
potamuses, two elephants, a rhinocerus and a giraffe. The cost of
transporting such exotic creatures from Africa to Rome, just to be
killed by the young emperor, was as exorbitant as his behaviour
was excessive.

Commodus practised his gladiatorial skills at home, lopping off
ears and limbs as he killed or maimed compliant slaves (or so we
are told). He even took part in preliminary bouts in the arena
itself, though with blunted swords. As emperor, he always won.
Proper Romans were disgusted by this imperial display. He even
planned to be inaugurated formally as consul while dressed in
gladiator costume. But he was assassinated first, strangled after a
drinking bout (and not stabbed while fighting in the Colosseum
as the film *Gladiator* depicts it). The gladiator, sexy hero of manly
virtue and base slave whose life hung on the gesture of a thumb,
embodied a paradox of Roman ideas of power. When the emperor
acted as a gladiator, the tension between high and low, power and
expendability, desire for honour and shameful display, became
too intense for the Roman mind to negotiate comfortably.
Commodus was a scandal.

The gladiatorial games were very serious entertainments that produced story after story, image after image. The Roman obsession with manliness and violence, hierarchy and displays of power, found its perfect emblem in the gladiator. The mosaic floor in Figure 41 is one of many which represent gladiators. It decorated a wealthy villa but is typical of the pervasive representations of gladiators in the Roman visual world. This was an image for a good Roman family to live with.

41. Gladiator mosaic

The gladiators are named, and each pair shows a clear winner and loser. In the bottom pair, the death stroke has been applied, and the heroic victor is posed above his dead and still bleeding rival. The spilled blood, discarded sword and closed eyes of the distorted body of the victim contrast with the firm stance of the victor, eyes raised towards the heaven of imperial authority. In the upper pair, the death blow is about to be delivered. The victim faces the blow with open eyes. His name is Cupido (which means 'Desire' in Latin, a good name for a gladiator); under the name is the Greek letter, theta, which is the first letter of the word *thanatos*, or 'death'. It is the mark which indicates that the death sentence has been passed by the sponsor of the games. The helmeted executioner holds his sword aloft for the *coup de grâce*. Above both pairs, the black stretcher waits to carry out the dead bodies. The violence of the arena was not just for the crowd's adrenalin-filled excitement. It is also part of the domestic furniture of Roman family life. Even a baby's bottle may be decorated with an image of a gladiator.

The bell-pull in Figure 42 shows one of those gladiators who fight wild beasts. He has a drawn sword and is fighting an animal, which rises out of his erect penis. This is meant to be funny (I take it), but it cuts to the quick of Roman ideas about sex and violence with the gladiator. Is the gladiator fighting to conquer desire – 'the beast below the waist', as Shakespeare put it? The gladiator's training for a noble death is a paradigm of self-control. Or is this a way of cutting the sexiness of the gladiator down to size? Is the bestiality of aggression inside a man or his enemy? The dividing line between man and beast has become here a fusion of self-destructive violence. This is an everyday object to hang by a house door. But it is an image whose expressiveness is hard to tease out. Gladiators were represented all around the Romans because their spectacular per-

42. Gladiator bell pull

formances were central to how Romans conceptualized violence, sexuality and power.

From their beginnings at aristocratic funerals, through to the massive displays of the emperors, the gladiatorial games were always a scene of political theatre. The games were offered as part of the power displays of the elite, and the people played a crucial role in this spectacle. Under the emperors, there were far fewer opportunities for political activity for the Roman people (and a restricted role even for the elite). Consequently, the games where the massed populace gathered before the emperor could be a dramatic encounter of the ruler and the ruled. Emperors were adept at carefully controlling their appearances, and had the power to stage their own appearances as celebrations. But to display this too overtly or aggressively could easily become a sign of tyrannical violence. Domitian pulled back the canopies which shaded the crowd from the burning sun (one of the most amazing technical achievements of the Colosseum), and forced the crowd to sit and suffer. The games became a place visibly to express the social tensions of Rome.

At the games, the massed populace found a voice which they lacked in other formal political settings. So the crowd appealed to Caligula at the Circus to cut taxes. When he refused, they kept shouting till he sent soldiers into the crowd with orders to kill anyone caught shouting. The crowd fell silent, seething. This scene, according to the Jewish historian Josephus, helped motivate a band of conspirators to plot to assassinate the emperor. The Emperor Tiberius, on the other hand, faced by the anger of the people because he had taken a well-known (and evidently much loved) statue from the public baths to his private palace, complied with their wishes and agreed to return it.

On such occasions, the power of the emperor came up against the collective mass of popular will. But the most regular display of imperial authority was more direct. At the end of a combat, the victorious gladiator appealed to the man who had given the games. Was he to kill his opponent or spare him? The crowd yelled its view; and the emperor, signalling with his hand – thumbs up for death, thumbs down for mercy – decided the fate of the defeated man. This repeated performance visibly demonstrated the emperor's power of life and death. The thrill of the games is deeply interwoven with the thin and arbitrary line between death and life, the turn of a thumb, and the opportunity for everyone in the crowd to shout his or her own death sentence. As the poet Juvenal bitterly observed, 'Even those who do not kill want to have the power to do so.' At the moment of climax, the whole crowd and the performers focused on the emperor; and in that instant the very preciousness of life hangs on the emperor's gesture. It would be hard to construct a more intense and insistent spectacle of power.

The games were also part of the politics of punishment. Criminals were publicly executed there. The form of execution varied in spectacular brutality. Criminals could be thrown to wild animals, who had been starved in preparation. (This, of course, is the favoured image of Christian martyrdom, being 'thrown to the lions'.) Or they could be used as cannon fodder in set battles. Perhaps most bizarrely, they were used also to enact grizzly deaths from the stories of myth. Hercules had been burnt to death on a pyre, and this scene was re-enacted with a criminal dressed as Hercules. Pasiphae had slept with a bull (and thus produced the Minotaur). So a woman was forced to copulate with a bull till she died. Violent public punishment, like beheadings or being hung, drawn and quartered, remained common throughout European history, but the grotesque tortures of mythological re-enactment were special to Rome.

Animals were also set against each other, and were hunted by trained hunters. The elegant carving in Figure 43 captures something of the thrill of such occasions. Although the rarity and expense of the beasts and the skill of the hunters were what kept Roman interest, the highly symbolic struggle between humans and animals is basic to the power relations on display at the games. Treating men as flesh for animals to tear and eat is part of the humiliating reduction of criminals to non-human status; the hunting of animals reasserts the boundary between man and beast. The watching audience thrills and shivers in its secure recognition of the potential fragility of human domination over the natural world.

This background gives the most famous story from the games its charge. Apion, according to Aulus Gellius who records the story, was in the Circus that day and saw this event with his own eyes. Androcles was a slave who had escaped from the governor of Africa. He was eventually recaptured and sentenced to death by wild beasts at Rome. But the fierce and ravenous lion, instead of attacking Androcles, licked his feet and hands, and they seemed to greet each other like old friends. Caligula was the emperor in

43. Relief of gladiators fighting lions

charge of these games. He called Androcles to his box to explain the prodigious sight. Androcles narrated how he had hidden in that very lion's cave while on the run, and while there he had removed a thorn from the beast's foot. The lion seemed not to want to savage him afterwards, so Androcles had stayed three years in the cave. When he left, he was recaptured. Now he had met the same lion again. The emperor had the story written on placards and carried around the arena for everyone to appreciate. This fable-like story of exchange and gratitude between man and beast stands in stark counterpoint to the expected violence of the games, the deliberate dehumanization and destruction of its victims. This is one reason why modern audiences have loved to retell this story as an antidote to the games.

The skilled brutality of the gladiators and the crowd passionate about slaughter provide an enduring image of imperial Rome. The stratified audience, in their best robes and special seats, the imperial power on display, the dynamics of ruler and ruled, the constant noise of ritual, chants and scandals, turned this into an occasion when Rome made a spectacle of itself. Romans them-selves saw the games as an aspect of Rome's militaristic society, its commitment to discipline and manliness as virtues. But the games can also be viewed in a more psychological frame as a form of exor-cism for the prevalence of early death in pre-industrial society, and for the powerlessness of the citizen in a vast, threatening world. In the games at least the crowd is always the survivor.

But what has most fascinated and excited Western society since the Renaissance is the very fascination and excitement of the Roman crowd – the baying, feverish, vibrant mass fixated by the spectacle of human death. Like all in the Colosseum, we are as absorbed in looking at the spectators as we are in looking at the staging of death. The mixture of eroticism and violence that so attracts and repels the modern audience is sharply imagined in Simeon Solomon's *Habet!* (Figure 44), which pictures the moment of a gladiator's death reflected in the women's different bodily expressions of desire and power. Solomon's manipulation of the Victorian obsessions with female desire, death and the ancient world acts like a mirror for the viewer. As we stare at Solomon's painting, we catch sight of our own desire to gaze at the spectacles of Rome.

The strangeness of the games – the violence of the bare chest turned to the sword, the crowd yelling for death, the emperor's thumb sealing a man's doom, the smell and sight of human blood and smashed flesh – is felt at every turn. Feeling that otherness is part of what helps us define modern Western civilization, to define ourselves. We like – we *need* – to see the games as 'utterly

44. Habet! *by Simeon Solomon*

alien and almost unimaginable'. It provides a surety of our own civilized societies. It is a consolation.

Like most consolations, this comfort depends also on a measure of self-denial. It depends on not thinking too hard about the violence, symbolic and real, of modern society. Public executions are no longer the sensational excitements that they were for most of European history. But state executions in America must have members of the public present, and can be bought on video for repeated viewing. Pornography happily displays violent and degrading acts both in live shows and on film and video. The more real, the more pricey. There is a thriving video business in 'real disasters' from car crashes upwards. On television, 'real murder' and 'real crime' shows continue to have huge ratings, and Jack the Ripper remains a commercial success. In the reporting of war or of terrorist acts, no modern news programme is complete without the image of a dead body being carried out or covered up. The footage of the 11 September atrocities in New York again and again showed people jumping to their death. The second Gulf War had cameras following soldiers through battle and journalists under fire.

This list can be painfully extended, both with institutionally supported events and with more socially marginalized activities: bull-fighting in Spain; boxing; bare-knuckle fighting; the obsessive and repetitive violence of Hollywood action films; the more baroque violence of art-house films; the huge spread of video games; the exhibition of flayed and plastinated corpses by Gunther von Hagens across Europe's cities. Modern society also loves to show violence; it too gathers its passionate, or cruelly dispassionate, crowds for entertainment; it is fascinated by lurid displays of flesh, sliced, twisted or just humiliated. If a society is known by its entertainments, modern Western society has a long way to go before it can boast of having repressed the dark and vicious underbelly of civilization.

Gladiatorial games *are* different, importantly so, from all of our contemporary spectacles, not least because of their commitment to 'status bloodbaths' in such a civic, public arena. It would be foolish to suggest otherwise. But if the difference of ancient games produces only a sense of comfort with our own civilized entertainment, then an element of self-reflection seems to have been rather worryingly submerged. *Spartacus* and *Gladiator* are huge successes partly because of their audience's frisson at the thought of the games as entertainment – of being there, at the real thing. The lure of such feelings is also more directly fostered by the gigantic entertainment industry, which produces its many levels of military, sexual, personal violence. The vicarious pleasures of watching violence to the human body are scarcely 'wholly alien and unimaginable' in our society.

The spectacle of the gladiatorial games is shocking still, but the shock should not lead just to the question 'How could they?' It should also help us see how fragile are the boundaries of what we pride ourselves in seeing as modern civilization. The question raised by the spectacle of gladiators is a question that the modern world also needs to face, and all too rarely does: what does it say about us that we like to watch such things in the name of entertainment?

4
The Last Supper

Jews across the world celebrate the Passover – the exodus from Egypt, as narrated in the Bible. The main form of celebration is the highly ritualized meal known as the Seder, where the Haggadah is read. This book tells the story of the escape of the people of Israel from Egypt, comments on it, adds psalms for singing, and ends up with children's folk songs. It was this meal that Jesus and his disciples were celebrating in the 'last supper'. During the Seder, it is required that everyone drink four glasses of wine, and the Haggadah instructs that everyone should do this while reclining – though not many people these days take this injunction literally and provide couches for all the guests at the table.

A Greek citizen from the classical city, or a Roman from the Empire, would find much of this occasion surprisingly familiar. For the Seder follows in its customs many elements of the symposium, the Greek drinking party familiar from the sixth century BC onwards in the Mediterranean. The symposium was an especially Greek form of entertainment, in Greek eyes, but it spread throughout the Empire, especially among the Greek-speaking elite who dominated upper-class circles across the 'Greek East', an area that included at least modern Egypt, Turkey, Iraq, Iran, Syria and Israel. The symposium was one of the defining signs of a cultured Greek life.

Lying on couches was the normal style for a symposium, usually three to a couch. The amount of wine drunk and its strength were determined by the 'symposiarch', the elected leader of the party. Drinking four glasses while reclining is typical of the symposium, not just because it is more wine than usual and is drunk lying down, but also because it is a set amount for all. At a symposium, a slave would wash his master's hands (and so today still the head of the Seder has his hands washed), and the evening would progress with stories told, games played and alliances made. The more intellectual symposium often had set speeches on a particular topic, or asked light-hearted if obscure questions to test the company. The Seder too follows the same procedure of question, debate and explanation, usually with each person around the table taking a turn. Its most famous passage of liturgy is the 'four questions', traditionally asked by a child.

In the ancient world, as the wine flowed more freely, the symposium would break into raucous songs, and finally the young men might go out into the night for the sort of partying young men usually get up to on the streets. The Seder ends with the singing of folk songs, but the final formal act is the eating of a concluding piece of unleavened bread, the 'aphikoman'. The word is meaningless in Hebrew (and most people are happy not to know where it comes from). But it is a corruption of the Greek words *epi komon*, which means 'to the *komos*', that is, the drunken party that leaves the house on the razzle. It marks the end of the evening proper (and the proprieties of the evening).

The Seder took the basic form it retains to this day during an era of Greek cultural dominance in the eastern Mediterranean. It is a celebration of freedom, and of the luxuriousness and benefits of a life of peace. But even though the Seder is a major ceremony of Jewish self-definition, its shape and its emblems of freedom are taken from the surrounding Graeco-Roman society. These emblems are still followed by Jews all around the world, for all that few are fully aware of this Greek heritage piously transmitted across the generations – and for all that some would repress that knowledge for less than satisfactory ideological reasons. The Seder is a perfect example of the remarkably long and sustained inheritance of Greek and Roman entertainment in modern culture. What is extraordinary is the continuity of such ritual forms over thousands of years. Those who celebrate the Passover, whether they know it or not, are living out a history of cultural borrowing and emulation.

The Christian iconography of the last supper replays this ceremonial with new significance. The unleavened bread and the wine, signs of freedom, become signs of the different Christian religious mystery, a different promise of freedom: the body and blood of Christ offering freedom from this material world. The Lamb of God replaces the lamb of the Paschal offering: Jesus' blood as a sacrifice will save and free the Christian world, just as the blood of the lambs, painted on the doorposts of the Israelites, saved the Jews from the Angel of Death and led them to freedom. For some Christians, 'Paschal' (*pascha* in Greek) was etymologically related to Christ's 'Passion' (*paschein*). For others, the 'Passover' became Christ's passing over into heaven. Yet this tradition too is no more clear about its Greek heritage: with an astonishing act of linguistic imperialism, Greek-speaking Christians used the word 'Greek' (*Hellen*) as the standard term for 'pagan' – the despised other.

The emulation of classical culture is all around us in the histories of our own art forms. It is most obvious in sculpture and painting, which self-consciously seek to recapture classical form. But that concern for classical proportion – and classical bodies – runs through ballet and the history of dance too, as it does in athletics, where the 'Olympic ideal' is so often expressed through the poised and perfect athletic images of the ancient world. The history of theatre and opera is full of attempts to recreate the glory of Greece and the splendour of Rome – from Wagner's Bayreuth festival back to the first opera and forward to modern theatre's love affair with Greek tragedy.

It is important to understand that our privileged forms of entertainment have a long classical genealogy and have often depended on their classical origins for authority, status and inspiration. It is also fascinating to see where those genealogies are forgotten and the heritage of the past comes to feel like our own culture – an unrecognized history inside us. A tragic love story can make us cry, even when it acts out the plot of Dido and Aeneas yet again. Every returning soldier plays Odysseus, even when Homer is unread.

The history of our entertainments needs classics to explore its genealogies and heritage. But these ancient entertainments also act as a mirror to reveal a harsher type of self-recognition – one where we observe more clearly the insufficiencies and self-deceptions of contemporary public culture. Thinking about modern entertainments through a classical lens also makes us aware of the blinkers, which allow us to be comfortably self-confident about the civilized quality of our pastimes. It lets us see ourselves more clearly.

What a society does by way of entertainment is always telling. But it is especially hard from the inside to reflect on what our entertainments reveal about ourselves. The very word 'entertainment' seems to wave away serious attention, even if we know that to understand ourselves is to understand what we do. As Plato and Augustine feared, entertainment is where we like to forget ourselves; and, as Freud showed, it is when we forget ourselves that we are most self-revealing. Theatre and the gladiatorial games, those archetypal entertainments of ancient Greece and Rome, are very much still inside us, either through the artistic tradition or in the popular imagination. Partly because of this, they turn out to be a particularly valuable route into reflecting critically on what *we* do. They give us a necessary vantage point to see ourselves. If you want to know what you think you are doing, the theatre and the games are a good place to do that thinking from.

V

WHERE DO YOU THINK
YOU COME FROM?

I

A Greece of the Imagination

When a child asks 'Where do I come from?', the answer is always a story. Parents may call their story 'the facts of life', but their words are always a highly edited version of what adults know. As children grow, stories about where they come from multiply. There are personal stories – family histories with all their myths and memories, trivialities and tragedies. There are the little anecdotes which all members of a culture share: how an apple fell on Newton's head (for the English), how William Tell shot the apple off his child's head (for the Swiss). Anyone who doesn't know those stories would be outside the loop of their own culture. There is the history of the nation, the community, the race, which produces the affiliations of social life. There are also the grand religious and scientific narratives, which set out to explain the Major Questions of the past, such as how the human race itself came into existence – Adam and Eve, or the Big Bang and Evolution. Myth and history construct the past for us and in us. Our sense of the here and now is formed through the stories we tell of where we come from.

If we want to understand modern society, we need to look carefully at the historical narratives that lead people to live the sort of life they do, to hold the beliefs they hold, and to take the actions that make a difference in society. The conflict in the Middle East, for example, is fuelled by historical narratives. The most ancient history – the Bible and the existence of the Jewish Kingdoms, until their destruction in the Roman Empire – has been repeatedly used to provide a significant justification for claims and

counterclaims to territory. The more recent past is equally obsessively and stridently fought over. It's hard to imagine a discussion
of the current political situation in the Middle East which did not
quickly and passionately revert to the role of the British Mandate
of 1920–47, the history of immigration and expulsion (complete
with family stories), the causation of recent wars or uprisings, and
mutual accusations of past terrorism, coupled with heated claims
to the right of freedom. These are life-and-death stories. People
fight over them – and for them. Such stories provide the motivation for murderous violence and self-righteous hate – and everyone across the globe who takes part in such discussions inevitably
gets entwined in the work of retelling those histories, however
naively, insultingly, gently or intelligently. It matters, it matters
crucially, how these stories are told.

'Where do you think you come from?' is a question which
today seems unfailingly to incite political turmoil. It lies at the
heart of so much current violence and conflict, from the brutal
dissolution of the former Yugoslavia to the insidious or vitriolic
rows about immigration and national identity that still dominate
the European political debate; from the aggression of institutionalized apartheid to the nasty hostilities of day-to-day racism and
prejudice; from the confused scientific arguments about genetics,
nature and nurture to the social implications of those new bio-
logical understandings. Reflecting on the power of the question
'Where do you think you come from?', its power to mould and
influence lives, has never been more necessary than now.

Generations of European and American writers, politicians and
artists have repeatedly found one fundamental, idealistic answer to
the question 'Where do you think you come from?' – the classical
past. The very distance of the classical past allows for an *ideal*
picture to be developed and utilized, and the ideal image of Greece
in particular has again and again fuelled the most stirring cultural
and political revolutions of Western society. Greece is seen as the
fountainhead of Western values. It has been a banner to march
under, a spur to revolutionaries, an inspiration and aspiration.

Ancient Greece and Rome have provided a story of the past which has changed lives. When Karl Marx said, 'The French Revolution was enacted in Roman dress,' he meant that the lines of thought, the models of behaviour and, above all, the political ideals which together made the French revolution possible were essentially formulated through its leaders' study of classics. He's right, too: without that longing gaze backwards, the revolutionary progress which convulsed eighteenth-century Europe, and made modern Europe, could not have happened as it did. This idealized image of the classical past, and usually the Greek past, has been absolutely central to Western culture and politics. It affects even the ways we now understand our inner lives. Sigmund Freud found an Oedipus inside everyone. For Freud, the story of Oedipus – that archetypal Greek myth – explains where we all come from. He too needed an ancient Greek image to explain the modern mind.

Marx and Freud have had an inestimable impact on the culture of the twentieth century and on our society today. However shocking their theories were, their turn back to a Greece of the imagination would have surprised none of their contemporaries. The age in which they wrote is the era which witnessed the most intense, widespread and passionate engagement with the ancient world, in politics as much as in art, in music as much as in literature. Freud's Oedipus and Marx's Roman-dress revolutionaries speak directly to the intellectual commitments of nineteenth-century men and women.

Nineteenth-century culture may have produced Marx and Freud, twentieth-century heroes. But contemporary society has defined itself against that culture of the nineteenth century above all. One place we come from – all our yesterdays – is inhabited by ladies in long crinolines, gentlemen in top hats, and ubiquitous servants. 'The Victorians' are leading actors in our story of the past. How we understand the Victorians and their picture of things is a foundation of our self-recognition. To explore the history of the Greece of the imagination – how the myth of

Greece and Greek myths themselves have helped form Western culture – there is no better place to start than the long nineteenth century, when the rulers of the British Empire sailed to govern the colonies with classical texts in their hands, when Greek and Latin were the core of education across Europe, and when the touchstone of artistic idealism was the glory that was Greece. To find out where we come from, we need to visit the Greece of the imagination.

2

Founding Fathers –
From Keats to Hollywood and Back

Shelley's Swim and Oscar's Clothes

The museum is an enshrined story of the past, and none captures the West's fixation with the glory that was Greece as powerfully as the British Museum in London. The Elgin Marbles, the friezes that once adorned the Parthenon on the Acropolis of Periclean Athens, are the central exhibit of a display which encapsulates both the symbolic power of the British Empire and the European longing for a Greece of the imagination. The British Museum embodies the aspirations of nineteenth-century England, and the Elgin Marbles are a fitting jewel in that crown because from the Romantic era onwards English culture obsessively turned its longing gaze towards ancient Greece.

When these remarkable carved marbles first made their precarious way to England in 1816, they were exhibited in a rather ramshackle hall, where they were visited by all the great cultural figures of the age. Keats went, and captured his response in a sonnet. The young poet is reduced to 'a most dizzy pain' by the 'Grecian grandeur', its 'shadow of magnitude'. 'I must die', he swoons, 'like a sick eagle looking at the sky.' With a typical indulgence of sensuality, he found it gratifying to sob before these images of the past: ''tis gentle luxury to weep'. The marbles embody the idealism towards which Keats aspires but of which, as a poet, he tearfully finds himself falling short.

Keats' poetry records his lifelong absorption in the classical past. This longing for Greece is most vividly articulated in his

'Ode on a Grecian Urn' (1819), another poem which dramatizes Keats in front of an ancient work of art. Keats did not come from the upper classes (as did the poets of the period) and consequently he actually knew no Greek. (Byron called his work 'piss-a-bed poetry' and worse, insulting what he saw as Keats' lack of masculinity – by which he meant his lack of education and class as much as any effeminacy.) But these days, through hours of schoolroom analysis, this poem is a standard by which the English quest for a lost Greece is epitomized.

The poem is structured as a series of rhetorical questions addressed to the images on the vase, dramatizing the poet's attempt to penetrate the mystery of the silent scenes. Keats' questions have him transfixed before the urn's beauty, but longingly unable to enter and participate fully in its ancient setting. The fourth stanza famously begins:

> Who are these coming to the sacrifice?
> > To what green altar, O mysterious priest,
> Lead'st thou that heifer lowing at the skies,
> > And all her silken flanks with garlands drest?

The story goes that these lines were inspired by the Elgin Marbles, and specifically the image in Figure 45 in which a heifer's head is indeed turned towards the skies, mouth open, on its way to a sacrificial death. The 'Ode on a Grecian Urn' at one level stages in an intense form that sense of the overwhelming attraction – and yet the baffling otherness – of this Greece, a land of the imagination caught in a still and opaque image.

In this love of Greece, Keats was absolutely typical of the cutting edge of English culture. A whole generation of Romantic artists in Britain were absorbed by 'Graecomania'. While the poor Keats languished artistically in London, Lord Byron, forced by scandal to flee London, became a superstar poet writing from abroad, but entered the pantheon of Romantic artists by dying for Greece. Like many writers and thinkers, he was galvanized by the fight for Greek freedom from the Turkish Empire. It was a fight that gave a fully politicized agenda to the ideological idealism of the artistic turn towards Greece. Byron may in reality have achieved next to nothing and have died – rather more mundanely – of fever. But he became a heroic symbol of Romantic commitment to the cause of freedom (artistic, political, sexual), which made Philhellenism – a passionate love of Greece – an essential credo of the age.

45. Parthenon frieze

Shelley too was passionate about the Greek fight for independence, and many of his greatest poems link the struggle to escape the dulling shackles of social convention and political oppression with the ideal image of a free Greece. Prometheus was a figure to whom Shelley returned again and again: the chained creative spirit who suffers for truth and mankind, and yet longs for freedom and justice – a very definition of the Romantic artist as much as a Greek Titan. Shelley also died young and abroad. He drowned off the coast of Italy – a death that has been invested with less mythic nobility than Byron's. Strangely, however, even swimming was touched with the glamour of the classical. It's hard now to appreciate that swimming was rediscovered as a pastime only in the late eighteenth century, and as a sport much later still. Although Greeks and Romans swam as a leisure activity, there is a long gap in its history – people don't swim in medieval and Renaissance Europe. It was taken up again with a conscious look backwards towards the ancient love of exercise and training the body, especially by Romantic Philhellenes, who fancied swimming the Bosphorus, like Leander of Greek myth, towards a lover of their own. To swim was to sport and strive like a Greek or Roman hero. Shelley's death by water – his last swim – becomes part of his self-mythology of Greekness.

For Byron, Shelley and a host of intellectuals – the Romantic giants of the first quarter of the nineteenth century – Greece was an intellectual rallying call. A generation of English intellectuals defined themselves aesthetically and politically by turning towards an idealized Greece. They were committed to a revolutionary politics and a revolutionary poetics, and in both areas they found the image of a free Greece inspirational. Shelley raised the banner for his whole generation when he proudly declared: 'We are all Greeks.'

These Romantic Philhellenists set the agenda for the century that follows. Greece courses through the artistic and cultural life of England with a continuing obsessiveness. For the educated classes, it was an integral part of the construction of a personal and cultural identity. In Figure 46 we can see Oscar Wilde, flamboyant as ever, on his first trip to Greece, which he made with his tutor from Trinity College, Dublin in the 1870s. This picture gives a good sense of the self-construction involved in such a trip. Dressing up as a Greek for the camera, a self-confident smile, and foot poised on the ancient rocks of Greece, in a carefully posed image for friends at home or university, is a highly coded self-projection, with the same flair for spectacular self-presentation that marks Wilde's later career. He had written to his tutor in Oxford to ask permission to be late for term because a visit like this to Greece was so educational. Certainly Wilde was learning.

46. Oscar Wilde in Greece, 1877

Wilde was acting out what it meant to say 'We are all Greeks,' and he knew well the intense charge of such a claim in the circles in which he was already moving. He found himself at home with a group in Oxford and London known as the 'Aesthetes'. These Aesthetes offer a distinctive flowering of self-conscious transgression. The group was a self-selected and shifting collection of individuals, linked by their commitment to an extreme aesthetic principle where 'beauty' mattered above all. All aspects of life were submitted to that criterion. And for all of them Greece provided the very paradigm of a world infused with beauty.

Wilde's later notoriety has eclipsed a line of more serious scholars, including the art historian Walter Pater, poets such as Algernon Swinburne and essayists like John Addington Symonds, who had a profound influence on a generation of young men both by their publications and by personal contact in the elite world of Oxford University education. Greece ran through their debates on beauty – and on sexuality. Pater, the movement's high priest, wanted his pupils to rediscover all around them 'a world of exquisite craftsmanship, touching the minutest details of daily life with splendour and skill, in close correspondence with a particularly animated development of human existence' – which was how he defined Greek art, his model and hope.

Symonds, however, had a more specific liberalizing sexual agenda. He saw the cultural ideal of Victorian Hellenism in terms of his own socially stigmatized desires. *His* Greece of the imagination is summed up like this: 'Like a young man newly come from the wrestling-ground, anointed, chapleted and very calm, the Genius of the Greeks appears before us. Upon his soul, there is no burden of the world's pain . . . nor has he yet felt sin.' For Symonds, a longing for Greece is pictured as a beautiful boy without – for once – the feeling of sin. Greece promised a pre-Christian, guilt-free paradise. Unsurprisingly, it was Symonds rather than Pater who was scathingly attacked by Oxford conservatives for what they all-too-vividly imagined he was thinking of when he demanded that 'we must imitate the Greeks'. Wilde knew what he was doing when he dressed up as a Greek.

Wilde himself shows his growing engagement with this Greek love in his notebooks and commonplace books, where he collected a series of passages from Pater, Symonds and his other reading. Platonic philosophy and the *Symposium*'s praise of male love play a special role here. These phrases show Wilde's Grecian style as it is being formed: 'We wrestle to embrace and embrace to wrestle,' he wrote, lovingly dwelling on a mixture of homoeroticism and dialectical philosophy. He added a catchphrase from Pater: 'to do philosophy with desire'. So strong was the 'Grecian' aspect of doing philosophy that 'being of a philosophical disposition' became a euphemism for someone with whom you could talk of homoerotic feelings.

Wilde tried to capture those intense conversations between young men in a single principle: 'the refinement of Greek culture coming through the romantic medium of impassioned friendships'. The romance of his impassioned friendships needed the veil of the 'refinement of Greek culture', and in particular Plato's discussions of desire offer an ideal image to live up to. Hellenism was the medium of homosexual expression for this high-profile and influential intellectual milieu. It's not by chance that the lead character of Wilde's best-known novel should allude to a scholarly world of Greek feeling. *The Picture of Dorian Gray* hesitates to mention 'the love that cannot speak its name', but through the odd name 'Dorian' it alludes knowingly to the Spartans, the Dorian race *par excellence*, and thus to a Spartan pederastic tradition, which made male love part of manly warfare, and not a sign of effete softness. This sort of hint and smirk is typical of the insider talk of these aesthetically minded teachers and pupils, writers and artists.

For the educated classes in Victorian Britain, Greece was a fundamental route to understanding the world and, above all, for expressing one's own place, intellectual, moral, sexual, within it. This is partly why the long-running argument about the place of classics in the school and university curriculum was so heated. This political debate ran throughout the nineteenth century and stretched well into the twentieth. Nor has it finished yet today. But in the nineteenth century the argument started with the question of whether anything else but classics and the Bible should even be taught to children, once they could read and write. For most of the century, classics took up a good 80 per cent of the time in the classroom. The familiarity with Greece and Rome begins with this institutional foundation.

Politicians and educationalists throughout the nineteenth century made educational reform and the place of classics in it a matter of intense *national* concern. One of the most influential figures in this long debate was Benjamin Jowett. At the same time as the Aesthetes were strutting their stuff on the streets of Oxford and London, Jowett – who was friendly with many of them, especially Swinburne – was fundamentally changing the educational system in Oxford, starting with Balliol, the college where he was master.

Jowett also took Plato as his master-text, but in a quite different way from those who poured over the *Symposium* as part of their crushes on beautiful boys. Jowett established the one-on-one class or 'tutorial' as the mainstay of his educational policy – classes deliberately set up like Plato's portraits of Socrates with a friend, doing philosophy together. He himself translated all of Plato into English, and made Platonic philosophy a guide for those in public life – something Plato would have appreciated well. Jowett educated his students with Plato to rule the Empire, and, from the study in Oxford to the corridors of power across the Empire, this education was remarkably effective.

It was helped by a civil service exam that awarded many more marks for success in classical papers than any other subject – even the languages spoken in the areas to be governed. Classics was a training to rule, and the best and brightest who went from public school to university to government were educated in ancient texts. The role of the civil service in ruling India had been formulated by Thomas Macaulay back in the 1830s. When he travelled out to India first by boat, he carefully read – and reread – much of Greek literature including nearly all of Plato, and the *Iliad* and the *Odyssey*, along with Cicero and other Roman writers. This was his preparation for ruling an empire. When Alexander the Great conquered the known world, he slept with a copy of Homer under his pillow, as he strived to achieve the immortal glory of the Homeric heroes. The pursuit of empire – cultural conquest – is fed by classical dreams.

The dominance of this educational model was pervasive, and Jowett's Oxford formed the apex of a far broader educational commitment in England. From the first schooldays to ruling the Empire to a quiet retirement reading Homer in the evening, classics was integral to the formation of the nineteenth-century gentleman.

These snapshots of poets, aesthetes and educational grandees give a good flavour of how varied the passionate lovers of Greece in Victorian Britain were. What such vignettes cannot capture is how pervasive and broad this passion was. The figures I have focused on are the cultural heroes for nineteenth-century England. They set the cultural agenda which was absorbed and followed by vast numbers of the educated classes. The Romantic poets and their self-conscious revolutionary Hellenism, the Aesthetes with their self-consciously transgressive Hellenism, and the Oxford-educated elite with their self-aware commitment to Hellenism as an education for Empire, take very different roots towards an ideal Greece, and use their Greece in very different ways. Yet each group is empowered by their understanding of Greece, and their understanding informs their whole lives. Their interest in Greece is not just one intellectual hobby among others, but a way of responding to the world and existing in it. It is an integral part of the construction of their personal and cultural identities.

A Greece of the imagination informs Victorian culture. In the last hundred years, modern British culture has spent a tremendous amount of energy trying to show how it is different from Victorian society – while recognizing its roots in it. It's one of the obvious places contemporary Britain *comes from* – and anxiously explores, rejects, fantasizes about. In England, unlike, say, the USA, there are plenty of Victorian buildings in towns and cities around the country. Victorian novels are still a mainstay of our education in English, and of television adaptation. Margaret Thatcher demanded a 'return to Victorian values'. Nostalgia for the days of Empire, or a more sombre recognition of the tensions of our new post-colonial society, flood popular culture, from newspaper discussions of what cultural identity is to lush films of balmy Victorian afternoons with long dresses. There is something important at stake in understanding Victorian culture for modern Britain.

Yet what Victorians themselves thought to be the basis of any cultural formation – the study of classics and the absorption of the Bible – is increasingly being whitewashed out of contemporary perceptions. Education is a battlefield in any society experiencing cultural change, because education is formative: it makes the citizen. Education for those Victorians who progressed through the education system – an elite if ever there was one – meant the classics. They learnt by heart, they shared and they took for granted the Greek and Latin languages and the literature written in those languages, along with the Bible – which was also written in the classical languages of Greek and Latin and Hebrew, of course. That was their furniture of the mind. If we do not try to appreciate that furniture of the mind, how can we appreciate their culture?

Just as Keats was mocked by Byron for his ignorance of the Greek language, a whole horizon of expectation of Victorian culture is closed off from the modern historian if that classical training is silenced. The point is not to reproduce, to support or to regret the passing of 'Victorian values', Victorian prejudices or Victorian elitism in today's society. It's a question of what sort of a picture of Victorian society is helpful, if we want to know where we come from. The danger is that *all* we do when we look at the past is to hold up an opportunistic mirror for our own interests. The hope is that by understanding better where we come from, we might understand better why we are what we are. A blanched and thin picture of the Victorian cultural imagination can't help that process of understanding: we need the classics to give our picture of Victorian culture any real colour and depth.

Washington's Toga and Bush's Cicero

Britain's growing passion for Greece through the eighteenth and nineteenth centuries shows a cultural identity under construction. For Americans in the eighteenth century, the classical past meant Rome more than Greece. The founding fathers' engagement with classics was profound too, but had a different focus. In America, the turn to classics was an integral element in fomenting a *political revolution*.

The founding fathers of the American Republic read classical history and classical political philosophy as a way of enabling themselves to do the job of founding a republic. When John Adams visited Paris in 1778 to help Benjamin Franklin achieve an alliance with the French, crucial if the revolution against the British was to succeed, he took his sons John Quincey Adams and Charles Adams with him. As soon as he landed in France, he enrolled them in a Latin grammar school. On the boat home – the ship was called *Alliance*, aptly enough – he sat down and read Cicero's speech against Cataline with John Quincey – a great speech for a political revolutionary, with its tales of blood and plotting in the service of the Republic. When all three returned to Europe in 1780, Adams wrote to his son, 'My wish at present is that your principle Attention should be directed to the Latin and Greek tongues.'

Adams was not alone. Thomas Jefferson wrote that classics was 'the foundation preparatory for all sciences', and he said he read 'one or two newspapers a week, but with reluctance to give even that time from Tacitus and Homer'. He fills his letters with so many Greek annotations that even John Adams – out-cultured – exclaimed, 'Lord! Lord! What can I do with so much Greek.' Even George Washington, who on his farm had lacked the formal classical education of Adams and Jefferson, boasted when he was a grandfather how, thanks to his purchase of books and his educational zeal, his grandson Jack had begun Latin as soon as he could speak. With such educational ideals, these founding fathers were following European examples, and even proudly trumping them. Like the Europeans, the Americans were dazzled by the classics.

But it is in their politics that their reading of the classics leaves the most obvious and lasting fruit. Classical heroes and in particular the military and political leaders of the Roman Republic provided models to live up to and bandy about. Essays were signed by Latin and Greek pseudonyms – 'Publius', 'Metellus', 'Tully', 'Aristides', 'Horatius'. Classical stories were used in order to model careers: George Washington loved the figure of Cincinnatus. Cincinnatus was a farmer ('George' conveniently means 'farmer' in Greek) who left his plough to become military and political commander-in-chief in Rome. He did his duty for the state, eventually winning a glorious victory and driving the enemy from the soil of Italy. At that point he immediately resigned from his illustrious position and returned to the farm to live again his life of rustic peace, until another call should come. And so a toast, offered on 4 July 1788 in Wilmington, Delaware, prayed for 'farmer Washington – may he, like a second Cincinnatus, be called from the plough to rule a great people', and, on the other side of the Atlantic, the revolutionary Lord Byron celebrated Washington as 'the Cincinnatus of the West, whom envy dared not hate'. Stories, stories from the past, mould how events are lived and told.

No surprise then that Washington was repeatedly portrayed in Roman costume, as he himself repeatedly used a Rome of the imagination to express his country's fight for freedom. Figure 47 is a copy of a statue by Canova. Washington is wearing Roman military dress, but is writing what his lofty expression suggests is one of his more stirring addresses. He has now, as 'father of his country', laid down his sword (it is on the floor) and taken up his pen. A hero of the Roman Republic, reborn.

But the classics played perhaps its biggest role in giving the founding fathers an ideal of a political system to strive for. Samuel Adams prayed that Boston might become a 'Christian Sparta'.

47. *George Washington in*
Roman military dress

This image cannot be pressed too hard. Sparta's famed militarism, communal male living and sexually dodgy practices would be hard to integrate smoothly into a Puritan Christian community, even in Boston. But in Sparta Adams did find an ideal of frugality, selflessness, valour and patriotism which he could use more happily. Jefferson, less impressed, called the Spartans 'military monks', and John Adams, not one for communism, thought the Spartan practice of communal ownership of goods 'stark mad'. It was Rome and above all republican Rome that inspired – and aroused anxiety.

Rome's governmental system prompted a great deal of discussion around the forging of the American constitution. Rome's constitutional checks and balances between the people and the ruling Senate with its elected consuls was contrasted with the despised monarchy of Britain – but the contrast worked in more than one way. Rome's military triumphs were admired; but at the same time Rome's treatment of its provinces stimulated more unpleasant analogies. One of the founding fathers, James Otis, in 1764, wrote, 'The conduct of Rome towards her colonies and the corruptions and oppressions tolerated in her provincial officers of all denominations, was one great cause of the downfall of that proud republic.' Alexander Hamilton upped the stakes in 1774: 'Rome was the home of freedom. She was celebrated for her justice and lenity; but in what manner did she govern her dependent provinces? They were made the continual scene of a rapine and cruelty.' Greece treated her colonies well, and if England had been more like Greece, less like Rome, what might have been avoided? 'The truth is we have been forced into it,' wrote another founder of the revolution, 'to guard our country and posterity from the greatest of all evils, such another infernal Government (if it deserves the name of Government) as the provinces groaned under in the latter Ages of the Roman Commonwealth.' As victim, America was a colony crushed and forced into rebellion by the cruel despot, like the Jews or Christians resisting the tyranny of Rome.

Rome, the mother of all empires, was a fantastic model for the American founding fathers to use in order to think through the invention of their Republic. The founders of America may have come from Britain, but the revolution made the question of what such descent might mean something of a political conundrum. In the swirl of ideas in which the constitution was formulated, classical models provoked and stimulated and inspired the founding fathers. Both the symbolic authority of these classical models and their active political philosophy provided an inspiration for the fathers and their own political aspirations.

America was not alone in this turn to the republican values of Rome. Marx's dictum that the French revolution was 'enacted in Roman dress' was made in part because every leading intellectual figure who helped foment the revolution claimed a classical source of inspiration, made constant reference to classical ideals in their speeches and pamphlets, and used classics to articulate the model of a new political system. Typically, Jean-Jacques Rousseau, perhaps the most influential intellectual guide for the revolutionaries, declared that his 'free and republican spirit, that indomitable character, impatient with the yoke and servitude', was forged by reading Plutarch as a child. (Bernard Shaw, many years later but with the same reforming zeal, proudly called Plutarch 'a revolutionist's handbook'.) Classical texts made the revolutionaries what they were.

But Marx also saw how individual heroes of the revolution *enacted* their classics. Charlotte Corday is one of the figures who make up the myth and the history of the French revolution. She was an ordinary country girl, the story goes, who preserved the true spirit of the revolution by an act of extraordinary heroism. It was she who stabbed to death the tyrannical and murderous Marat in his bath, in the name of liberty, equality and fraternity. This assassination and her subsequent trial became an icon of the revolution, which is still part of every French child's history lessons. Charlotte Corday, as Karl Marx recognized, acted in classical dress: not only did she play out the role of the ancient historians' favourite hero, 'the tyrant-slayer', but she was said to have read Plutarch all day before she undertook her heroic deed.

For both the French revolution and the American revolution, the classical past was a stimulus, a provocation, a means to develop foundational political ideals. The study of classics provided the intellectual framework in which their republican politics were worked out. The verbal and artistic imagery in which their revolutionary ideals were articulated drew on the full authority and repertoire of the exemplars of ancient Greece and Rome. The Greece and Rome of the imagination were instrumental in the shaping of modern Europe and America.

This role of Rome has returned to American culture via twentieth-century Hollywood, but in a negative rather than a positive light. Throughout the twentieth century, and in particular in the decades surrounding the Second World War, Hollywood made a series of often very successful films on Roman topics – *Spartacus* (1960), *Ben Hur* (1959), *Cleopatra* (1963), *Quo Vadis* (1951), *The Sign of the Cross* (1932), *The Fall of the Roman Empire* (1964) – and many rather less successful ones too. Many of these films, like *Ben Hur* and *Quo Vadis*, are based on nineteenth-century novels or plays. Others like *Spartacus* are taken from contemporary novels and more strikingly reflect their genesis in Cold War America. All, however, use Rome to talk about America, its ideology and its power in the world. During both the Second World War and the subsequent Cold War with the Soviet Union, the film industry used classical antiquity to *do* politics.

In the Hollywood world of goodies and baddies, there is no doubt on which side Rome stands. Its negative image is repeatedly established from the opening shots of a film. The Romans stand for a brutal militaristic regime whose ruthlessness and efficiency are only undone by its excessive sexuality and perverse corruption. Rome is the Evil Empire – and not a civilization capable of attracting the admiration which the founding fathers had demonstrated. The Roman general Marcus Crassus sums this up in a famous speech in *Spartacus*. As the Roman army, all leather, metal and bristling weapons, marches out of the city, he reflects with suitably grand tones: 'There, boy, is Rome – there is the might, majesty, the terror of Rome: there is the power that bestrides the known world like a Colossus. No man can withstand Rome, no nation can stand her – how much less a boy . . . there's only one way to deal with Rome, Antoninus – you must serve her, you must abase yourself before her, you must grovel at her feet, you must – love her.' According to Shakespeare, Julius Caesar 'doth bestride the narrow world like a Colossus', but the complexities of power and individual ambition in that play are subordinated in *Spartacus* to the image of an oppressive military might. In the uncensored version of the film, which was released forty years after it was made, the previous scene had involved the general Crassus trying to seduce Antoninus, played by Tony Curtis, with what is a particularly shocking moral licence, especially for 1960. This gives the requisite sexually corrupt edge to the display of power and, as this is a Roman general speaking to a slave, adds bite to the words 'you must abase yourself . . . you must grovel . . . you must – love'. Rome is power incarnate, a power which corrupts.

This makes the opposition to Rome a cinematic necessity – from Cecil B. de Mille's blockbuster epic films back in the 1930s right up to *Gladiator* in 2000. The form of the opposition is what counts, however, for the ideological force of these movies. The Christians are archetypal revolutionaries in the struggle against Rome. The voice-over prologue to *Spartacus* begins, 'In the last century before the birth of a new faith, Christianity, which was destined to overthrow the pagan tyranny of Rome and bring about a new society, the Roman Republic stood at the very centre of the civilized world.' Christians might be revolutionaries, but they are fighters whose victory is assured not just by history but by the rhetorical portrayal of the enemy as a 'pagan tyranny' – because both 'pagan' and 'tyranny', we know, invite crushing in the Hollywood scheme of things. The idea of Rome as the 'centre of the civilized world' is easily dismissed when it is called a 'pagan tyranny'.

The Sign of the Cross begins with Rome burning while Nero, lyre in hand, plots to blame the Christians. We cut to a Roman street, where two thuggish and hairy men discuss catching Christians to win a reward from the emperor. Two old men meet in the street: one makes a line in the dirt with his staff, the other completes it into the sign of the cross. After they leave, the sign is seen being trodden over by the feet of passing Romans, but never rubbed out. It's clear where history is travelling here – towards the Christian kingdom on earth, with which the American spectator is encouraged to identify. The sign that can't be destroyed.

Christianity here is not only a morally just resistance to corrupt power. These films also make their heroes discover the sort of proper family love and personal integrity which American society promotes. In both *Quo Vadis* and *The Sign of the Cross*, Christian conversion and, of course, romance with a good woman, that ever present Hollywood motivation, allow one individual Roman to escape the brutal totalitarian regime into a true heroic narrative. Hollywood's Christianity in Rome gives us heroes who are both a plucky, small band of underdogs and unequivocally on the side of world history, righteousness and truth. The audiences of these films are overwhelmingly attracted by such a winning combination.

From the late 1930s right up to the 1960s, there is also a more pointed political use of Rome, however, to promote fascism in Italy and oppose it in America. Mussolini, the leader of the Fascist Party in Italy, was explicit in his aim to re-establish a Roman empire. 'We dream of a Roman Italy,' announces one of his early published speeches, 'that is to say, wise, strong, disciplined and imperial. Much of that which was the immortal spirit of Rome is reborn in fascism: the *fasces* are Roman; our organization of combat is Roman; our pride and our courage are Roman: *civis Romanus sum* [I am a Roman citizen]'. In his grandiose new designs for the city of Rome, he reclaimed the tomb of Augustus, the memorial of the first emperor of the Roman Empire, and built round it, constructing a monument to himself. The very word 'fascism', as Mussolini declares, comes from the *fasces*, a bunch of sticks carried by Roman officials as a sign of office, and it was used by fascists precisely for those associations with ancient power. It's not by chance that the Italian government funded an epic film about ancient Rome's triumphant campaign in Africa – as the Italians fought there themselves. The new Italian Empire was glorified through the images and narratives of the old Roman Empire.

The Roman Empire looks very different from America. Romans, in Hollywood at least, salute each other with a raised arm and shout 'Hail Caesar!' The parallels with the Nazi salute and 'Heil Hitler' were drawn as early as 1935, when the educational pack which was distributed with the film *The Last Days of Pompeii* asked school children 'what form of salute is used by the Romans? In what countries are similar salutes now demanded by the Government?' The very phrase '*demanded* by the Government' works to set American freedom against European totalitarian regimes. John Huston was explicit when he started preliminary work for *Quo Vadis*: it was to be 'a modern treatment about Nero and his fanatical determination to eliminate the Christians in much the same manner as his historic counterpart and fellow madman, Adolf Hitler, tried to destroy the Jews 2000 years later'.

The great epic *Ben Hur* in particular, whose hero is a Jew forced into opposition against the masters of Rome, draws fully on these fascist associations of Roman power. Messala, a former friend of Ben Hur, who becomes the military representative of Roman cruelty and power, tells him that the emperor 'wishes Judaea to be a more obedient and disciplined province'; he asks Ben Hur to 'persuade your people that resistance to Rome is stupid. It's worse than stupid – it's futile. For it can only end in one way, extinction for your people.' The move from requiring order and discipline to threatening the extinction of the Jewish people uses Rome to mirror the history of German fascism. The pointed political edge is clear and powerful.

The grand, spectacular scenes of the massed forces of Rome, scenes which are a staple of these epics, take on a different light after the Nazi rallies of the 1930s, especially as lovingly recorded by Leni Riefenstahl, the most seductive innovator of German documentary film-making. Even such normal parts of Roman society as slavery became reframed by this politicization. The Nazis seemed to have learnt how to treat what they called 'alien subject races' from a distorted version of the Nietzschean ideology of the Superman, which required the crushing of weaker races into slaves. This made every film which talked of 'freedom' a political statement of American values. The founding fathers who fought for freedom found their republicanism through Rome. For those 'fighting for freedom' in the twentieth century, Rome had become an image of the totalitarian enemy.

Rome has never left American popular culture, whether in the Las Vegas hotel Caesar's Palace or in a comedy musical like *A Funny Thing Happened on the Way to the Forum*, or at a student toga

party. But for the forty years around the Second World War
Rome was a space of the imagination where American values were
visualized and discussed in a very specific and significant way.
Perhaps *Spartacus* shows this best. In the nineteenth century, the
story of Spartacus had been used as the plot of one of the century's
most popular plays, *The Gladiator*, written in 1831 by Robert
Montgomery Bird. The play had won a competition for a five-act
'American tragedy' in which the hero was 'an original of this
country'. The early reviews commented with 'pride and satisfaction' that the play was very well suited indeed 'to the genius, to
the taste, and to the literary enterprise of the American people'.
It will be little surprise that the Roman authorities in this play act
as an all-too-easy symbol for British imperialism, and Spartacus
fights for freedom and for his family and home, just as the grand-
fathers of the audience had done. As 'an original of this country',
Spartacus becomes a story of where the American Republic
comes from – what the later film version of *Spartacus* called in its
press pack 'the age-old fight for freedom'.

By the 1950s, however, with the tension of the Cold War, and
with the House Un-American Activities Committee avidly pur-
suing any sign of communism, a story which celebrated the rising
up of the downtrodden had different associations. Karl Marx –
founding father of communism – had written to Engels, fellow
founding father, that 'Spartacus comes across as the most excellent fellow in the history of antiquity . . . a real representative of
the proletariat of ancient times.' When the communists led by
Rosa Luxemburg attempted a coup in Berlin in 1919, their group
was called the Spartakusbund, 'The League of Spartacus'.
Howard Fast, who wrote the bestselling novel *Spartacus* on which
the film is based, was a member of the Communist Party of
America. He was actually imprisoned for contempt by the House
Un-American Activities Committee, and began to draft the novel
while in gaol. The book is clear in its ideological stance. Spartacus
calls to the other gladiators in a version of the words of the
Communist Manifesto: 'To the slaves of the world: rise up and

cast off your chains.' Rome is seen as a capitalist machine destroying its slave labour. Roman leaders cynically manipulate the false consciousness of the Roman citizens. To take the book *Spartacus* for a Hollywood film was not an obvious choice.

All those involved in the project were aware of how dangerous it was. Kirk Douglas, the main creative force behind the film, as well as its star, met with Richard Nixon, then vice-president, to test the waters. How would the administration react to them using a black-listed writer and on a film like this? (In the light of subsequent events, that meeting would itself make a great play.) The film-studio bosses were keen to silence any political message, to protect profits more than any other motive. Others involved had their own ideas, their own hesitations and their own defensiveness. The resultant film is certainly quite different from a Marxist tract. It makes the bonding together of the gladiators a triumph of the human values of integrity, loyalty and self-determination. It leaves the family as a secure centre of value – even when the final image is of the dead Spartacus' wife and child being driven into the distance. From the prologue, it holds out Christianity as the salvation which will undo both the 'disease called human slavery' and 'the age of the dictator'. This film was the biggest box-office success of the year, as well as a critical triumph, and it spoke a welcome message to a large American audience. Yet it is still a film which shows the dangers of how power corrupts an empire's rulers, and how an empire depends on oppression and violence. Perhaps there is at least the hint of a question left waiting to be asked, as America headed towards the presidency of Richard Nixon.

For Hollywood, Rome is a way of avoiding the censor. When a film is set in ancient Rome, it can use the authority of the classical to show scenes of violence, sadism, sexuality or spectacle, which would be otherwise regarded as dirty, cruel or unpleasant. At the same time, Rome can be used to explore politics or the themes of power and authority or the role of the individual against the state in a way often resisted with a contemporary setting. Ancient Rome acts like a veil: it makes decent *and* lets us see what would otherwise be hidden, or too exposed.

It will be fascinating to observe how twenty-first-century Hollywood continues its love-affair with Rome, as America continues to formulate its view of its own modern Empire. The global success of the film *Gladiator*, with its wholly traditional story of the brave individual fighting against the might of the corrupt Empire, and, of course, standing up for the values of loyalty, the family and justice, will provide one stimulus to further film-making. But when America reflects politically on its own Empire and its own military campaigns it may turn back to the Roman Empire with new eyes. A host of projects on ancient themes have been announced since the terrorist destruction of the World Trade Center buildings in 2001, mainly focusing on the need to stop dictatorial despots. A spokesman for the American government also duly informed the world that President George W. Bush anchors his political ideas not just in great religious teachings, but specifically in 'the thinking of the ancient Greeks and Romans and in the principles of the founding fathers'. Aristotle and Cicero apparently are key inspirations for George W. The point is not exactly *how* Cicero inspires the president so much as the desire to make that sort of classical inspiration public. It seems that American public life will continue to articulate its political discourse through Rome. We need the past to tell the story of the present.

3

Finding the Fatherland –
Where Freud's Oedipus Comes From

In the nineteenth and twentieth centuries, there has been one country whose love-affair with Greece has flamed with especial intensity – Germany. In the German-speaking world, not only was the education system structured to promote classics above all, not only were artists and writers obsessed with classical models, but also classics played a major role in the ideology that constructed the new German state, an ideology that linked nationalism and racism in a way which has helped forge modern Europe through war and still-continuing violence. It is a story that is fundamental to the history of modern Europe.

The question 'Where do you think you come from?' intimately links this history of German nationalism with the love of the classical past. For Germany found a particular link with the glory that was Greece: the Germans knew that they came from Greece. The general turn to Greece that had dominated German culture in the nineteenth century led to a more specific and startling genealogical claim. New Germany is the heir and descendant of old Greece.

It is within such a context that Sigmund Freud took a figure from Greek myth to explain where we all come from, psychologically. Freud's theories are part of how we all understand ourselves in modern society. Putting Freud's Oedipus back into the German-speaking context from which he comes connects two fundamental twentieth-century histories: the horrific political consequences of making 'where you come from' the key issue of national identity, and psychoanalysis' radical new understanding of the self which sees knowing where you come from as the key to self-understanding. The German struggle to found a fatherland created a unique family tree reaching back to Greece, and Freud's new sense of the psychological drama within the family went back to Greece to explain the violent passions within us all.

Throughout the nineteenth century, Greece acted as the ideal model for Germany with an all-embracing power that is difficult to appreciate today. What has memorably been called 'the tyranny of Greece over the German imagination' can be seen at every level of activity. Greece, in Hegel's idealistic vision, was 'the focus of light in history'. Ancient Greece was the only place to be: 'in the name of Greece, educated men in Europe, and especially we Germans, feel at home'. 'With the Greeks we feel ourselves so completely at home, that we are on the soil of the Spirit.' A generation later, Nietzsche, full of high Romantic alienation and longing, expresses what is recognizably the same idealism: 'one is no longer at home anywhere; at last one longs for the only place in which one can be at home, because it is the only place one would want to be at home: the *Greek* world'. Poets take on the same allegiance. Hugo von Hofmannsthal, when he wanted to sum up what epitomized the true German poet, wrote: 'His soul yearns for the land of the Greeks.' Or, at the very beginning of the Philhellenic movement, Schiller encouraged his fellow writer Goethe to find a Greek homeland inside himself to compensate for his northern life: 'Now that you have been born a German, now that your Grecian spirit has been thrown into this northern world . . . produce your Greece as it were from within.'

These quotations express the passionately held credo of some of the great figures of German writing; and these masters had innumerable disciples. To long for Greece, to find in Greece a true home, was a sign of the great German soul. Ancient Greece was an inspiration and an aspiration. This was particularly true in the arts, where, as Hegel authoritatively states, 'In Art, Greek Art in its original form furnishes us with the best models.' This meant much more than sterile classicism. Plenty of dull classical scenes in painting and many a wispy poem peopled with Greek figures were produced: there was a ready market for these too, and they spoke with feeling to a broad audience. But more interesting is the way that the most revolutionary art of the century took Greece as its guide and lodestone.

Wagner is undoubtedly the most important German cultural master of the nineteenth century. His operas not only revolutionized music and drama in Europe, but also became a banner for a new political fervour of German nationalism. 'No boy could have had a greater enthusiasm for classical culture than myself,' he writes, with his customary self-dramatization as hero. He describes how when he read Aeschylus, 'the intoxicating effect of the production of an Athenian tragedy was brought before my imagination', and 'the effect on me was indescribable. Nothing could equal the sublime emotion . . .' From that first encounter with Aeschylus, he 'lived in an atmosphere so far removed from the present day that I have never been really able to reconcile myself with modern literature. My ideas about the whole significance of drama and of the theatre were, without a doubt, marked by these impressions.'

So Wagner begins his first published work on the theory of music with this credo: 'In any serious investigation of our art today, we cannot take a step forward without being brought face to face with the art of ancient Greece.' And, like Nietzsche and Hegel, Wagner emotes: 'I felt myself more truly at home in ancient Athens than in any condition the modern world has to offer.' Wagner knows that 'only *revolution* not slavish *restoration* can give us back the highest art work.' But the aim and model of this revolutionary art is still wholly defined by the ideal of Greece.

Wagner's credo was not just a theoretical stance or windy self-promotion. It was fully instantiated. The festival of Bayreuth was explicitly conceived to imitate the festivals of theatre in ancient Athens. Wagner worked through Greek ideas in the plotting of his greatest operatic work, the *Ring* cycle. He even saw his music as an instantiation of Greek ideals. The orchestra and its use of Leitmotifs – musical ideas associated with particular characters – were described by him as playing the role of the chorus of a Greek tragedy. 'Greek tragedy denoted the culminating point of the Greek spirit,' wrote Wagner, and he hoped his opera would provide such a culmination for German culture. And in the eyes of his many wildly enthusiastic devotees, he succeeded in this aim.

What Greece meant as an ideal for the arts was fought over from the moment that eighteenth-century archaeologist Johann Winckelmann, one of the founders of modern art history, first praised Greek art for its 'noble simplicity and serenity', and thus set the agenda for the next generations. But the notion that Greece provides *the* ideal for artistic production is an idea that linked German artists for more than a century.

But this 'tyranny of Greece' was evident not only at the level of the arts. The whole education system was reorganized to match this fervent Philhellenism. From high school to university, Classical Studies and Greek in particular dominated the curriculum. It was the privileged and central subject. The politician Karl von Humboldt laid down how the educational system was to work in the German-speaking world at the beginning of the nineteenth century. His credo is clear: 'Knowledge of the Greeks is not merely pleasant, useful or necessary for us – no, in the Greeks alone we find the ideal of that which we ourselves should like to be and produce.' In the best schools, as in England, Greek and Latin could take up as much as 80 per cent of the timetable, and all the best students were automatically streamed into Classical Studies. By the middle of the nineteenth century, as one rather hopeful historian gushes, 'the Utopia of the sixteenth century, a world of Latin-speaking dentists, Homer-reading lawyers, and Sophocles-quoting merchants, had become a reality'. By the end of the century, the Kaiser himself felt bound to enter the debate on education and say a word for Germany: 'We should raise young Germans, not young Greeks and Romans,' he lamented.

His very public intervention is testimony to just how deeply *formative* classics was in nineteenth-century German culture.

One fundamental force that forms a bridge between the artistic fervour, the educational reforms and the broader politics of culture is German nationalism. I've been using the phrase 'German-speaking' not only because Freud comes from Vienna, and Austria should be recognized as a different political and social environment from Berlin or Munich. The broader historical perspective is also crucial here. This period, which stretches from the birth of Romanticism at the end of the eighteenth century to the outbreak of the First World War in 1914, sees the battle-scarred formation of the Austro-Hungarian Empire, and Germany fighting to become a nation state. Greece holds a unique place in the history of German nationalism.

Many of the leading writers, artists and thinkers of the German-speaking world were explicit that their work is dedicated to the formation of this new nationalism. Writing history goes hand in hand with the construction of national identity. Hegel saw his history as creating a 'new national spirit', and described four stages of the history of mankind, where the 'German Spirit' is the fourth and culminating stage. Wagner set an inscription on the printed score of the *Ring* which dedicated his masterpiece 'in trust to the German spirit'. Nietzsche speaks intensely of 'German Music', 'German Philosophy', 'German Nature' – and even 'German Bodies'. 'Germanness' was an obsessive concern – a concern which became hugely instrumental in the war-dominated history of twentieth-century Europe.

The study of Greek was essential to the formation of this national character. The dominance of the study of classics came at the same time as the education system was expanded to include many more children of quite different social backgrounds. The upper-middle-class social groups who were so committed to the ideology of Romantic Hellenism were politically weak, and highly conscious of the need to build a nation. Greece offered an ideal of a society and a culture which the nascent state could strive for, and which it could begin to establish at grass-roots level in its educational policies. Greece provided the ideological glue that bound together those struggling to form a national character and a nation. Where the Americans dream the American dream, the Germans' dream was Greek.

It was this heady mix which made the family connection between Germany and Greece so potent. Many arguments were developed to make the genealogical case convincing. One particularly significant approach is the invention of the Race, the People – or, in German, *das Volk*. The true spirit of a Nation is found in its People. Even where politics and wars may not have created a state, the People – the Race – carries the essence of the Nation over generations. There has always been the German People.

A major figure in this story is Johann Gottfried von Herder, whose writings at the end of the eighteenth century were immensely influential across the German-speaking community. He laid down the criteria by which a People or a Race could be defined: *das Volk* must have a shared body of myths, a shared language, a shared homeland and even a shared body type. Myths were distinctive to a People and a People must have its myths – which is one reason why Wagner's Nordic tales could have such an impact: it answered the need of a German myth for a German People. The shared physical characteristics of the German people also fitted this Nordic legend. The stereotype is familiar: tall, blond, muscular and blue-eyed. Such descriptions of early Germans could be found in the Roman historian Tacitus, which proved with classical authority the eternal truth of the stereotype of the German physique. The shared homeland was Germany – the fatherland. The race has a name: it is the Aryan Race: its German branch, the Teutons.

Language too is central. This produces another part of the genealogical argument, in the form of an eighteenth-century academic, whose influence was most strongly felt in the nineteenth century. Sir William Jones was a British linguist and Orientalist.

He discovered – or proposed – an original language which existed in the far-distant past and which explains some of the apparent linguistic connections between the languages of Europe and the languages of the East. He called this original language Indo-European, and it's still fundamental in the modern study of languages. This language offered scientific proof that the Aryan *Volk* was a dominant power in the past – for Indo-European was the language of this race – and, as importantly, it provided a link between the Greek and German tongues, which otherwise might look very different indeed. Greek and German are both descendants of the same Aryan language of Indo-European.

A further element of the argument was put in place by Karl-Otfried Müller, who published a book in 1824 called *The Dorians*. The Dorians were an ethnic group of ancient Greece, a group which included the Spartans and the Corinthians (the Athenians were Ionians). The Dorians were said to have invaded Greece from the north and successfully to have colonized it. The material about the early Dorians is largely mythic stories told by much later Greeks themselves, in order to justify their political and territorial conquests, or their own alliances. But the image of 'the tribe from the north' became a German fixation. The so-called 'Dorian migration' is one of the subjects of Müller's book, and, of course, the origin of the Dorians in the north is particularly useful for his linking of Greece and Germany. One of Müller's pupils shows the full ideological pull of this story when he feels moved to argue the extraordinary case that a language as beautiful as Greek *must* have originated in the north and could not possibly have come from the Mediterranean.

But Müller found a Nordic character not only in the language of the Dorians but also in the shadowy early Dorian people, for whom he imagined a culture to admire. Dorians, he writes, are full of moderation, simplicity, frugality and steadfastness – all good German Protestant values, of course. And he develops at length an opposition between the Dorians and the Ionians in terms that seem now obviously slanted. Dorians, for example, developed a sense of freedom, whereas Ionians are easily enslaved to another's authority. Or the Dorians act cautiously and after suitable deliberation, while the Ionians are impetuous and rash. The Dorians from the north who have such Germanic characteristics provide a happily precise family-tie. The Germans are the New Dorians.

Strange as it may seem now, belief in this genealogy was extremely widespread and passionately held. Greece was not just the origin of Western culture in general; Greece had a specific and integral *blood* connection with the Germans, its descendants and heirs. The tyranny of Greece over the German imagination had its ancestor cult. The search for 'pure' and 'uncontaminated' blood – a search which produced such horrors in its worst racist forms – is a fundamental part of this genealogical construction: a blood-line.

Wagner presents just one example of this bizarre family tie in action. He celebrates Winckelmann and Lessing, two of the greatest Philhellenic scholars, precisely for helping Germans understand their blood-lines back to Greece: 'Hail Winckelmann and Lessing, ye who beyond the centuries of native German majesty, found the Germans' real and original ancestors in the divine Hellenes!' Trailing clouds of glory, the Germans come from divine Greece which is their home.

Knowing where you come from is a real question for German ideology in the nineteenth century, and the answer to the question is resounding: Greece. The journey of the People may have a long and complex history, but there are two fixed points: the birthplace of the German spirit in Greece, and its fulfilment in the contemporary – or future – nation state. Our image of nineteenth-century culture will be a hopelessly inadequate picture if we do not try to understand how this nationalist myth was forged out of a longing for Greece. The passions of the past may fade, and leave a new generation confused and unknowing, like children faced by their parents' desires, but the influence of those past passions continues to be felt. The distorting and violent fantasies of nationalism and the blood-line are scarcely fading into twenty-first-century politics. One good reason why we should take the question 'Where do you come from?' very seriously indeed is the long and continuing history of violence and prejudice, which has resulted from answering it with a misplaced and self-assertive certainty.

It is therefore especially disturbing to see in the first years of the twenty-first century a similar process of searching for antique origins still at work. In 2001–2, a new exhibition of archaeological discoveries from Troy travelled through Germany, where it was seen by 850,000 people. Its title, ironically enough, was 'Troy: Dream and Reality'. It claimed to show that Bronze Age Troy was really a trading centre between West and East. The catalogue of the exhibition came with an address from the President of Turkey (the location of the site of Troy), in which he declared that from this archaeology we could clearly see that 'the strongest roots of European culture' – capitalism – 'were to be found in Anatolia', along with an equally political reply from the President of Germany. This heavyweight politicized introduction to an archaeological catalogue was produced, with transparent opportunism, as Turkey was trying to gain admission to the European Union, and Germany was controversially changing its citizenship laws to allow new rights to Turkish resident workers in particular. The image of Troy as a link between East and West also prompted a national radio discussion in the now reunified Germany – which attracted an enormous audience and led German academics to come to blows! How are the East and the West linked economically? What did this new Troy mean in and for the new Germany? (Ironically, 'New Troy' was how that great imperial trading nation, Elizabethan England, had also styled itself.) The dream of Troy, of Greece, remains very much part of the reality of German political ideology, as the search for foundations in antiquity goes on.

At the turn of the twentieth century in Vienna, it was perhaps inevitable that Freud should turn to a figure of Greek myth to express his revolutionary comprehension of the psychology of the self, which so changed how the modern world answers the question of where we come from. There's no escaping Freud today. Everyone now lives in a cultural environment deeply influenced by Freudian theory. The subconscious, repression, the Freudian slip, the Freudian symbol are part of what society knows, however scandalous his theories may have seemed to his Victorian audiences and no matter how much modern critics have questioned his propositions. Freud's Oedipus has become part of how we all understand ourselves.

Freud made an anxiety of self-knowledge central to his therapeutic principles. The inability to escape what the past does to each of us, and the need to pursue a new knowledge of that past, are founding principles of Freudian psychoanalysis. If you do not know how your childhood development is formative, you are destined to spend your life locked into your unresolved childhood problems (to rewrite Cicero again). What happens to the child and how the child resolves the tensions of his infant life make the adult what he or she is – and the failure to resolve those tensions destines the adult to an infantile state. Knowing where you come from is the pursuit of analysis. For Freud, Oedipus was the figure who epitomized that anxiety of self-knowledge, and Freud made out of Oedipus a master-narrative for the development of the modern mind and modern sexuality. Through Oedipus, Freud found the nasty secret of a sexual past in everyone's mind. Without Oedipus, psychoanalysis would look very different indeed.

So why did Oedipus play such a role for Freud? Two answers immediately suggest themselves. First, the name of 'Oedipus' conveniently summarized the violent, ambivalent emotions of desire between children and parents that Freud saw as the emotional crisis in any child's early development. Second, he recognized in Greek tragedy the type of exploratory and powerful conversation which psychoanalysis demanded. Freud was explicit about this debt. The action of *Oedipus the King*, he writes, depicts 'a process that can be likened to the work of psychoanalysis'. Oedipus' painful, obstinate search for his self, which moves through questioning of the past back towards his engendering, reminds Freud of the work of analysis. The repeated language of 'solving riddles', 'tracking the traces', 'hunting the truth', in which Oedipus' search is described, was also an obvious attraction.

But, more oddly still, Freud saw *himself* as Oedipus. He identified with Oedipus, the solver of riddles and tragic searcher for self-knowledge. The typically opaque words of Nietzsche – 'Who of us is Oedipus? Who is the Sphinx? It is a rendezvous, it seems, of questions and question marks' – could stand as an epigraph to Freud's lifelong obsession with Oedipus.

On the occasion of his fiftieth birthday in 1906, Freud was presented with a medallion by some of his students and followers. On one side of the medallion was engraved the master's own portrait in profile. On the other side, there was an image of Oedipus answering the riddle of the Sphinx (Figure 48). No doubt every-

48. Freud's medallion

one thought that it was a neatly fitting and even rather witty token. A line of Greek verse was added from *Oedipus the King*: 'Who knew the famous riddles and was a most mighty man.' The line, taken from the last speech by the chorus (now usually thought to be spurious), sums up Oedipus' life. But no one had suspected quite how fitting a gift it was. Ernest Jones, Freud's biographer, was there, and he records that Freud 'became pale and agitated . . . as if he had encountered a *revenant*' or ghost. It turned out that as a young student Freud used to stroll around the great arcade of the University of Vienna where there were set up busts of famous professors. He used to fantasize that one day his head would be up there, and when he fantasized like this he always thought his bust would be 'inscribed with the *identical* words he now saw on the medallion'. It was a fantasy come to life. Only for Freud would this uncanny embodiment of a dream be quite so apt and frightening.

In 1873, Freud had made a special study of *Oedipus the King*, part of which he had to translate in one of his student exams. References to the Sphinx dot his correspondence. He gave one of his patients 'the present of a picture of Oedipus and a Sphinx' to thank him for his help in Freud's self-analysis – though we don't know how the patient interpreted the gift. Around his consulting room as an analyst, he kept statues of ancient figures that he collected avidly. The photograph in Figure 49 gives a great sense of the jumble of his office (though the dog, Jofi, is rather distracting). The Sphinx is clearly placed on top of the cabinet, proudly standing, facing the camel over the bowl. Higher on the shelves were busts of the great Greek tragedians, including Sophocles. Freud also had a whole cabinet dedicated to little terracotta statues of Eros, the winged boy, god of desire (Figure 50). The symbolism of *that* may not need a Freud to interpret it. But the reasons why Freud was so drawn to ancient Greek mythological models to express his new science of psychoanalysis do need attention.

The reading of Greek, the collection of statues, the naming of the Oedipus complex, all indicate Freud's deep and abiding involvement with the classical past. His engagement with antiquity is made most vividly – physically – evident by those ancient

49. Freud's office

statues around his consulting room. Throughout Freud's life, classical archaeology was one of the most explosive and trendy of disciplines. It captivated his imagination and that of his contemporaries. Schliemann had discovered Troy, the foundational battle-site of the conflict of West and East, the city where Hector, Paris and Helen had walked. He had excavated Mycenae, and his soundbite 'Today I have looked on the face of Agamemnon' was a triumph of self-publicity. Sir Arthur Evans had discovered the great Palace of Minos on Crete, home to the Labyrinth and the Minotaur, a discovery which seemed to bring the monsters and mysteries of myth to physical life. Freud was passionate about

50. *Freud's cabinet*

archaeology, as were many of his patients. The model of excavation, layer by layer, back to an ancient truth, was particularly stimulating – both the technique itself, and the antiquity, originality and authenticity of the discovered truth. The glamour of discovering those buried cultural treasures in the soil of Greece easily transferred to Freud's probing beneath the surface of the mind, and made Freud's turn to ancient Greek models a way of justifying his new method of investigation.

But when Freud says that 'Oedipus' fate moves us only because it might have been our own,' or when other critics in the same tradition make such statements as 'in some sense Oedipus is every man and every man is potentially Oedipus', another appeal is being made too – and it is deeply connected to the question 'Where do you think you come from?' Writing at the pinnacle of the German-speaking world's love of Greece and its nationalist fervour, Freud is uncovering the dirty secret of desire and violence in the family history of the race. He is exposing a scandalous truth that threatens Germany's national myth of a pure white origin in Greece. Greece, for Freud, provides the story to explain where we come from – but it is not a story of glorious ancestry. Freud's theories were a deep provocation to a German sense of identity.

The German context is of fundamental importance to Freud's Oedipus. When Freud called his discovery 'the Oedipus complex', the name has a sort of instant authority from its classical status. Greece was so important to the West's idea of its own development that a Greek hero was an immediately attractive figure for a new model of human psychological development. And, along with the Unconscious and the Freudian symbol, the Oedipus complex is probably still the most instantly recognizable indicator of a psychoanalytic approach. At the same time, Freud's theories were really scandalous. He discovered that even children have sexual feelings, and that everyone's sexual desires were at a deep level transgressive – a position even less popular in nineteenth-century Europe than today. Greece, in his hands, became a more primal, bloody and disturbing place than in most German schoolrooms. The provocation of Freud's writing also knowingly exploited the lustre of the Greek.

Tracing Freud's German Oedipus has overlapped several versions of the question 'Where do you think you come from?' Freud worked to find where the self comes from, and located the turning point of development in infantile desires. There is in every human a buried history which makes us what we are. He named this model after a Greek hero whose story is the archetypal quest to find where he came from – a buried history which also finds its turning point in transgressive sexuality. At the same time, Freud was writing for an audience engaged in a growing nationalism which ensured that the genealogical search for roots became a passion. Blood, the purity of the race, made where you came from a different sort of question. German nationalism, at all levels of culture, found a symbolic home and birthplace in ancient Greece, and put that claim into action in its education system, opera houses, literature – its general cultural life. And for the twenty-first century Freud himself is one of the origins of a modern sense of identity – we are all Freudians now. Our sense of self is mediated through a century of talk of Freudian slips, the subconscious, repression of sexual desire, psychological health – even when Freud's own writings may not have been studied in themselves.

The intricate story of Freud's German Oedipus reveals how many layers there are to the question 'Where do you think you come from?' Digging down through those layers uncovers just how intimately the history of the modern idea of the self and the political history of Europe are intertwined with the Greece of the imagination.

4

The Mother of All Stories –
The Greek Oedipus

Freud knew what he was doing when he chose Oedipus as his model of the necessity and anxiety of self-knowledge. For when it comes to worrying about where you come from, the mother of all stories belongs to Oedipus. It is one of those stories which few people can remember the first time they heard it (one good sign of myth in action). But who doesn't know that Oedipus killed his father and slept with his mother? Here is the founding Greek story of the man who did not know where he came from – and was destined to live out the very worst narrative of a child. Oedipus has haunted the Western imagination's pursuit of self-knowledge, and interwoven that pursuit with the horror of self-deception and self-destruction.

In the ancient world, and in the modern too, there is a long roll-call of different Oedipuses. For the stories that are called 'myths', by ancient intellectuals as well as modern, are told and retold for different purposes in different contexts and in very different ways – tragic, comic, philosophical, idiotic, with drawings – often with a changing cast of heroes and wildly varying plots and outcomes. There is no authorized version. Although modern readers tend always to hanker after the one original take, the world of myth lets a thousand stories bloom.

Yet, for all that variety, some versions, some tellings, grew so popular and so influential that they became increasingly authoritative and dominant over other possibilities. Everyone knows them, and knows them best. Homer's story of Achilles in the *Iliad* or Virgil's Aeneas are such examples, as is Shakespeare's Hamlet. And Sophocles' tragedy *Oedipus the King* is another.

Sophocles' play has proved so influential in European culture that it must be our guide to the Greek Oedipus. The good reason why this tragedy has had such power is evident. For it is Sophocles' drama which makes Oedipus a profound response to the question of 'Where do you think you come from?', rather than merely a sad tale of incest or mistaken identity. *Oedipus the King* is one of the most impressive and lasting works of Western culture. This version is a truly tragic dissection of the search for an origin. There are many reasons why the ancient world is worth studying: it shouldn't be forgotten that the sheer intensity, subtlety and emotional power of its literature is one good reason why the classics are called the classics, and deserve our attention. Sophocles' dramatic insights into the questions of identity speak to a modern audience with shocking precision and intensity. Freud was right when he made Oedipus a model for every human being: Oedipus' search for himself, his journey to discover where he comes from, is the paradigmatic example of how we must look back for self-knowledge, but also of how disturbing and painful that necessary process can be.

Oedipus the King was for Aristotle the perfect tragic plot: it summed up his principles of the gradual unfolding of inevitability that crushes a good man through his own miscomprehension. As with so many Greek tragedies, the plot line can be retold quite simply, though it does have more twists and turns than others. Greek tragedy does not have formal act divisions, but the five scenes of the play, separated as they are by choral odes, give the play an easy structure of action to follow:

ACT I
The city of Thebes is wracked with plague. Oedipus, its king, receives an oracle from Apollo that the city is polluted, because the killer of its previous king, Laius, has not been found and punished. Oedipus curses the murderer, and pledges to hunt him down.

ACT 2

Scene 1: His first step is to summon the seer Teiresias. The seer, at first grimly silent, is bullied by the king into making a pronouncement – in which he declares Oedipus himself to be the murderer. Oedipus, outraged, accuses the seer of plotting with Creon, Oedipus' brother-in-law, to take over the throne. Teiresias leaves in high dudgeon.

Scene 2: Oedipus accuses Creon of treachery. Their argument is interrupted and quelled by Queen Jocasta. As they talk, it emerges that when Oedipus first travelled to Thebes from his home in Corinth he *had* killed a man whose carriage had driven him off the road. Oedipus was fleeing his home in Corinth, because of an oracle which had warned that he would kill his father and marry his mother. If the man he had killed was in fact Laius, Oedipus reasons, he has inadvertently cursed himself. There had been only one survivor of Laius' final trip, who had said at the time that the royal entourage had been attacked by a band of robbers. This man must be summoned to clarify the story of the former king's murder.

ACT 3

Before this shepherd appears, however, a messenger arrives from Corinth to announce the death of Polybus, Oedipus' father, and to offer Oedipus the throne of Corinth. Oedipus, though saddened, is relieved because now he cannot kill his father. The Corinthian messenger, in order to relieve him of his worry about the rest of the oracle, tells him that actually Polybus was not his real father, nor was Merope his real mother. Oedipus was a foundling given to the king and queen of Corinth. This is a bombshell. Oedipus now becomes desperate to find out the identity of his true parents. It turns out that the self-same herdsman who was the witness to Laius' death was also the man who had passed the baby to the fellow who had passed it on to the royal house of Corinth. Jocasta knows the shepherd and immediately realizes what this all means – that it was *her* child. She has slept with her son. She exits in desperation to her bedroom, where she will kill herself.

ACT 4

But Oedipus, still in ignorance, awaits the shepherd's arrival. The man arrives and is forced into a confession of the truth. The child was given to him by Jocasta and Laius. Finally, all has become clear. The oracle has been fulfilled. Oedipus has killed his father and slept with his mother.

ACT 5

Oedipus rushes into the house to find Jocasta already hanged; he takes a pin from her dress and stabs out his own eyes. And the play ends with Creon entering as regent to take control of the city – and with the blind, bloody and broken Oedipus awaiting the next stage of his grim fate.

The question 'Where do you come from?' motivates this celebrated plot at each crucial juncture, and Sophocles makes it echo insistently through the play to shattering effect. When Oedipus first goes to the oracle at Delphi, it is because a drunken chap at a feast had teased him that he was not the child of his parents. The anxiety of not quite trusting the answer to the question 'Where do I come from?' is an experience that so many children know. From Shakespeare's *Winter's Tale* to Dickens' *Oliver Twist* to *Star Wars* and *Harry Potter*, the discovery of the true parent is one of the masterplots of Western fiction. Oedipus, however, is not given the answer he wants from Apollo. At the shrine, he is told he will kill his father and sleep with his mother. Terrified by this, he runs away from what he knows is his home – and because he thinks he knows where he comes from, namely Corinth, he runs directly towards where he really comes from, namely Thebes. With extraordinary layers of symbolic resonance, Oedipus meets and kills his father precisely 'at the place where three roads meet'. It is at a crossroads, that point of choice and transition, that Oedipus takes the decisive action that fulfils his destiny. The crossroads gives a physical, spatial form to the question of 'Where do you think you are coming from – and where are you going?'

Here Oedipus is knocked off the road, and takes the irreversible step of killing his father. A crossroads dramatizes the question of whether you know what route your life is taking.

The next person to taunt Oedipus for his ignorance is Teiresias. The seer always tells the truth, although his riddles undo rather than help his listeners. When Oedipus sneers at the prophet for not helping the plague-ridden city, he bursts out in challenging and dismissive tones:

> You have eyes and do not see your terrible condition,
> Neither where you are nor with whom you make house.
> *Do you know where you come from?*

As Cicero might have warned, because Oedipus does not know where he comes from, he is destined always to be an ignorant child, in the most horrific way possible. He does not know why his life – who he lives with and where – is a disaster. The king cannot see his own terrible condition, says the blind prophet. It is uncanny to watch how Teiresias hooks Oedipus by his own anxiety:

> Teiresias: I may seem foolish to you,
> But to your parents who bore you, I am sensible.
> Oedipus: Who? Wait! Who sired me?

Even though Oedipus is angrily dismissing Teiresias, this jibe stalls him. Even in his rage, Oedipus still has a desperate need to know for sure who his parents are. He cannot say with certainty where he comes from. And this ignorance stops him in his tracks. It is a crossroads in his story.

Sophocles plays out Oedipus' anxiety a third time with brilliant and distressing irony. When the messenger from Corinth reveals to Oedipus that his true parents were not the Corinthian king and queen, Oedipus demonstrates just how passionately he cares to know where he comes from. Jocasta begs him with increasing desperation not to search for his origin: 'No, by the gods, if you care for your life at all, don't try and divine this.' But Oedipus will not be thwarted. In a scene of painful misunderstanding, he assumes that Jocasta, who has by now worked out his actual identity, is upset because he might turn out to have lower-class parents. The clash between his assumption of her snobbery and her absolute terror is excruciating. All she can do, before rushing off, is to wish fervently that he should never know who he is. Nothing will stop me, asserts Oedipus with blind certainty: 'I must know my origin.' And he *will* know, as he pursues his identity to the point of self-destruction.

For Oedipus, not knowing where he comes from is a burning anxiety and a source of disaster. He ends up in the wrong city, his own city; in the wrong house, his own house; and in the wrong bedroom, the bedroom in which he was born. He tries to discover the answer to the question of his origin. Yet finding out where he comes from only brings horror and self-mutilation. The multiplying ironies of Sophocles' play all take place within this paradoxical framework of a man caught between the disaster of not knowing where he comes from and the disaster of finding out.

This plot line is grimly fascinating and drags the audience into a horrified gaze at the self-destruction of a man. But what takes *Oedipus the King* to another level is the language of Sophocles' poetry. It opens to us a profound sense of what it means to be a person, and how the words we use play an integral role in defining a person – and in defining ourselves. The play does not just ask, 'Do you know where you come from?' It also provokes a painful question about knowing who you are. And it does this by an extraordinary dismantling of the language of identity.

Two fundamental examples illuminate this process. First, the word 'child', which can stand in for all the similar terms we use to indicate family relationships. A person's biography – a sense of self – is mapped out by those kinship terms. Any life-story uses them as a grid – 'my mother', 'your father', 'our children' and so on. Sophocles takes apart this map. But the most particular token of identity is the proper name. The name 'Oedipus' is my second example. Sophocles passes these crucial markers of identity through the destabilizing twists of his plot of incest and ignorance, and leaves them – and us – shattered.

Oedipus' first words, which are the first words of the play, and Oedipus' first surviving words in Western literature, are 'O my children'. He is addressing the people of Thebes as their ruler, 'the father' of the state. His final words in the play, addressed to Creon, are 'Please do not take my children from me.' He wants to keep his daughters with him to salve his anguish. But Creon takes them away. Between Oedipus' first and last words, the play traces how he loses not just his children, but the very possibility of using that most simple of vocabulary. Oedipus' children are also his brothers and sisters, as his mother is his wife. In incest, the usual language of self-definition implodes. Oedipus laments that the marriages of his family 'have revealed fathers, brothers, children, family blood, brides, wives, and mothers . . .' A person should be placed on a social map by the network of blood-ties, but in this tumbling list of relations the map has become a jumble of family blood, where none of the categories does its work any more. For Oedipus, finding his origin means losing his place in the order of things, and becoming merely the sign of collapsed family values.

This should make us hear the very first words of the play with fresh foreboding. When Oedipus opens with his regal 'O my children', he has already shown the horrific doubleness of his position – as saviour and polluter of the city; both the king who solved the Sphinx's riddle and the murderer for whom the word 'child' summons so awful a story. Since Aristotle, tragedy has been seen as the story of a good man who has a fearful and pitiful downfall through his own error. But Oedipus was always on a path from concealed horror to revealed misery. The chorus captures this journey in one of the most haunting lyrics in tragedy:

Alas, you generations of men.
I count you in your life
As equal to
Nothing.
For who, what man
Wins more happiness
Than a semblance, which slips away from seeming.

When Oedipus opens the play with 'my children', we can immediately hear with a shudder the 'semblance of happiness' starting already and inevitably to 'slip away from seeming'. The word 'child', from the first, is a fissured sign of Oedipus' tragedy.

The very name of 'Oedipus' becomes part of the slippage, this dangerous failure of language to do its job, as incest infects the system. What does 'Oedipus' mean? One traditional version understands the name as 'Swollen Foot'. Oedipus' ankles were pinioned at birth, by his parents when he was exposed to die, and he limped throughout his life from this primal injury. The messenger from Corinth tells us that this is precisely why the king is called 'Oedipus'. But Sophocles also writes a whole series of strange word-plays into the name 'Oedipus' – *Oidipous* in Greek – mostly involving the word *oida*, 'I know', and the word *pou*, which can mean 'where'. Oedipus may not know 'where he comes from', but his name seems to shout 'I know where'.

The most emphatic set of disruptive word-plays comes as the messenger from Corinth enters. Jocasta has just prayed to Apollo for 'release'. The messenger arrives on cue like an answer from god – a bitterly ironic answer, since the 'release' he kindly offers undoes them all. This, then, is a turning point in the play's fascination with knowing, concealment and revelation. And as the messenger enters, he says lines which always sound transparent and dull in translation:

Strangers, may I learn from you
Where the house of Oedipus is?
In particular, can you tell me where he is, if you know?

In Greek, though, they are astounding: for the verse has been turned inside out, so that each of the three lines ends with a jingling, obsessive rhyme:

> . . . *Mathoim' Hopou* ('may I learn where?')
> . . . *Oidipou* ('of Oedipus')
> . . . *Katisth' Hopou* ('do you know where?')

The word 'Oedipus' is made to resound with 'know where'. His very name asks out loud, 'Do you know where you come from?'

In the *Bacchae*, when Dionysus tells Pentheus that he does not know who he is, he answers with his proper name, his mother's name, his family – a position in society. In *Oedipus* each one of those markers is systematically dismantled: Oedipus' name, his relationships, his position, all fragment into unstable differences. His identity is pulled apart as fully and vividly as Pentheus' body.

This would be a grim enough view of things, but Sophocles gives the whole one more twist of the ratchet. For Oedipus himself, from the beginning of the play, is characterized not as a bad or corrupt man but as an intelligent, focused and highly energetic figure, who is fighting with all his human skills to control what is going on around him. He is man empowered by his knowledge and respected for it. The play associates such knowledge with blindness, and the blindness of the seer Teiresias with the only knowledge which counts. Oedipus struggles to assert control, but other forces – call it fate, or chance, or divine patterning – lead him along a different road. He wants – and who doesn't? – to control the narrative of his life. And he does what a man can do in pursuit of such control. Yet the concluding lines of the play, delivered with finality by Creon to Oedipus, declare: 'Do not seek control in all things. For what you did control did not accompany you in your life.' The bitterest irony of all is that those telling sentiments are also Creon's attempt to assert *his* control over things.

Those who know Antigone's story will hear the desperate fragility of Creon's attempt to have the last word.

What *Oedipus the King* shows to its audience is the failure of human control over human life, the inability to see one's own life-story clear and straight and in order. It challenges every reader to see himself or herself in Oedipus – every reader, that is, who seeks control over the narrative of his or her own journey through the world. I don't know any reader who hasn't wondered why the hyper-intelligent Oedipus does not appear to notice the 'coincidence' that Jocasta was given an oracle that predicted her son would marry her, and that he was given an oracle that predicted he would marry his mother – and put two and two together. Why doesn't he ask why his feet were maimed? Why, after an oracle like the one he was given, didn't he just avoid killing anyone or sleeping with anyone older than himself? It's easy enough to ask those questions of Oedipus. What the play shows, however, is how hard it is for anyone to ask the right questions in their own lives. When you think you have solved the riddle, is it leading you to disaster? When you reach the crossroads, do you know which road you are following?

The most shocking drama in *Oedipus* is not that we have to watch a man come to the recognition that he has killed his father and slept with his mother, brutal and painful though that must be. Most shocking is the play's insistent and disturbing claim that it is exactly at the moment that you think you know where you come from and who you are that you are most open to a tragedy of self-deception.

This is a play designed to provoke its audience into self-reflection. Just as Teiresias' questions stop Oedipus in his tracks, this drama should stall anyone's self-confidence with the hesitation of anxiety. The issue is not so much that you might kill your father and marry your mother, nor even, as Freud would have it, that you might subconsciously *want* to kill your father and marry your mother. The play no doubt offers complex psychological lures, as Oedipus hunts out his true parents and tries without success to avoid living out the horror of his family's fated story. But the nagging, destabilizing effect of this play is most forcefully felt elsewhere. Oedipus is a reader of riddles, a solver of problems and a pursuer of knowledge – and every moment of success leads him further into disastrous self-destruction. Wanting to know and being good at finding things out – *Oedipus the King* undermines these essential human qualities. Especially for an age which prides itself on the ability of humans to control the world, Oedipus raises a disturbing spectre. Freud's choice of Sophocles' Oedipus to explore the self of the modern era has proved painfully prescient. An arrogance of control and a misplaced certainty of knowledge have contributed all too tragically to the miseries of the history of the last century.

Oedipus may be the mother of all stories when it comes to worrying about where you come from. But what makes Sophocles' play so powerful a drama is its insistence that it is the 'knowing' as much as the 'where from' which is the problem. 'Where do you think you come from?' is a difficult question. As *Oedipus the King* insists, it is difficult to *know* properly about the past and how the past is making sense of the here and now. The paradox of the play is that it both demands and exposes man's attempts to have control over things through such knowledge. The grimness of the tragedy of Oedipus – what indeed makes it tragic – is that you cannot escape the past, the buried life that makes you who you are, and you cannot know until too late precisely how that past is coming into your life.

It is one of history's ironies that in the modern world Oedipus began to be such a powerful image when nationalism and racism had begun to dominate political conflict. For all the self-confident ideologues of national and of racial heritage, personal or political, for all those who think it is easy and certain to answer where they come from, Sophocles' play demands that the generations of men should 'Look at Oedipus, and bewail.'

5
The Myth of Origins

In the face of a play as profound and disturbing as *Oedipus the King*, it is a sad irony that 'Greek myth' is today so often treated merely as a cartoon subject for schoolchildren. But it is not by chance that so many discussions of 'myth' lead to Greece. On the one hand, Greek myths are particularly intertwined with the myth of Greece, which has so dominated the cultural and political imagination of Europe. On the other, 'myth' was invented in ancient Greece. The idea of 'myth' as a category was articulated first in the fifth century BC in Greece at the same time that the practices of history and science were also inaugurated. To talk of 'myth' and 'history' is to rehearse one part of our intellectual inheritance from the ancient world. To look at where myth comes from, however, is also to investigate at the most general level how and why we tell stories of the past, and it shows why there is still power in the myth of Greece.

The Elgin Marbles, in front of which Keats swooned, have always been a story about the glorious past – the lost age we come from. These friezes from the Parthenon, built in Periclean Athens to celebrate the city itself, depict a familiar mythic, heroic time. When the Athenian citizen looked up at the west end of the building, he gazed at fourteen panels depicting the battle of the Greeks with the Amazons. The Amazons, wild, horse-riding, man-hating, property-looting women, invaded Attica (he could tell you) and were defeated by Theseus. Theseus was the king of Athens, the good king, the man who had brought all the villages and homesteads of Attica together into the city-state called

Athens. He was the founder of the city. That's why Athens is Athens. Defeating the Amazons was part of the story of the foundation of the state. The citizen could look out from the Acropolis across the city and point out the Areopagus, one of the other hills of Athens, where the high court now sat: this is where the Amazons camped before their defeat. History is laid out before you.

The Amazons are the epitome of everything the crop-growing, patriarchal, orderly Athenian men are not. They have to be defeated, just like the centaurs, those bestial half-man half-horse creatures on the north side of the building, or just like the Trojans depicted on the south side of the temple, or the giants on the east side. All round the building are stories of Greek and Athenian triumphs over the forces of disorder. This state-funded temple, which still dominates the real and imaginary landscape of Athens, has a strong architectural message, a programme about how to be a good Athenian and what needs to be crushed to maintain the order of the state.

The Elgin Marbles tell an Athenian story about where the Athenians come from. Its unique power over the Athenian mind arises because it is a story of the past which is taken for granted. It is part of the furniture of the mind. The very repetition of myth helps make it one of the familiar expectations of thought. One idea this story takes for granted, for example, is the natural properness of male superiority over the female, a principle that can be found in almost any Greek piece of writing or any Greek temple sculpture, and lived out in every Greek household. Myths are a machine to make a culture's view of itself seem natural, proper and inevitable. Here on the Acropolis we can see civic myth in action, telling the Athenians where they came from, as a state, as a people.

Such a sculptural programme puts the past before the citizens' eyes to be absorbed. Homer's epics, performed and reperformed again and again throughout the centuries, put the past in their minds through words. The *Iliad* and the *Odyssey* told the Greeks where they were from. The heroes were the ancestors that later families and states honoured and traced their roots to, and in their fight against Troy the heroes readily enacted for future generations not just the proper manly pursuit of military glory, but also the fight of the hardy Greeks against the corrupt and splendid world of the barbarians of the East. Troy was in Persia, the home of the barbarians, the constant enemy of the Greeks and of all that the Greeks hold dear. Homer's *Iliad* with its tale of the glorious Achilles, fighting to take revenge on the city of Troy for Paris' snatching of Helen, and fiercely arguing with his fellow Greeks about honour and status, was a privileged account of how to be a real Greek man. So Achilles, ever the man's man, also killed an Amazon, their queen Penthesileia, whose dying beauty inflamed him with desire, even as he killed her. In Homer, Greeks found a tale of national and cultural identity. The heroic past grounds the here and now.

The *Iliad* already knows about how stories of the past work. 'Ten men of today could not lift that rock that Hector lifted with ease,' says Homer, reminding us how the heroes of the Trojan War are fitter, faster, stronger and more beautiful than anyone listening to the poem. What's more, even the characters in the poem sing of lost generations of great men who provided examples to live up to or warnings of what to avoid. 'You're not half the man your father was,' Athene taunts a battling warrior. 'Learn from the example of Meleager of old,' Achilles is warned by his tutor. This sort of fame is what heroes want. They fight not simply for honour or for victory but to win 'undying glory', the fame that song gives. A hero fights to become a legend – the sort of story men sing about when they want to celebrate the great deeds that make the man worthy of the name of hero. A hero always wants to make himself into a mythic figure, for future generations to know and marvel at. Epic is that memorial of the past.

Standing before the Parthenon, Homer in mind, the Athenian citizen was grounded in his culture and history. Or so it should be, according to traditional cultural expectations. It could be the case, however, that the citizen who guides us around the Parthenon is one of those young intellectuals who had studied with the new and trendy thinkers of the fifth century called sophists, and who knew the latest thinking on religion and its stories. Where a traditional Athenian would happily tell you these stories as the history of the foundation of Athens, this more pushy intellectual guide might adopt a rather self-consciously critical line on these stories and dismiss them as 'myths' – stories for the populace to follow, but not to be accepted at face value by educated men.

Once they start to become argued about, once they start not to be taken for granted, myths can become a battleground for how we think about the past. The fifth-century Greeks give us the tools for thinking about what happens when 'myth' stops being the stories which everyone knows and agrees to tell. These tools are the very ideas 'myth' and 'history'.

'Myth' is a gift of the Greeks. It was in the classical city of Athens that 'myth' was first developed as an idea. The fifth century BC is often described as the 'Greek Enlightenment' – or, in more Romantic days, as the 'Greek miracle'. This period is unique because in a very short time, and primarily in a single city, so much of what the West prides itself on came into being. Athens invented a democratic constitution, and with it came the law courts with their juries of ordinary people. The theatre produces the tragic masterpieces of Aeschylus, Sophocles and Euripides, and the comic genius of Aristophanes.

But the fifth century is called the 'Greek Enlightenment' especially because it was in this period that science, philosophy, history and medicine came into being as disciplines. People have attempted to cure sickness or injury ever since humans have been sick or injured. But for the first time in the fifth century there were recognized experts, trained in a school, who engaged in self-conscious discussion of techniques and principle, and debated the physical causes of disease, and experimented, and tested their results, and published their findings. Some people have been 'political' ever since there was a group to win power over. But for the first time in the fifth century there were political theorists who argued about the theory of different constitutions, and about the abstract nature of power and the city's institutions. This development of self-conscious, theoretical, abstract thought, along with new institutions of education and regulation, makes 'medicine' and 'political philosophy' *disciplines* for the first time.

These new forms of intellectual activity began as radical innovations, and were immediately seen by more conservative forces as threatening. Each of these new disciplines, as they fought to become established, needed to distinguish their own authority. One key rhetorical strategy for each discipline was to disparage or diminish its opponents by calling them purveyors of myth. 'Myth' becomes the name for what these new disciplines *don't* do. 'What I offer', claims one physical scientist, 'is a true picture of the world scientifically observed and described. I can tell you how the physical world works. Those old stories about how things came to be, they are just myths.' Myth can no longer mean simply an inherited story of the old days, let alone an authoritative tale. Now 'myth' is opposed to true 'history'. Or it is something to be dispelled by real 'philosophy'. Or replaced by objective 'science'. This negative colouring, which develops during the fifth-century Enlightenment, still tinges the concept of 'myth' today: we still say 'mere myth', 'just a myth'. With final dismissiveness, myth has come to mean a silly or pernicious tale whose false enticements you should beware.

The Greek Enlightenment successfully set out to debunk old authorities, and the new discipline of 'history' in particular aimed to change how the past is understood. Herodotus is 'the father of history'. His great work, circulated in the 430s BC, is the first to call itself 'history' – *historie*, or 'investigation' in Greek – and he has been taken as the founding father of history by ancients and moderns alike. His topic is the Persian Wars. The Persian Empire was the greatest power in the Mediterranean and it twice invaded Greece in the middle of the fifth century in order to conquer it for the Great King's Empire. Twice, the far-outnumbered Greeks won and pushed back the Persians. It was a stunning and inspirational event for the Greeks. Indeed it was a defining moment for the Greek nation. Before the Persian Wars, there was little awareness of a shared cultural identity of 'being Greek'. After the Wars, the Greeks, rather than being just a series of cities which shared the same language, became aware of a national identity.

Herodotus' history investigates not just the famous battles by which the Persians were defeated and the invasions turned back – Thermopylae, Marathon, Salamis and the like. He also travels the whole Mediterranean – and beyond – exploring the differences between different cultures. Tellingly, Herodotus too tells us about the Amazons, now to be found in Scythia, and discussed from an anthropological perspective as a still-existing tribe of women, who breed with nomads of the steppes. He explains the defeat of the Persians by showing how the Greek culture of the West is superior to the Persian culture of the East. Xerxes, the Persian king, is forced to learn 'what true men are', and one concluding moral of the whole history is that 'soft countries produce soft men'. Rugged Greece, by contrast, is 'a fit nurse of men'. Herodotus is the founding father of the West's view of the Orient as a dangerous, wealthy, degenerate, sly and threatening other which must be defeated. His image of the Orient still fuels modern Western politics. The conflict between West and East is the subject of the *Iliad*, the first surviving poem of the Western tradition. But it is Herodotus who gives this conflict the rhetorical slant familiar still in contemporary ideology. In its rhetorical opposition to the East, this is truly a history of where the modern West comes from.

Herodotus writes the history of the victory of Greece – and the victory of Greekness. But he is far more subtle than that gung-ho bias might suggest. Egypt, for example, is depicted as a country much older than Greece and with a range of knowledge and expertise that makes Greece seem like a Johnny-come-lately. 'Greek claims of superiority are laughable,' writes Herodotus, in the face of Egyptian antiquity. Other cultures too hold up a mirror for the Greeks in which they can find similarities and differences – and not just see their own superiority reflected. Herodotus maps the variables of cultural difference, with a keen analytical eye and with critical investigation. Every element contributes towards understanding and evaluating cultural norms. The positive and negative images construct a kaleidoscope – precisely a shifting pattern of mirrors – in which Greekness is viewed and intellectually reflected on. The boundaries of what is normal are explored through all these variations. What it means to be a Greek, rather than Persian or anything else, becomes a topic of historical *investigation*. The Greek reader is engaged in a fascinating process of self-recognition. Herodotus provides a guide which encourages the reader to place himself or herself within a matrix of social, moral and political markers – a map to find ourselves. His history is the story of the invention of Greekness: a critical answer to the question of where we think we come from.

Herodotus is worth caring about today, however, not only because his is a founding text of conflict between the values of the West and the values of the Orient, although that is a story of opposition which shows no sign of ending in contemporary ways of thinking. How he makes us look at the world is also crucial. Herodotus is called 'the father of history' because he wants to make historians of us all. That is, rather than tell the old stories which have power because they are taken for granted, he writes as a critical, analytical investigator, who shows exactly how he *isn't* taking stories for granted. He demands we understand the causes of events, and doesn't just record events. He constantly shows his workings for us: 'I cannot exactly say what language the Pelasgians spoke, but if we were to argue from inference . . .', 'From my own enquiries, I have discovered . . .', 'What they say is not convincing to me . . .', 'The second explanation offered is less scientific.' His account is dedicated to explanation and analysis. Of course his narrative, like all narratives, takes many things for granted, and uses many forms of rhetorical persuasion. But what Herodotus parades, and demands of us, is the ideal of investigation and criticism. He asks us to think hard about where events come from, and what makes us who we are.

Thucydides, the cynical, sharp and brilliantly analytical leader of the next generation of historians, wrote of the great war between Athens and Sparta, and he takes Herodotus' principle of investigation to the highest methodological level. 'For most people,' he declares, 'searching for the truth is an indifferent activity; they incline to what is simply available.' We should not trust 'poets who decorate and exaggerate in their songs . . . and chroniclers who compose more to attract listeners than to find the truth. Their evidence cannot be tested, and most of it, because of the passage of time, is untrustworthy and passed into myth.' Thucydides' acid rhetoric highlights the invention of myth at work. Ordinary people, people not like us, simply take what's on offer, and foolishly trust writers who merely want to pleasure the listener and offer stories which can't possibly be tested. Those sorts of stories, hallowed by time, should be dismissed as *mere myths*. Instead, claims Thucydides, there is an intellectual duty to commit yourself to truth – which means precision, accuracy and testability. He demands scientific history – history that sets itself to *dispel myth*. Critical analysis of the past is also a lesson from classical antiquity. Part of cultural tradition is the dissection and analysis of the past, and a drive towards self-awareness – towards an active recognition of one's place in an ongoing history. We need that critical history to understand where we think we come from.

This clarion call of Thucydides has inspired generations of historians. He called his history 'a possession for all time' and so it has proved. As the first Gulf War started in 1990, the BBC did something quite extraordinary. It cancelled part of its evening schedule and replaced the programming with a set of dramatic readings from Thucydides on the Sicilian expedition – the doomed imperialist mission of the Athenian state. It was an extraordinary event not just because it happened at all, remarkable though that remains, but also because the commentary was

so much more pointed and painful than any of the political discussion that was on offer elsewhere. The critical analysis of the
'possession for all time' once again proved timely.

From the very beginning, even in Homer, Greece already had a
'Greece of the imagination'. We have always turned to the past
for images and explanations of how things are as they are – and
we keep doing so today too. We too have our epic past (the battle
of Britain, storming the Bastille, crossing the Potomac), our civic
myths (the village green in England; the 'sansculottes' in France;
the American Dream in America), and we have our histories too
(which, like Herodotus, are also accounts of burgeoning national
and cultural identity, as with Winston Churchill's *History of the
English-Speaking Peoples*). But the Greeks also invented 'myth' and
'history', our privileged ways of telling the story of the past and
of constructing 'where we think we come from'. Greece provides
us with our paradigms for thinking about the past.

It is easy to oppose myth and history. Thucydides and his
modern heirs demand that we choose scientific history as the only
real route to the truth of the past. Few would prefer to be a slave
to the false consciousness of myth rather than 'committed to the
truth'. But it is difficult to imagine either myth or history without
each other. The categories of 'myth' and 'history' mutually define
each other. But, more importantly, a cultural imagination will
always use its repeated and accepted stories, however much it
believes in analysis or critical enquiry. Historians cannot cure us
of myth-making (as the current Middle East shows all too
vividly). However many histories are written, Winston Churchill,
Abraham Lincoln or Joan of Arc will still be figures to tell national
myths with. We *need* to tell stories of where we come from,
though we should be prepared to analyse those stories carefully
and critically. Indeed it's because we need those stories so much,
in order to make sense of the here and now, that critical history is
also necessary – if we do not wish to spend our lives as children,
wide-eyed and spell-bound before a tale of the old days.

We are inevitably both slaves of our inherited stories and analysts of the buried lives that make us who we are. There's a dynamic tension between myth and history in how we understand the past, and that is what makes the question 'Where do you think you come from?' so pressing.

The Elgin Marbles are still a place where myth and history collide. Melina Mercouri, with whom this book began, is most famous for her campaign to bring the Elgin Marbles back to Greece. Many years after her death, her picture still graces the website of the Ministry of Culture in its continuing campaign, as she stands in front of the Parthenon, waving, not swooning. It is striking, and sad, that amid all the arguments, good and bad, for where the Marbles should be housed, the rhetoric of nationalism, which has so scarred the last centuries, is still the trump card: the Marbles are the symbol of the Greek nation, the aspirations of a people. The myth of Greece flourishes here still. It may be taken as a sign not only of how often the myth of Greece has played a role in the politics and culture of Europe, but also of how the power of such myths of origin continues to dominate the political and cultural imagination of today's world.

Looking at where 'myth' and 'history' come from, looking at their invention in Greece, may allow us to see the power of both of these ways of telling stories of the past, in our lives today. While myths of origin continue to have such force in nationalist rhetoric, political policy and religious violence, a more self-conscious awareness of how the myth of Greece has functioned and continues to function might help us see why the question 'Where do you think you come from?' needs focused and critical attention in our contemporary society. There is a lot at stake in the stories we tell of where we come from.

6

History Today

Nineteenth-century Britain was a culture experiencing radical change. The artistic revolution of Romanticism cannot be separated from the Philhellenism of its leading writers. The educational practice and theory which formed the minds of the rulers of Empire, as well as the leading figures of public life at home, were wholly engaged with the place of classics. Greek and Latin provided the furniture of the Victorian mind.

The French revolution and the American War of Independence made Rome the republican ideal to strive for and used classical politics as a way of thinking through the principles and practices of reform. It is not by chance that America has its 'senators' and France its Roman law.

Nineteenth- and twentieth-century Germany found not just a cultural identity in art and literature through 'the tyranny of Greece over the German imagination', but also a nationalist fervour. The search for origins – where the Germans thought they came from – in the twentieth century has had murderous consequences of the most horrific kind. (Not all revolutionary change is good.) The pursuit of classical origins and the power of nationalist myth continue to distort political life throughout Europe.

The classical past does not just sit there, nor does the study of classics simply flow smoothly across the generations. The ideal of Greece and the model of Rome have repeatedly flared into significance – as a banner for revolution, as an inspiration for political and artistic change, as a space for intense self-reflection. A

Greece and Rome of the imagination have been absolutely foundational at these key junctures of political and cultural history in the West. Seeing what all these founding fathers made of their classics and what their classics made of them is a fundamental story in the history of where we come from.

What is most remarkable in the face of this constant revolutionary inspiration provided by a Greece and Rome of the imagination is the image of classics that all too often is circulated in the contemporary media. The most radical figures in politics, art, music, poetry, thought and sexual behaviour have taken classics as a moving force of their idealism, but it is hard, in England at least, for classics to be mentioned, without the cliché that it is an elitist subject, a conservative subject which, even if once fashionable, is surely now only for the few, and, of course, of limited relevance to the modern era.

This is a very narrow view indeed of why classics matters, not least because there is a good reason why studying classics has been so instrumental in the West's most radical thought. For thinking hard about the past reveals the buried life of the present, its potential for change, for being different. Looking back critically at where we come from is a revelatory education about the present.

The simplest point that emerges from looking back at how the myths of Greece and Rome have functioned in the history of European culture is this: the past matters. It matters because in psychological, social, intellectual, artistic and political terms the past is *formative* of the present. It is the person's or culture's deep grounding. It matters *how* the past is understood or told. Stories change lives. They make foundations, they build hopes and they can kill. A self-aware appreciation of the past requires reflecting on the myths and the histories, the story-telling and the critical analysis, which make sense of the past – and thus the present. The shibboleth of 'living in the present' is no more than an infantile fantasy – the destiny of those who do not know how the past runs through them. To understand the present – as opposed to just living in it, like a child – requires a critical look backwards. And the person who does not understand the deep grounding of culture can only be a shallow person.

At a further level, however, the past of classical antiquity has mattered immensely and with specific force to generations of the founding fathers of the political, intellectual and artistic traditions of the West. Our fathers and mothers have cared passionately about Greece and Rome, and made their images of Greece and Rome fundamental to their cultural imagination. They used their classics to change the world. If we fail, like children, to understand our fathers' and mothers' passions, our view of the past will be wholly inadequate and, perhaps worse, little more than a dull mirror of our own concerns. 'Relevance' is a contemporary idol. But 'relevance' should not mean just revelling in the blinkers and trivia of the here and now, nor does it mean responding only to the stories and images which are just like ourselves. It also means understanding and learning from the *otherness* of the past, and its continuing influence on the present. Understanding the past also requires that we understand how previous generations thought of the past, were stimulated and inspired by it, rebelled against it, denied it. Classical antiquity has constantly been reinvented as the privileged model of the past, and it has been thus a force for comprehending – and changing – the present.

In order to understand and be part of the cultural tradition of the West, we must appreciate that repeated reinvention of the past through Greece and Rome. Of course, this is not all that's necessary. But it is one essential strand of what has made the West what it is. If we do not recognize how classical antiquity furnished the imagination, stimulated and structured thought and acted as a banner of artistic and political revolution, our view of our own cultural tradition will be necessarily distorted. But, most importantly, this cultural tradition is what makes *us* who we are. We cannot understand who we are without understanding where we have come from. Without the Greece and Rome of the imagination, that journey of understanding must be halting and inadequate.

Classics is interesting for its own sake; and it is instructive because it helps us understand how previous generations have understood and responded to the world. But it *matters* because you cannot properly answer the question 'Where do you think you come from?' without it.

Such historical self-consciousness is a crucial element of self-understanding. I rather admire Cicero's scorn when he declares, 'If you do not know where you come from, you will always be a child,' and find Socrates' declaration that 'the unexamined life is not worth living' both seductive and inspiring. Knowing how we have come to be what we are is a necessary step for understanding what matters in the world, and how we might act in it. The history inside us makes us who we are. We need to understand this history to be ourselves fully and with fulfilment.

Notes

All translations are my own unless otherwise noted.

A Life in Ruins

p.3   A very free rendition of Cicero *Orator* 120.13.

p.7   Euripides *Bacchae* 906–7; 1118–21.

Part I: Who Do You Think You Are?

p.15   Plato *Charmides* 153a–b; *Lysis* 203–4.

p.16   Lucian *Anacharsis* 25.

p.21   Hippocrates *Regimen* III 73.

pp.22–3   Xenophon *Memorabilia* III 12.

pp.25, 28   F. Nietzsche *Werke. Kritische Gesamtausgabe* ed. G. Colli
               and M. Montinari vol. VII 3, pp. 412–13 fr. 41 (4).

p.43   Aristotle *De Generatione Animalium* 716a17ff., and else-
               where.

p.49   Aeschylus *Choephoroi* 600–1; Sophocles *Antigone* 791–2.

p.50   Seneca *Dialogi* II 7.4.

p.53   Plutarch *Erotikos* 750d–e.

p.56   Aeschines *Against Timarchus* 135.

p.57   Theognis 1335–6.

pp.58–9   Plato *Charmides* 155d–e.

p.59   Euripides *Hippolytus* 525–6; Aeschines *Against Timarchus*
               139–40.

p.62   Plato *Palatine Anthology* V 78; Xenophon *Memorabilia* I 3.

pp.72–3   Plato *Symposium* 216d; Plato *Symposium* 218c.

Part II: *Where Do You Think You Are Going?*

p.97   T. S. Eliot *Essays Ancient and Modern* (London, 1936) 174.

pp.104–5   *Life of Simeon Stylites* trans. F. Lent *Journal of the American Oriental Society* 35 (1918).

p.109   Anthony *Letter* 1 p.5.

p.109   Ps. Athanasius *De Virginitate* 7; Terence *Eunuchus* IV 5.6; Jerome *Letters* 54.9.

p.110   Homer *Iliad* XXIV 131–2.

p.112   Prudentius *Crowns of Martyrdom* X 562–70: St Romanus.

p.112   Homer *Iliad* XXI 108.

p.123   Synesius *Letter* 105.

p.125   Jerome *Epistles* 22.5.

p.128   Jerome *Epistles* 22.30.

p.130   Clement *Protrepticus* 4.

p.131–2   Prudentius *Contra Symmachum* I 501–5.

p.134   Justin Martyr *Second Apology* 10.

p.136   Achilles Tatius VI 21.

p.140   Clement *Protrepticus* 6.

p.140   Tertullian *De Praescriptionibus Hereticorum* 7.9–12; *Apologeticum* 46.18.

p.141   Synesius *Epistles* 105.

p.142   Augustine *Confessions* III 5.9.

p.145   Erasmus *Epistles* 335 [II 88 Allen]; 335 [II 86 Allen].

p.146   Erasmus *Epistles* 396 [II 215 Allen].

p.147   Erasmus *Epistles* 149 [I 353 Allen].

pp.150–1   Wallace, R. *Antitrinitarian Biography* 3 vols (London, 1850) II 272–80.

pp.152–3   Erasmus *Epistles* 456 [II 321 Allen].

p.153   Erasmus *Epistles* 1062 [IV 182–3 Allen]. Thomas More *Responsio ad Lutherum. Yale Edition of the Complete Works of Thomas More* (New Haven, 1963–) V 1.683.

p.154   Erasmus *Epistles* 769 [III 210 Allen]; 844 [III 332 Allen].

pp.154–5   Thomas More *Selected Letters* ed. E. Rogers (New Haven, 1961) 96.

Part III: What Do You Think Should Happen?

p.164   *Letters of the Wordsworth Family from 1787 to 1855* ed. W. Knight (London, 1907) I 66.

p.171   Scolia 893 (Campbell *Greek Lyric Poetry* [London, 1967]).

p.180   Thucydides II 40.

p.181   Thucydides II 41–2.

p.182   Thucydides II 40; Aristotle *Politics* 1275a 22–4.

p.186   Demosthenes xviii 265; Aristotle *Politics* 1253a 19–21.

p.187   Aristotle *Politics* 1253a3.

p.188   Euripides *Phoenissai* 391–2.

p.189   Herodotus VII 104.

p.190   Aeschylus *Persai* 212–14.

pp.191–2   Lady Winifred Anne Henrietta Gardner Burchlere *A Great Lady's Friendship: Letters to Mary, Marchioness of Salisbury, Countess of Derby 1862–1890* (London, 1933) 128–9; A. Patchett Martin *Life and Letters of the Right Honourable Robert Lowe, Viscount Sherbrooke G.C.B., D.C.L.* (London, 1893) 287–8.

pp.196–7   A. Patchett Martin *Life and Letters of the Right Honourable Robert Lowe, Viscount Sherbrooke G.C.B., D.C.L.* (London, 1893) 323; 330–1; 273–4.

p.198   Plato *Republic* VI 493a–d.

p.199   Plato *Republic* VIII 558c10–562a2.

pp.206–7   Richard Crossman *Plato Today* (London, 1937) 300. George Grote *Plato and the Other Companions of Sokrates* (London, 1865) vol. III, 240.

p.207   Aeschines *Against Timarchus* 173. Plutarch *Life of Cato* 23.

Part IV: What Do You Want to Do?

pp.229–30   Homer *Odyssey* III 306–10.

p.237   Pliny *Panegyricus* 33; Cicero *Tusculans* II 41.

pp.237–8   *Corpus Inscriptionum Latinorum* IV 1474; Juvenal *Satire* VI 112.

p.244   Aulus Gellius *Attic Nights* V 14.

p.245   Keith Hopkins *Death and Renewal* (Cambridge, 1983) 5.

pp.250–1   Hippolytus *Treatise on the Passover*; Origen *Treatise on the Passover*.

Part V: Where Do You Think You Come From?

p.259   John Keats 'On Seeing the Elgin Marbles' (1816).

p.262   Percy Shelley 'Preface to *Hellas*'.

p.264   Walter Pater *Greek Studies* (London, 1922) 224; John Addington Symonds *Studies of the Greek Poets* (London, 1873) 399.

p.264–5   *Oscar Wilde's Oxford Notebooks* ed. P. Smith and M. Helfand (New York, 1989) 146–7, 115.

p.269   *Adams' Family Correspondence* ed. L. H. Butterfield (Cambridge 1963) 4.48; Jefferson's *Literary Commonplace Book* ed. D. L. Wilson (Princeton, 1989).

pp.271–2   James Otis 'The Rights of the British Colonies Asserted and Proved' (1764); *The Papers of Alexander Hamilton* ed. H. C. Syrett (New York 1961–79) 1.53; *Papers of George Mason* ed. R. Rutland (Chapel Hill, 1970) 1.435.

pp.272–3   Jean-Jacques Rousseau *Confessions* ed. C. Kelly, R. Masters and P. Stillman (Hanover and London, 1995) 8.

p.276   Speech quoted in *Il Popolo d'Italia* 21 April 1922.

p.277   John Huston *An Open Book* (New York, 1980) 175.

p.278   *Karl Marx, Friedrich Engels: Collected Works* ed. R. Dixon (New York, 1975) 41.264–5.

pp.281–2   G. Hegel *The Philosophy of History* trans. J. Sibree (New York, 1956) 87; 223; F. Nietzsche *Werke. Kritische Gesamtausgabe* ed. G. Colli and M. Montinari vol. VII 3, pp. 412–13 fr. 41 (4).

pp.282–3   F. Schiller *Briefwechsel zwischen Schiller und Goethe in den Jahren 1794 bis 1805* ed. H. Hauff (Stuttgart, 1856) ep. 4; G. Hegel *The Philosophy of History* trans. J. Sibree (New York, 1956) 47; E. Foerster-Nietzsche ed. *The Wagner–Nietzsche Correspondence* (New York, 1921) 125; R. Wagner *My Life* (London, 1911) 46.

pp.283–4   *Richard Wagner's Prose Works* trans. W. Ellis (London, 1892–9) I 32.

p.284   R. Wagner *My Life* (London, 1911) 412; *Richard Wagner's*

Prose Works trans. W. Ellis (London, 1892–9) I 53; I 43; H. von Humboldt *Humanist Without Portfolio* ed. and trans. M. Cowlan (Detroit, 1963) 79.

p.285 W. Jens 'The Classical Tradition in Germany: Grandeur and Decay', in E. Feuchtwengler ed. *Upheaval and Continuity: A Century of German History* (London, 1973) 69. G. Hegel *The Philosophy of History* trans. J. Sibree (New York, 1956) 75.

p.288 *Richard Wagner's Prose Works* trans. W. Ellis (London, 1892–9) IV 43.

pp.289–91 S. Freud *The Standard Edition of the Complete Psychological Works of Sigmund Freud* 24 vols ed. and trans. J. Strachey (London, 1953–74) IV 262–3.

p.291 F. Nietzsche *Beyond Good and Evil* trans. H. Zimmern (London, 1907) para. 1.

p.292 E. Jones *The Life and Work of Sigmund Freud* 3 vols (New York, 1953–7) 2.14.

p.301 Sophocles *Oedipus Tyrannus* 413–15; 435–7.

p.302 Sophocles *Oedipus Tyrannus* 1060–1; 1084–5.

p.303 Sophocles *Oedipus Tyrannus* 1405–7.

p.304 Sophocles *Oedipus Tyrannus* 1186–96.

pp.304–5 Sophocles *Oedipus Tyrannus* 924–6; 1521–2.

p.315 Thucydides I 20–1.

Further Reading

Part I: Who Do You Think You Are?

1. The Perfect Body

Andrew Stewart *Art, Desire and the Body in Ancient Greece* (Cambridge, 1997)
Robin Osborne *Archaic and Classical Greek Art* (Oxford, 1998)
Mary Beard and John Henderson *Classical Art: From Greece to Rome* (Oxford, 2001)
Catherine Johns *Sex or Symbol? Erotic Images of Greece and Rome* (London, 1982)

2. A Man's Thing?

James Davidson *Courtesans and Fishcakes* (London, 1997)
Kenneth Dover *Greek Homosexuality* (Cambridge, Mass., 1978)
Jack Winkler *The Constraints of Desire* (New York, 1990)

3. The Female Body – Soft and Spongy, Shaved and Coy

Helen King *Hippocrates' Woman* (London, 1998)
Thomas Laqueur *Making Sex* (Cambridge, Mass., 1990)
Susan Suleiman *The Female Body in Western Culture* (Cambridge, Mass., 1986)

4. His and Hers – A Love Story?

Anne Carson *Eros the Bittersweet* (Princeton, 1986)
Claude Calame *The Poetics of Eros in Ancient Greece* (Princeton, 1992)
Roger Just *Women in Athenian Law and Life* (London, 1989)

5. *Greek Love*

Michel Foucault *The Use of Pleasure* (New York, 1985)
Michel Foucault *The Care of the Self* (New York, 1986)

6. *A Man Is a Man Is a . . .*

François Lissarrague *The Aesthetics of the Greek Banquet* (Princeton, 1990)
Natalie Kampen ed. *Sexuality in Ancient Art* (Cambridge, 1996)

7. *Longing for Sappho*

Margaret Williams *Sappho's Immortal Daughters* (Cambridge, Mass., 1995)
Bernadette Brooten *Love Between Women* (Chicago, 1996)
Lynda Need *Myths of Sexuality* (Oxford, 1988)
Yopie Prins *Victorian Sappho* (Princeton, 1999)
Joan deJean *Fictions of Sappho 1546–1937* (Chicago, 1989)

8. *Doing What Comes Naturally?*

Michel Foucault *The History of Sexuality* (London, 1978)
Stephen Heath *The Sexual Fix* (London, 1982)
David Halperin *One Hundred Years of Homosexuality* (London, 1990)

Part II: Where Do You Think You Are Going?

2. *Superstars of the Flesh*

Peter Brown *The Body and Society* (New York, 1988)
Peter Brown *The Cult of the Saints* (Chicago, 1981)

3. *Sex and the City*

Ross Kraemer *Her Share of the Blessings* (Oxford, 1992)
Susanna Elm *'Virgins of God': The Making of Asceticism in Late Antiquity* (Oxford, 1994)
Kate Cooper *The Virgin and the Bride* (Cambridge, Mass., 1996)
Gillian Clark *Women in Late Antiquity* (Oxford, 1992)
Caroline Bynum *Holy Feast and Holy Fast: The Religious Significance of Food to Medieval Women* (Berkeley, 1987)
Virginia Burrus *Chastity as Autonomy: Women in the Stories of the Apocryphal Acts* (New York, 1987)

4. *What's Athens to Jerusalem?*

Jas Elsner *Art and the Roman Viewer* (Cambridge, 1995)
Peter Brown *Society and the Holy* (London, 1982).

5. *Greek Is Heresy!*

Lisa Jardine *Erasmus: Man of Letters* (Princeton, 1993)
Simon Goldhill *Who Needs Greek?* (Cambridge, 2002)

6. *Knowing the Answer*

Keith Hopkins *A World Full of Gods* (London, 1999)

Part III: What Do You Think Should Happen?

1. *Does Politics Need History?*

John Dunn *Western Political Theory in the Face of the Future* (Cambridge, 1992)
M. I. Finley *Democracy, Ancient and Modern* (New Brunswick, 1985)
Josiah Ober and Charles Hedrick ed. *Demokratia: A Conversation on Democracies, Ancient and Modern* (Princeton, 1996)

2. *Athenian Democracy – Changing the Map*

Robin Osborne *Greece in the Making 1200–479 BC* (London, 1996)
J. K. Davies *Democracy and Classical Greece* (Hassocks, West Sussex, 1978)
M. I. Finley *Politics in the Ancient World* (Cambridge, 1983)

3. *The Good Citizen*

R. K. Sinclair *Democracy and Participation in Athens* (Cambridge, 1988)
Ellen Meiskens Wood *Peasant, Citizen and Slave: The Foundations of Athenian Democracy* (London, 1988)
Nicole Loraux *The Invention of Athens* (Cambridge, Mass., 1986)

4. *The Critics of Democracy – Experts and Education*

Josiah Ober *Political Dissent in Democratic Athens* (Princeton, 1988)
Jennifer Roberts *Athens on Trial: The Anti-democratic Tradition in Western Thought* (Princeton, 1994)

John Rawls *A Theory of Justice* (London, 1973)
Karl Popper *The Open Society and Its Enemies* (London, 1945)

5. *A Question of Betrayal*

Sarah Kofman *Socrates: Fictions of a Philosopher* (New York, 1998)
Alexander Nehemas *The Art of Living* (Berkeley, 1998)
Melissa Lane *Plato's Progeny* (Cambridge, 2001)
I. F. Stone *The Trial of Socrates* (London, 1988)

Part IV: *What Do You Want to Do?*

1. *That's Entertainment!*

Peter Burke *Popular Culture in Early Modern Europe* (London, 1978)
Peter Stallybrass and Allon White *The Politics and Poetics of
Transgression* (London, 1986)
Robert Hodge and Gunther Kress *Social Semiotics* (Oxford, 1988)

2. *The Question of Tragedy*

Simon Goldhill *Reading Greek Tragedy* (Cambridge, 1986)
Simon Goldhill *Aeschylus: The Oresteia* (Cambridge, 1992)
P. E. Easterling ed. *The Cambridge Companion to Greek Tragedy*
(Cambridge, 1997)

3. *The Gladiator and the Baying Crowd –* *'At My Command, Unleash Hell'*

Keith Hopkins *Death and Renewal* (Cambridge, 1983)
Carlin Barton *The Sorrows of the Ancient Romans* (Princeton, 1993)
Thomas Wiederman *Emperors and Gladiators* (London, 1992)
Donald Kyle *Spectacles of Death* (London, 1998)

Part V: *Where Do You Think You Come From?*

2. *Founding Fathers – From Keats to Hollywood and Back*

Linda Dowling *Hellenism and Homosexuality in Victorian Oxford*
(Ithaca, 1994)
Frank Turner *The Greek Heritage in Victorian Britain* (New Haven,
1981)

Richard Jenkyns *The Victorians and Ancient Greece* (Oxford, 1981)
Carl Richard *The Founders and the Classics* (Cambridge, Mass., 1994)
S. Joshel, M. Malamud and D. McGuire ed. *Imperial Projections:*
   Ancient Rome and Modern Popular Culture (Baltimore, 2001)
M. Wyke *Projecting the Past: Ancient Rome, Cinema and History*
   (London, 1997)

3. *Finding the Fatherland – Where Freud's Oedipus Comes From*

Peter Rudnytsky *Freud and Oedipus* (New York, 1987)
Simon Goldhill *Who Needs Greek?* (Cambridge, 2002)

4. *The Mother of All Stories – The Greek Oedipus*

C. P. Segal *Oedipus Tyrannus: Tragic Heroism and the Limits of*
   Knowledge (New York, 1993)
J.-P. Vernant and P. Vidal-Naquet, *Myth and Tragedy in Ancient Greece*
   (Brighton, 1981)

5. *The Myth of Origins*

Simon Goldhill *The Invention of Prose* (Oxford, 2002)
Marcel Detienne *The Creation of Mythology* (Chicago, 1986)
Lowell Edmunds ed. *Approaches to Greek Myth* (Baltimore, 1990)
Wm. Blake Tyrrell, and Frieda Brown *Athenian Myths and Institutions*
   (Oxford, 1991)
Paul Cartledge *The Greeks* (Oxford, 1992)

Picture Acknowledgements

The author and publishers would like to thank the following for permission to reproduce illustrations: Figure 1, Museo Archaeologico Nazionale, Naples; 2, Trustees of the Wallace Collection; 3, National Archaeological Museum, Athens; 4, German Institute of Archaeology, Rome (photo Singer, 69.634); 5, Charles Atlas Limited, all rights reserved; 6, National Museums Liverpool; 7, Leni Riefenstahl-Produktion; 8, Peter Clayton; 10, Rheinisches Landesmuseum Trier; 11 and 20, Staatliche Museen zu Berlin, Antikensammlung; 12, 14, 38 and 42, Museo Nazionale, Naples; 13, German Institute of Archaeology, Rome (photo Faraglia, 28.26); 15, University of Wisconsin Press; 16, Villa Giulia, Rome; 17, Ashmolean Museum, Oxford; 18, 19, 22, 28, 29 and 45, The Trustees of the British Museum; 21, Staatliche Antikensammlung, Munich; 24, Manchester City Art Galleries; 26, The Walters Art Museum, Baltimore; 27, Louvre, Paris © Photo RMN/Hervé Lewandowski; 30, The Royal Collection © 2003, Her Majesty Queen Elizabeth II; 31, The Detroit Institute of Arts; 32, Robin Osborne; 33, German Institute of Archaeology, Rome (photo Bartl, 58.1789); 34, German Institute of Archaeology, Athens (KER16171/16172); 35, Brooklyn Museum of Art; 36, Harvard University Press; 37 and 39, The Metropolitan Museum of Art, all rights reserved; 40, Museo Archeologico al Teatro Romano, Verona; 41, Borghese Gallery, Rome; 43, Museo della Civilita Romana, Rome; 44, Private collection on loan to Bradford Art Galleries and Museums; 47, North Carolina Division of Archives and History, Raleigh; 48, 49 and 50, Estate of Sigmund Freud.

Love, Sex & Tragedy

Acknowledgements

Heartfelt thanks to my friends who discussed chapters of this book, especially Helen Morales and Miriam Leonard, to my agent Peter Straus, and most especially to my editor, Anya Serota: a real editor, without whose direction and support this book would never have happened.